110 STORIES

110 STORIES

NEW YORK WRITES AFTER SEPTEMBER 11

EDITED BY ULRICH BAER

NEW YORK UNIVERSITY PRESS New York and London

NEW YORK UNIVERSITY PRESS
New York and London

Library of Congress Cataloging-in-Publication Data
110 stories : New York writes after September 11 / edited by
Ulrich Baer.
ISBN 0-8147-9905-1 (acid-free paper)
1. New York (N.Y.)—Literary collections. 2. September 11
Terrorist Attacks, 2001—Literary collections. 3. American
literature—New York (State)—New York. 4. American literarature—
20th century. I. Title: One hundred ten stories. II. Baer, Ulrich.
PS549.N5 O13 2002
810.8'0327471—dc21 2002005615

New York University Press books are printed on acid-free paper,
and their binding materials are chosen for strength and durability.

Manufactured in the United States of America

10 9 8 7 6 5 4 3 2 1

CONTENTS

ACKNOWLEDGMENTS

In a dark and troubling era, a possibility remains of expressing thankfulness for help that has been offered.

I thank the authors for their work.

I also thank my wife Niobe Way, as well as Carol Mann, Eric Zinner, Art Spiegelman, Philip Graziadei, Jessie Labov, Martin Baer, Barbara Baer, Bella Brodzki, Betsy Bradley, Tina Bennett, Adrienne Brodeur, Gabrielle Civil, Alyse Dissette, Madhu Kaza, Consuelo Murtagh, Michael Lobel, Sina Najafi, Lorin Stein, Brenda Way, and Marvin Taylor.

All of the authors contributed their pieces without receiving compensation; Art Spiegelman also designed the cover free of charge. This book could not have been created without all these individuals' generosity.

The editor is donating his proceeds to the New York Foundation for the Arts.

INTRODUCTION

ULRICH BAER

The events of September 11, 2001, produced a flood of writing from commentators and journalists in the form of personal essays, political opinion pieces, and testimonials. But no single collection has yet recorded how New York writers of literary fiction, poetry, and dramatic prose—those for whom language has always been a vital concern—responded to September 11. This book attempts to fill this void.

The World Trade Center's twin towers rose 110 stories high. Just as each of these 110 stories was filled with individuals of every stripe, the contributions in this volume represent the diverse and multi-hued texture of New York City, its boundless complexity, polyglot energy, and spirit of confrontation and solidarity. This book offers a model for New York's perpetual self-reconstitution through metaphor and language that will prove as significant as the construction in concrete and steel around us. Like the two towers, this book contains 110 stories brought to life and spelled out by New Yorkers in New York.

The stories address the need for narrative in the wake of a disaster. In a recent essay, Don DeLillo identifies the task at hand: "to give memory, tenderness and meaning to all that howling space" caused by the towers' collapse. With *110 Stories*, poets, novelists, short story writers, script authors, playwrights, and artists enter terrain that needs not only remediation by engineers and clean-up crews but integration into the city beyond zoning and construction. Their stories explore the possibilities of language in the face of gaping loss, and register that words might be all that's left for the task of finding meaning in—and beyond—the silent, howling void.

While writers don't provide disaster relief in terms of food and shelter, they help to account for loss and make survival meaningful. Here they make a first wager on how to remember the destruction of the towers without numbing the reader, and without relegating the deed to the realm of the incomprehensible. As authors of fiction and poetry, they guide us in the effort to turn the event into a story without glossing over its shocking singularity. They are intimately familiar with the necessity of approaching an event from angles that are not merely uncomfortable but painful to contemplate, and of struggling to find the words for an experience so complex that it mocks the black and white simplicity of printed paper.

The 110 authors create an index to measure the absences that now define New York City: absences initially confined to Ground Zero but quickly rippling outward to ever-wider circles of the bereaved, and ultimately affecting everyone who distrusts simple answers, ready-made and precision-bombed solutions, and the arrogant and foolish certainty of having the correct response to a severe collective trauma. Like archaeologists of the present, these writers provide scale to what dwarfed the imagination before its destruction, and now stumps us in its absence.

Developers, city planners, and construction crews wielding torches and cranes continue to physically repair lower Manhattan; they will undoubtedly incorporate a memorial into the reconnected grid. In the first days after the attack, the astounding efforts by rescue workers found a symbolic echo in poems postered on walls and fences: first in makeshift memorials, then delivered to inboxes all over the globe. This spontaneous burgeoning of poetry responded to a need—a need for words that then took the form of written scrolls hung on fences and walls along with donated pens and markers, allowing anyone to offer the language of poetry where little could be said. Sheets went up around the city like huge bandages soaking up grief, disbelief, and rage. *110 Stories* extends this original impulse that could have been neither predicted nor programmed and that testifies to the city's unshakeable tendency to write itself out, to give rise to stories that absorb and transform even its most violent transformations by shaping them into words. Poetry offered us guidance in the first uncertain days after the attacks; it also signaled the attempt to shape the way in which one's experience is written into history. Now, the literary imagination proves instrumental in attaching the scarred site to its surroundings, in tapping what remains unsaid in editorials and essays, but also in prying our minds from 9/11. Instead of providing solace, the work of fiction cauterizes the wound with uncomfortable questions and unflinching reflection. It sears the event into the collective imagination by embedding the initial shock in narratives, poems, theater, and tales.

September 11. The event has entered collective memory as that single date that we hope will not become the beginning of a larger story (the way Pearl Harbor augured World War II in the American imagination). The simple date *September 11* must be unraveled to reveal and spell out the many stories it contains—not all compatible, not all easy to absorb, not all welcomed by everyone, but neither morose nor sentimental. September 11 calls upon us to put into words the feeling of being at a loss, of not having an adequate expression for what happened. It also compels "us" to recognize how tenuous and dangerous the notion of a clearly defined "us" has always been.

With its admitted bias toward "downtown," experimental and avant-garde writers sharply skeptical of preconceived ideas, and willing to ask unwelcome questions and locate unwelcome truths, *110 Stories* offers 110 passages through silence to the first stirrings of a story, to the instant when event becomes tale, when loss gives rise to words. Since a city—and New York maybe more so than any other metropolis—lives and feeds on its stories, creates tall tales, half-lies and mythologies about itself on which its future then depends, I called to this forum particularly those writers who had participated in building the city, and asked them to lend their voice now to one of the gravest moments of New York's perpetual cycle of de- and reconstitution. Many of them have substantially shaped our understanding of the city's agglomeration of steel, cement, tar, and glass by extracting from it memorable images in startlingly original language.

Not all contributors address the events of September 11 directly. Some are searching for a kind of password that could unlock the truth screened by the cant around us, while others explore the central question whose answer informs every explanation of the events: has anything changed? Is there a "new normal" now, a post–9/11 world, another "New York state of mind"? Or were the attacks "only" a particularly spectacular instance in longer stories involving U.S.-sponsored violence? One of the disturbing effects of overwhelming trauma can be the stupefying sense that nothing has changed. After a great catastrophe, the destruction might appear so vast that the functions of language and thought necessary for remembrance and reflection seem permanently disabled. Even if it ultimately collapses into a stutter, or vanishes in a line break or ellipsis, the story of this new condition for making sense also needs to be recovered.

The writers in this book aim to detect but refuse to accept readily any new shifts in the way we now think about our lives and our deaths, and the lives and deaths of others. They address whether anything happened that could be termed a historical event, a psychic rupture in the world's imagination. They probe whether loss and pain, life and its joys, certainty and fear have been altered by what happened. Some head straight for Ground Zero, or relate a struggle to subdue the obsessive replay of a limited and blinding stock of disturbing images of the attacks and its aftermath. A few revise existing work that suddenly calls out in unexpected ways. But most invest stories, tales, poems, and dramatic dialogues with a subtle post-traumatic resonance to determine what, if anything, changed when the World Trade Center was attacked. The realm of literature here serves to determine where an individual's story and voice links up with, and where it contradicts, collective concerns.

Every one of the 110 stories in the World Trade Center's twin towers housed activity that sustained, furthered, altered, and affected life on the ground below. As with every skyscraper, these 110 stories were linked principally by their joint encasement in soaring glass and steel: each story sheltered lives that may have shared little besides stretches of time in the same tower. When these stories were cut off, the missing towers became monuments—invisible cenotaphs of loss and anger, of suffering and injustice, terrorism and fear, and the inarticulate grievance and brutal ideology that fueled the amateur pilots on their path to destruction.

All the stories told here recognize that there will be no single story to contain the event. They unfold in varied and complex idioms and genres and across a staggering range of accents and inflections. Literature is called upon here as the unconscious history-writing of the world: as a form of expression that uncannily registers subtle shifts in experience and changes in reality before they can be consciously grasped or have fully taken place. In opposition to the aim of political explanations, literature resists the call for closure. It is because there is no single story and no simple answer that orthodox adherence to the genre of short fiction would have been pointless. Hence the inclusion of short and longer poems in particular—the literary genre that hovers so close to loss without quite settling for either silence or full-fledged expression. But also included are postcards to the missing, unrealized film scripts, instructions for responses to disaster, imagined encounters with the bereaved, mini-whodunits, urban legends, scenarios of the unimaginable, paeans to the city, explorations of a terrorist's mind, downtown blues, anti-pastorals, several authors' own private 9/11's, and occasional defiant leaps into argument.

In the wake of the terror attacks on Lower Manhattan, the political discourses on both the right and the left seemed irreconcilable with what had happened. When I received a message on September 14 to hang a large white sheet out of my window, I had a visceral reaction of incredulity mixed with anger, frustration, even rage. To declare surrender—the standard meaning of a white flag—from the window of my then 1 1/2 year-old son's bedroom, days after the first jet had roared over us in the street and then hurled, in full view, into the first tower after passing a mere hundred yards from my building, to declare surrender seemed as incommensurate with the experience as the call for revenge.

I had witnessed the attacks from the safety of Washington Square Park, and watched the second tower go down from my son's window. In spite of my relative distance from the site itself, I was immobilized with fear. I became a kind of awestruck witness, unable to show a response lest my tears alarm the child I sought to shelter from what was happening. Until then I had believed that witnessing would remain a secondary act for me. While the north tower was still standing, I reached family in Germany to tell them—and to tell myself—that we were okay. Through tears, my father explained to me on the phone, to me who was thousands of miles away from him but only a mile from the Trade Center, that the events unfolding outside of my windows signaled the definite end of an era. The attacks, he instantly realized, would shape the course of the world for years if not decades to come, and thus for much of my son's lifetime. When he was speaking to me, he was already in the middle of what would be his last cycle of chemotherapy; two months later, he died. In early November, when he developed a sudden fever a week before his death, I took the first available flight to say goodbye, an option unavailable to those, like my student, who lost a loved one in the attacks. In light of my father's shock at the events of September 11 and the fact that in those first days he alone fully recognized how much the attacks had terrified me, I am convinced that he absorbed part of the blow in my stead. In reading the contributions for this book, I realize I am not alone in the feeling that the relation between unrelated personal losses, such as my father's death for me, and the events of September 11 became increasingly difficult to sort out. Like much of my city, I was saturated with grief. The season did not seem to end, and September 11 converged upon other losses in ways that proved overwhelming.

The exhortations for peace which clogged my e-mail and showed up on walls and flyers in the days after the attacks seemed at once sincere and naïve. I found equally alarming and even enraging the rhetoric of war and calls for revenge that I had been asked to protest; both doves and hawks, it seemed to me, failed to grasp the complexity of 9/11. In response to this inadequacy of available discourse, I turned to literature. Once traffic was restored to our neighborhood, once business began to approximate its former pace, I read continuously and only recall with difficulty what else I did that strange clear autumn; no rain, no cold, just blue sunny days unfurling from September 11 until year's end. In literature, I found neither consolation nor a substitute for grief but rather the foothold on reality from which I had slipped momentarily. Novels in particular, in their efforts to construct fully realized alternative universes, seemed navigable and inhabitable the way downtown was not, with the acrid stench and mysterious skin rashes, the urgent after-hour consultations with the pediatrician, the doctor's advice to keep children indoors or leave the area altogether on smoke-filled days. I admit it, I read literature as an escape: even novels about catastrophes seemed to provide the coherence that was missing from my life. In its ways of incessantly building and transforming a world, literature helped me confront reality without promising wholeness or denying absence, shock, and loss.

I also turned to fiction in order to gauge how our imagination would be expanded by the events, and how unwanted traumatic knowledge can be integrated into stories in a broader sense. Literature does not only measure our transformations; it grows as we grow. The attacks of September 11 hijacked our imagination, seized it irrevocably, and expanded it with a kind of knowledge and a series of images that no one had wanted to contemplate. A nail clipper at the airport unspooled images of force and destruction. During the course of every in-flight meal, the imagination was triggered to replay a scenario so horrible that it had to be kept at bay with great effort. Each plastic knife made us feel, wrongly, improperly, brashly, that our imagination had failed us before September 11; who would have thought that butter knives could be ominous? With the exception of severe neurotics, sociopaths, and, well, artists, no one had routinely assessed the propensity of everyday objects for great violence. It would be hard to put a limit on the invasive qualities of these intrusions. And sometimes it's just the body that remembers; sunny, blue-skied weather in Manhattan was for many more difficult than rain.

All of the authors were given broad license to fill two pages. In the months of soliciting contributions, I spent a good deal of time convincing authors who had difficulties writing in the wake of September 11 to search for a story, to begin to write again, to stop replaying in their heads the dead-end scenarios in and on the air. In order to write, one must feel deeply, and many tried to keep any hint of emotional or experiential intensity at bay. One author spoke of his sudden realization on September 11 that he had always thought of himself as a bohemian, rootless cosmopolitan for whom the word "home" held no meaning—until his home in Lower Manhattan came under attack. Another writer worried in a long conversation about the tempting and dangerous tendency for downtowners to take misguided pride in being more affected than others. Her advice in a difficult week: stay at home, cook, eat meals with friends. The fiction writers, on the whole, were slower to respond, and there is a story in itself about the origin of many of the stories included in this book. The poets, it sometimes seemed, went straight from their rooftops to the writing pads. Often I would receive a poem minutes after I asked for it, with the explanation that my then unrealized *110 Stories* was the destination the poet had been searching for when staring at the smoke and loss. Others responded by reshaping drafts or reviving texts that now seem eerily prescient or assume an unexpected resonance in this new context.

New York's capacity to interweave adjacent but otherwise unrelated lives into gripping stories is most breathtaking when it juxtaposes the utterly dissimilar. Read *110 Stories* by staying mindful of this beauty of accidental juxtaposition, just as scraps from two unrelated conversations can momentarily spark new meaning when they meet in the empty space just before a subway door slams shut, when the light changes, or before an elevator that has just disgorged one load of storied passengers is rushed by a new crop of stories pushing in.

1

HUMERA AFRIDI

Circumference

The woman has trained herself to wake up to precise images: aquamarine sea, limestone villas, sand the color of caramel custard. For a week now, she has awakened to this collage of all the beaches she has known.

Each morning the dream fills the barren plain that has been her mind since he left exactly one week earlier; each morning the dream dissipates more quickly. She uncurls herself from her duvet, reaches for the remote and turns on her radio. She has no television; she is still new here.

Less than a mile from where she lives there is a world destroyed, mangled, spitting the flumes of burnt steel, flesh and plastic. *The price of hubris*, the radio announcer posits. The woman slides her feet out of bed but keeps her head on her pillow and listens. Today has been declared a national day of prayer and mourning. The barricade north of Houston Street has been lifted. She is free to roam beyond the circumference of the five square blocks where she has been zoned for the last four days since the attack. Anxiety prickles at her, anxiety about this strange new freedom.

She will buy her first newspaper; she will buy sugar. She searches for her I.D. card, removes the stud from her nose.

Her lover—though after this last time, could he really be called that? said: *We should leave it at the level of skin. No telephone calls, no e-mail.* This woman who moved alone to the city three weeks ago cannot get her lover's words out of her head. She mutters them, remembering the breadth of him against her, wishing she'd said them first. She slings her surgical mask around her neck, rummages in her closet for a dupatta. She is not devout nor one to carry the baggage of tradition, yet she gropes about for a scarf to cover her hair.

She thinks of her husband. He will call soon from the home they had shared until three weeks ago. She will miss the call. On the fourth day after this world has been sabotaged, she knows that the other man, the one with whom she has this arrangement, this mutual exercising of lust, will not telephone. Each time, in the days following his visit, the sensation of his presence dissipates, but now she does not let him out of her head. To do so will mean creating space for the horror outside, the sinking in that this life is no longer a fiction.

Three people on her street—all Caucasian. Smoke belches and curdles from the site and subsumes the neighborhood in an acrid haze. She positions her mask over her face and walks north. Two people pass her and glare. Is she imagining it? On the first afternoon, a woman outside the deli said, *These fucking Arabs! I don't understand them.* Then, looking at her closely, said *You're not Arab, are you? I mean, you're not Palestinian?*

At Houston Street she shows her I.D. to a police officer. People cluster on either side of the blockade. As she crosses the street it feels as though she has left a country behind. Four men shove past her; one of them mutters something loud and incoherent.

Earnestness is not what the city is about and she wears her sin too close to her skin. She flags a cab. *11th Street and 1st Avenue, please,* she says. She does not say Madina Masjid. The driver peers at her through the rear view mirror. He is brown and complicit.

The woman feels she is driving through a palimpsest. People cluster around posters of the missing, learning the maps of their bodies. She wonders about the ones going from wall to wall with tape, watching the sky for rain.

The car stops at a red light. She cannot believe that the man who fucked her seven days ago hasn't bothered to e-mail, to call; she cannot believe she is thinking of him still and that she has thought more about him than at any other time, in any other year. She cannot believe she is becoming this sort of woman, the sort of woman who baffles her. A voice rasps through the window: *I'm going to fucking kill Osama. I want you to know I'm going to get him.*

Okay, okay, very good, the driver says like he's soothing a colicky baby.

The man at the window looks at her, says: *I'm telling this cabbie here I'm going to kill Osama.* He has a scruffy orange beard, a thin pasty face. The light turns, the tires screech, the driver swears under his breath in Punjabi.

Once out of the cab, she wraps her hair in her dupatta. She approaches a man in a mustard kurta-pyjama, asks for the women's entrance. He looks over the length of her body, tilts his head. *Why? Do you want to pray?* She disregards him and walks into the squat building. There is office carpeting, sheet rock walls; it smells like someone's cooking. There are only men. One says, *Yes?* as if she's a foreigner. It is evident to them she is not a mosque-goer; she lacks the protocol.

Where are the women, please?

No women here, he says abruptly and opens the door to let her out.

Standing in front of this mosque, she feels stripped to the bone: shameless; adulteress; wine-drinker. Her jeans seem to say this to the men as do her boots and the fact that she is here alone on a day when the women are secure at home.

You are here, she thinks, in this city, among things and people, vehicles and street vendors, but you cannot say a word. The sins of this life seem as flat as copper pennies ground under heeled boots, worthless as vanity, lost in dirt. There is a sudden newness to the street, there is a sudden stark separation of the soul from the world that sifts around and through the body. You are here, she thinks. When you awake tomorrow, and the day after and the day after that, this is where you will be.

2

AMMIEL ALCALAY

night of unity

It had long been the position of the United States that the warring parties could work out their own alliances.

—National Security Advisor Anthony Lake to Ambassador to the United States of Bosnia-Herzegovina, Sven Alkalaj, November 30, 1994

Rise, shining martyrs
over the multitudes
for the season of migration
between earth and heaven

—John Weiners

---

we swam the submerged body all the way to the boat before hoisting it on deck. We were fully dressed

---

Struck by her wisdom and intelligence, the king carries on long conversations with her—about God, politics, love, family, loyalty, betrayal and the will of the people. Along the way he reveals his insecurities. He wonders whether people will honor or desecrate his corpse after he dies.

"At work in both uprisings were the same material costs, the same first causes. Little had really changed in the intervening years. The same regency governed in the old manner, that is, as deemed fit, through the same narrow ring of privileged oligarchs, under the same thin pretense of constitutional politics. On occasion, as before, the parties, the publicists, the colleges, drew a breath. The regime had to concede that much to preserve itself. But, as before, the freedoms hesitantly granted were hurriedly snatched back, or allowed only in form and frustrated in practice. Those of the lower-classes, of the mud huts, still lived in squalor, ate polluted food and drudged long hours at impossible wages."

"The book is kind of a dirge. The king is talking about his death.

Every time I read the book I feel for the king."

"what is interesting and appealing to me is how you slow down the pace, how you use quotations as a model of reflection, a slow motion historical record, weighted and measured, where the isolated citations act as characters. They are cool and concise as if part of the written record. At the same time, they are ethereal, as if outside the record. As if they were/are from the warring factions—past, present and future—come to address us about the history they've witnessed."

"We stick with the plan," Mr. Thomas said. "We insist that the map be accepted." He added that "rumors" about the plan's being changed were untrue.

"One former director said gleaning facts from the avalanche of information was like trying to take a drink of water from a fire hose."

The cover of the novel says only that it is "by its author."

One night, while returning to her cottage from the king's palace, Zabibah is gagged and dragged into a forest where she is raped by a man who conceals his identity. He turns out to be her estranged husband. Afterward, Zabibah says to herself, "Rape is the most serious of crimes, whether it is a man raping a woman or invading armies raping the homeland." The enraged king vows revenge by opening a war "that will not end until victory or death." During the ensuing battle against the husband and his supporters, Zabibah is killed. Her husband, who is killed the same day, is buried beside her so that the people can throw stones on his grave to desecrate it on the anniversary of his death.

"It was just eight years after the end of World War II, which left American journalists with a sense of national interest framed by six years of confrontation between the Allies and the Axis. The front pages of Western newspapers were dominated by articles about the new global confrontation with the Soviet Union, about Moscow's prowess in developing nuclear weapons and about Congressional allegations of "Red" influences in Washington."

> "tribes, guilds and mystic orders lost cohesion or disintegrated; vast masses of people moved from the country and provincial towns to the big cities to enroll in the new army, bureaucracy or police force, or to find employment in the new businesses that supplied the needs of thcsc institutions, or to swell the ranks of the unskilled laborers and noticeably depress their earnings; old ties, loyalties, and concepts were undermined, eroded or swept away."

"lost to history,"

"the subject of fierce debate"

---

the operation's success was mostly a matter of chance

One by one, participants retired or died without revealing key details, and the agency said a number of records of the operation—its first successful overthrow of a foreign government, had been destroyed.

"I wanted to let Freedman know that I knew there had been involvement in the coup, but that I hadn't written about it," he said. "I expected him to say, "Jump on that story." But there was no response."

"He makes the proper sacrifices, and advances to the scales of justice. There he sees his own heart weighed against the ostrich-feather of Truth."

"Let this cave be Egypt"

---

the sentence, if this throne has a language:

---

kinetoscope reels the x-ray the wireless telegraph the mystery of radium

---

"dazzling as the wheels of Ezekiel"

"the sword like a stream of light
the moth that burns its wings in the lamp:"

"he says there is no substitute for time, the shadow it throws upon the screen:"

"it is a crude mind that would insist these appearances are not real, that the eye does not see them when all eyes behold them"

"they go to film after film till the whole world seems to turn on a reel"

"the reel now before us" "survives the shrinking and the warping"

"THE CHAPTERS ON COMING FORTH BY DAY"
"mysterious fourth dimension of its grace and glory"

"Half lies, half truths," the writer took "poetic license."
"Poetic license," he says, "drives me crazy."

"The field was filled with white specks and from a distance, they looked like mushrooms but when you moved up closer, you realized they were all skulls."

---

if we want to talk
about *things*:

I left my mattress
I left my mattress cover
I left my pillow
I left my plate and my cup
I left the clothing that I wore
I left everything and nothing

"these people down here, this is like an echo chamber, it's an echo chamber that resonates with the testimony of the living witnesses—and these people, these dead people are telling us the same story that the living witnesses have told us"

---

many people march toward the strange glorifying eye of
the camera growing larger filling the entire field of
vision disappearing when they are almost upon us
imagine a production that would chronicle the promise

"as a method of keeping the story from ending" "with the white glare of the empty screen:"

"darkness"

“on which we can paint” “the feeling of return:”

“THE QUESTION OF OUR DEPARTURE”

August 2001

3

ELENA ALEXANDER

Circum

The morning is full of storm
in the heart of summer.

The clouds travel like white
handkerchiefs of goodbye,
the wind, traveling, waving them
in its hands.

—Pablo Neruda, *Twenty Love Poems, and a Song of Despair*

1.

We are standing at the edge of a pond, a pond filled with lily pads. Swamp-matter grounds them at the root. Sun warms them. They stretch away in front of us; harsh, clear light. Space in all things. Green spade-face of lily pads, our shiny-white teeth, goofy smiles. Big smiles, tight smiles, big teeth, no teeth, and lips; generous lips; yes. Flesh is nothing. Space is all.

Wind moves from pad to pad making them dip, one by one in turn, giving their edges a barely perceptible darkness; stride. We turn to each other. Big smiles, no smiles, teeth, no teeth, and look. We've made lunch. We must have made lunch. It's there on the stove, cheddar-and-onion soup. Goop and gold. A generosity, and right there, on a round table, a salad: Red, yellow, green. Red, red. Please speak with your mouth full. I would love to hear; anything. You have to say.

2.

We are balanced on platforms the size of our feet. Our feet have smooth skin and high arches. Hunkering down in front of green leaves, that's what we're doing. Pinching leaves and talking. Pinching. Talking, talking and smiling. Pinching so that what grows will not go to seed and die.

3.

A large branch outside a window. We sit. Needles, piney and blue-green. They nod in the wind. We would love this spot. Quiet and green. Cloud-drift, silent as earth, that dark old receptacle; a generosity of bones.

Sky is everything, is all space implied. We sit in pools of ancient light and invisible water. Could be a pond, a tree, our teeth. We are situated this way, you, me, every one, and. Things.

A tree branch makes a shadow on a tiny slope. Not *now*. A moment ago. Clouds erase shadow; arms of wind go into motion. They swing from branch to branch, tree to tree. An invisible monkey with an invisible monkey-smile.

4.

There's a wasp outside our window. Okay, please. A wasp on wood. A potential sting, with all the hurt and pain that comes when you sit in the middle of a world. Love and no love. Water, wood, and lilies. You, me, goofy smiles, tight smiles, no smiles; teeth.

The clouds have drifted, wind pushes. Light, shadows, shade. The wasp flies away. It creases the space we never see, but know is there.

4

MEENA ALEXANDER

Aftermath; Invisible City

AFTERMATH

There is an uncommon light in the sky
Pale petals are scored into stone.

I want to write of the linden tree
That stoops at the edge of the river

But its leaves are filled with insects
With wings the color of dry blood.

At the far side of the river Hudson
By the southern tip of our island

A mountain soars, a torrent of sentences
Syllables of flame stitch the rubble

An eye, a lip, a cut hand blooms
Sweet and bitter smoke stains the sky.

(New York City, September 13–18, 2001)

INVISIBLE CITY

Sweet and bitter smoke stains the air
the verb *stains* has a thread torn out
I step out to the linden grove
Bruised trees are the color of sand.

Something uncoils and blows at my feet
Sliver of mist? Bolt of beatitude?

A scrap of what was once called *sky?*
I murmur words that come to me

Tall towers, twin towers I used to see.
A bloody seam of sense drops free.

By Liberty Street, on a knot of rubble
in altered light, I see a bird cry.

(New York City, October 17–November 3, 2001)

Note: "Aftermath" and "Invisible City" first saw the light of day on December 7, 2001. I read them while participating in a panel discussion "The Artist in a Time of Crisis" organized by the New York Foundation for the Arts at the Drawing Center, 35 Wooster Street.

JEFFERY RENARD ALLEN

5

It Shall Be Again

You can tear a building down
But you can't erase the
memory . . .
—Living Colour

Pennies rained from heaven in thick dirty color. Penny rain, ringing against parked cars, breaking windshields and windows, bouncing off concrete, rolling into sewers, spinning like plates. Sweat and work, Hatch played off-the-wall with a rubber ball against the ugly ribs of an old school building. In one motion, he caught the ball and shoved it deep into his pants pocket. He stood in the vacant lot and watched the world pass.

Open, coons chased pennies with brown grocery bags, coins cutting through. Coons abandoned their places in the lottery line and pulled at the sky with raised fists. Pennies spilled from windows and doorways. Coons fell from roofs with outstretched hands. Stud coons used they asshole for a purse, and bitch coons they pussy. Disbelief—awe—kept some rooted in shock. Not Boo. He plunged squarely into the business, clawing up coins like a bear fish. Stupid coon, Hatch thought. Never knew how stupid til now. Boo lived in a basement dark, damp and smelly like a ship's hold. Once a week Hatch boarded the ship—Ai, mate! Let's take to the seas, he teased. Hol de win, hol de win, hol de win. Don't let it blow—and tutored Boo in math and reading. Boo savored the sweetness of strength and gaffled his peers for their lunch money. Every day he ate two big ass slices of white bread (Hatch liked wheat), two lumps of mayonnaise (Hatch liked Miracle Whip), and two long rolls of pennies. To curry favor and keep Boo from beating his ass, Hatch had taught him this penny sandwich. Save for the future, he said. You'll always have something in your stomach.

Save. He bagged and transported groceries for HI LO FOODS. Seven, he earned a third of a man's salary, but could out think anybody thirty times his size and thirty-three times his age.

Boo was at the other end of the vacant lot, open mouth aimed at the sky. He swallowed his fill of pennies, full to the stitches like the Pillsbury Dough Boy, then headed home, slow and heavy. Vomiting pennies, shitting pennies, pissing copper.

Old ladies ran out the stained glass doors of the Ambassadors for Church of God in Christ, the Elder Milton Oliver, pastor. (They sat on pews all day, hoping to levitate the building with their waving fans.)

If coons are this worked up, surely the white folks downtown must be really showing out. Hell, I ain't gon chase no pennies. Be rich some day. His confidence was grounded in a structural vision. Heaven Incorporated. "Try Jesus-You'll Like Him." Dial 1-900-OMYLORD and talk to Jesus directly. (Free Blessing with every call!) $500 will buy you a train ticket to heaven. One time offer. $50 for your key to the kingdom (24k gold). $100 yearly membership for the Angel Club. (Purchase your wings first! Available in nylon, satin and silk. White or off-white.) $25 to reserve your bed in the upper room. He would build big ass churches the size of football stadiums, rising on every street, on every corner, in every neighborhood. Churches big as cities rising above county, state, and country. Hell, I might even put some on the moon. Hire me the best preachers: Sterling Pickens of the First Baptist Multi-Media Church, Rich "Ducets" Allen (Lay de foundation; build a home in dat rock; lift up this hammer; Gawd'll put you to work), Stallion Blade (It ain't bout the salary, it's all bout reality). Five dollar cover charge or yearly $10,000 membership. Bucket-deep collection plates. Yes, I'm gon be all money someday. Head flat as a dime. Diamond fingernails. Jeweled three-ton suit. Gold cane fat like an elephant's dick. Clockin dollars.

Knuckles, pennies punched through faces. Dragon's teeth, chewed up hands and feet. Sprayed brownstones clean. Leveled new houses and coppered old ones with squat layered covering like armored trucks.

In a burst of thunder (God's fart), the sky closed.

The once hollowcheeked were now frog-jawed with pennies. Green eyes were greener. Coons cradled coins in arms like children. (One bitch coon rocked her bundle back and forth.) The dark streets glowed copper paths. And under the streetlights, yellow blue red things, twitching or still. Some dressed, some naked. Some with calm faces, others with wide looks of terror.

Maybe the next time it will rain nickels, dimes, quarters, half-dollars and round dollars. Maybe the sky will pave streets in silver. Level steel skyscrapers and mold them into tracks. Forge the entire city into a massive silver railroad. Guess who gon be the conductor? Choo choo! Whistling and weaving.

No sooner had he thought this when it began to rain again.

He knew all the names for his people and recited them. Chocolate drops, coons, niggers, niggas, nigras, jungle bunnies, moolies, tarbabies, sambos, spooks, spades, spear chuckers, darkies, geechies, coloreds, negroes, Negroes, blacks, Blacks, Afro-Americans, African-Americans. Falling like bad dancers. Flopping like fish.

6

ROBERTA ALLEN

The Sky Was So Blue

"The world is coming to an end!" my friend Irina screamed into the phone, just after the first attack.

She was crying hysterically when I broke in, "What happened?"

"Turn on the TV!" She continued sobbing.

I turned on the television and saw a reporter on Twelfth Street and Fifth Avenue, the World Trade Center in the distance. The second plane had just struck the north tower. I don't want this to be a TV event, I told myself. I hung up the phone and ran down the stairs and out to the corner of Sixteenth and Fifth Avenue. The towers *were* burning. As I walked down Fifth, crowds gathered around a few parked cars and taxis with radios blasting the news. I was at Twelfth Street when the first tower fell. It folded so gracefully. A movie-ready image. Was it a movie? I had walked down to Washington Square to see its absence better when the second tower collapsed. Clouds of dust and smoke rose in its place. This is impossible, I thought. Where is God? What kind of God would let this happen? I seemed to be the only one crying. Why weren't the others crying? I felt suddenly alone, in a world without God. Then I remembered my writing student Julie. She would be calling at 10:30 from the suburbs in Pennsylvania to read me her story for our weekly session. I must go home to get Julie's call. I must not miss it, I told myself, and ran home. As soon as I entered my apartment, my boyfriend Craig called from the subway. He was on his way over. When he arrived, I cried hysterically in his arms, I forgot about Julie. While I cried, Irina called. She didn't want to be alone.

We found her sitting on the stoop with a jar of scotch when we came downstairs to meet her ten minutes later. The hair stylist Farida was sitting on the stoop too. Irina was ranting, hysterical, drunk. "She escaped from Rumania," I said to Farida, as though that explained everything. Craig, Irina, and I walked to the Village. The sky was so blue. It seemed to me the sky had never been that blue. I realized suddenly how alive I felt. I felt that sense of aliveness whenever I was at risk. One time I had a suspicious cyst that might have been breast cancer but thankfully wasn't. In that period of uncertainty I felt the same energy, the same life all around me that I was feeling now. So many people outside on a work day under that incredible sky made it seem like a perverse sort of holiday.

Irina decided to stay in a bar in the Village where the TV was playing. Craig and I continued up Sixth Avenue and sat down at an outdoor café, watching the crowds. How clear the world looked. The sight of that sky, bluer than I had ever seen it, the sight of those people so alive brought God back to life for me, made me feel that this disaster was part of something larger, part of a plan in the universe our consciousness was too limited to see. I thought of some lines from a fifteenth century poem:

> *The gloom of the world is but a shadow.*
> *Behind it, yet within our reach,*
> *is joy.*

I had not yet heard from the friend who had seen blood and body parts strewn all over the roof of his high rise. I had not yet seen pictures of people jumping from the upper stories to their deaths, nor seen on TV the woman leaning out the window, alone in the tower, black smoke billowing around her, looking up, down, behind her, to each side. Sitting in that café, I did not know my beliefs would be tested over and over again.

7

JONATHAN AMES

Womb Shelter

Yesterday, I was watching the girls play tennis.

I was trying to catch glimpses of panties beneath the little skirts.

Meanwhile, bombs were being dropped in Afghanistan. But the girls were still trying. Serving, running, volleying. Bending over. Yeah. Bend over. When I was fifteen I'd be alone in my basement watching Chris Evert on the television, my hands in my pants, waiting for her to bend over.

I also liked Tracy Austin's ass and Evonne Goolagong's. What a name. Goolagong. I think she might have been an Aborigine. You know she had a sweet pussy. A brunette pussy. I wish I could lick it right now. Even if she's fifty. To hell with writing. I'd like to lick Evonne Goolagong's pussy, right now!

Anyway, the girls were playing. Six courts. Twelve girls. End of the day fall light. Very pretty. Clean air. College! Hope! Young people! Flyers on bulletin boards!

Go tennis team! Blonde pony-tails. Long legs. Smooth legs. Twelve sweet pussies hidden somewhere in those skirts. Lots of bending over. Bombs dropping.

I was getting this delicious display of young bottom because I'm Writer-in-Residence for a month at this all-girls college. It's deep in the South. They have me up on a hill in a house, behind some trees, hidden. Like Anthony Perkins in *Psycho*. Down below is the soccer field and the tennis courts.

The tennis match was against Sweet Briar–Fur-Patch College, and I have to say those girls were blonder, richer, classier. You could see it in their strokes. Their sneers. Oh, to have one of them in bed. This thin blonde with a good net game comes to mind. She was wearing glasses! Glasses on a girl can be very sexy.

One time, years ago, late at night on Rue St. Denis in Paris, which is lined with hundreds of whores (it's legal in Paris), I wasn't tempted by any of the women. I enjoyed looking, it was fun, sure, but I was impervious—wasn't going to waste my money, wasn't going to risk getting crabs or who knows what, even with a condom. So I watched the parade of my fellow men. The lonely suckers. There were probably a thousand men marching up and down the street for three hundred hookers. I was in the parade, but I was above it all. A voyeur. A writer observing life!

Then I saw this one wearing glasses. That did it. Had to have her. She was dark-haired and short. A sexy body. Full tits. A pretty face. But it was those cat-shaped black glasses. Oh, those glasses.

So we climb three flights to her horrible room. Low-ceiling. Slanted floor. Walls so thin you could trace a drawing; something like that. The room had seen too much sad fucking. I gave her the money. She told me to undress. I did what she told me. Then she washed my cock with a wet rag. Probably spread diseases on it. Anthrax. Put anthrax on my cock. Wait, this was 1989. That wasn't popular back then.

After the cock cleaning, she undressed. Her body all trussed up in bra and girdle and hoses and clamps and hidden steel beams came melting out. Tits all dead. A Caesarian scar and stretch marks on her belly. But I had already paid. She yanked my thing to life and put a condom on it. We lay down. I caught a glimpse of her bush underneath a roll of fat. She took her glasses off, remembering at the last moment, and put them on the little night table. No! I could handle the scar, the fat, the yanking, but I needed those glasses for my hard-on.

But I was too embarrassed to ask. I was young then. Now I know to ask for what I need. Especially when it comes to the hard-on. I deflated, but she grabbed my soft thing and got it in her. She gave a couple of fake moans and kicked her heels in my ass like a jockey. I squeezed a boob and pinched a tired brown nipple. I put my mouth on the nipple and it hardened. This little spark of real life from her, even if involuntary, made me get hard and when I got hard I came. It had lasted sixty seconds. I looked at the glasses on the night table. There's nothing worse than bad sex. Except bad sex that you've paid for. If only she had kept the glasses on.

Anyway, the blonde from Fur-Patch College. She had glasses. Thin gold frames. If I had her here in my little house right now on the hill, I'd take her from behind. That tennis lesson ass would push back far more intuitively. Yes, sweet girl. Push back for it. You sweet beautiful girl. I forgive you your sneer because you're a doll in bed.

Look over your shoulder at me with those glasses. You dear thing. You're wearing glasses but you're on your belly with your gorgeous ass in the air and your pussy taking me in. You're a beautiful female animal. We're play-acting at making babies. I love you!

Anyway, these Sweet Briar–Fur-Patch girls were beating my girls pretty handily. Wouldn't you know I end up at a poor man's all-girls college. But what the hell. Better to be here than not to be here. An all-girls college feels like a pretty safe place as we go to war.

I only reported here for duty two days ago. They needed a writer at the last minute. Well, a month ago. But for academia that's the last minute. Somebody recommended me and so they hired me without reading my books. They only read the resume, which looks good: Leon David, Yale '86, three novels. But they should have read the novels before letting me down here. I took the job because it's a one-liner for my friends. "I'm spending a month as writer-in-residence at this all-girls school." Gave everybody a laugh.

But I don't know if it's a laugh. I've masturbated nine times in 48 hours. That's way too much at my age, three years shy of 40. I look like I have two black eyes. I'm losing too much semen. All my nutrients are going out my cock. To hell with Afghanistan, I need the government to drop some food on *me*. Drop it on my cock. I'm so horny because I'm Jewish. Jews know their life is in danger all the time, that's why we're so horny. It's distasteful. We're about to get it in the neck again, I'm sure. I think Jews must have alien blood in them. Some alien screwed a sexy Jewess in the desert five thousand years ago. That's why we're hated. We're part alien. How else do you explain Einstein, Freud, Gershwin, and Lewinsky?

If Lewinsky hadn't been so horny and brainy, she never could have sucked Clinton's cock. Granted, he was a fairly easy target, but still, it took a lot of brains and chutzpah and sex drive to give the President of the United States a blowjob. She's the Einstein of sex. And if he hadn't been dealing with his blow-job impeachment, maybe he could have done something in the Middle East and we wouldn't be going crazy right now, bombing and getting bombed.

Well, it's all too much for me. And now it's lunch time. I've been writing for two hours, imagining Goolagong's pussy and remembering that French pussy and wanting that Fur-Patch girl's pussy. So I'm going to the dining hall where I'll be surrounded by 600 real vaginas. Not imaginary. Real. Delicious. Beautiful. All being sat on while the girls eat. Incredible. I'm in a womb shelter. Bring on the bombs.

8

DARREN ARONOFSKY

A First Kiss

How long does a first kiss last? In September 1997 it took 107 floors. How deeply I dug that girl. My heart beat fast, threatening to burst free. And that kiss was a wildfire. It exploded like a lit firecracker in your hand with an alarmingly short fuse.

I met her at a party, pre–dot com insanity, at a grungy pad on Park Avenue. Yes Park Avenue, no doorman, no luxury, the last of the great apartment finds before real estate prices downed too many lines of speed. Fifty slackers sucking on cheap drinks and seedy joints wondering if there was something better going on.

She was standing in the back of the room sucking on a hand-rolled cigarette. I should've guessed then that she was French. My stomach dropped. A moist sweat broke my brow.

I knew then that it would be another night of regrets. Meaning: I would never get the courage to even introduce myself. I watched her eyeing some other guy. All I could do was nervously play with the ripped lining of my granddad's old jacket. It had seen better decades but I couldn't seem to let it go. And now, it was my crutch. If I couldn't play with her, I could play with my coat.

But somehow it happened. I can't recall how. Suddenly, I was shaking her hand. Trying to decipher her broken English. And then, searching for a pen for her number.

Wednesday we planned to meet again. Wednesday. I wanted to show her this city I deeply loved. She was here for a week and I wanted to give her the night of her life. But how? Wednesday? What to do?

The solution is easy when you have Manhattan as an ally.

There was one great thing to do on Wednesday. Windows on the World, which as a kid was a stuffy over-priced nightmare, had somehow earned its hip wings. They pumped out a fantastic mix of tunes and the crowd was a deep blend of all kinds of New York characters.

The dance floor was filled with hipsters, foreigners, brokers, just about anyone you would expect on the D-Train crossing the Manhattan Bridge into Brooklyn.

And if the crowd failed, there was always the view.

Our first pecks happened while staring out a wall of glass. Even though we could only see gray clouds, the view was infinite. I draw her New York, Manhattan, Brooklyn, Coney Island, my home on a bar napkin. She draws me Paris in return. On the dance floor we connect.

There is magic and we need to escape. Time to hit the streets.

As we head for the exit I look for the coat check. But then, the elevator pops open. It is empty. Empty, not a soul. My granddad's coat. The coat check. You know what, it's really just a shitty coat. I grab her hand and rush the elevator.

"But . . ." she starts. Our eyes cut her off. Lips like magnets. The doors ease shut and we fall into each other as we fall to the lobby. 107 floors, ears popping, we kiss and we kiss. All I can do is laugh. Laugh. But still we kiss.

When the doors ping open the late summer chill hits our face. We separate for our first breath. She asks why I was laughing. Simple. Our first kiss was perfect. The perfect first kiss because it would've lasted forever if the earth didn't exist.

I never saw that jacket again. Sorry granddad.

C'est bon.

9

PAUL AUSTER

Random Notes—September 11, 2001, 4:00 P.M.; Underground

RANDOM NOTES—SEPTEMBER 11, 2001, 4:00 P.M.

Our fourteen-year-old daughter started high school today. For the first time in her life, she rode on the subway from Brooklyn to Manhattan—alone.

She will not be coming home tonight. The subways are no longer running in New York, and my wife and I have arranged for her to stay with friends on the Upper West Side.

Less than an hour after she passed under the World Trade Center, the twin towers crumbled to the ground.

From the top floor of our house, we can see the smoke filling the sky of the city. The wind is blowing toward Brooklyn today, and the smells of the fire have settled into every room of the house. A terrible, stinging odor: flaming plastic, electric wire, building materials.

My wife's sister, who lives in TriBeCa, just ten or twelve blocks north of what was once the World Trade Center, called to tell us about the screams she heard after the first tower collapsed. Friends of hers, who live on John Street, even closer to the site of the catastrophe, were evacuated by police after the door of their building was blown in by the impact. They walked north through the rubble and debris—which, they told her, contained human body parts.

After watching the news on television all morning, my wife and I went out for a walk in the neighborhood. Many people were wearing handkerchiefs over their faces. Some wore painters' masks. I stopped and talked to the man who cuts my hair, who was standing in front of his empty barber shop with an anguished look on his face. A few hours earlier, he said, the woman who owns the antique shop next door had been on the phone with her son-in-law who had been trapped in his office on the 107th floor of the World Trade Center. Less than an hour after she spoke to him, the tower collapsed.

All day, as I have watched the horrific images on the television screen and looked at the smoke through the window, I have been thinking about my friend, the high-wire artist Philippe Petit, who walked between the towers of the World Trade Center in August 1974, just after construction of the buildings was completed. A small man dancing on a wire more than a mile off the ground—an act of indelible beauty.

Today, that same spot has been turned into a place of death. It frightens me to contemplate how many people have been killed.

We all knew this could happen. We have been talking about the possibility for years, but now that the tragedy has struck, it's far worse than anyone ever imagined. The last foreign attack on American soil occurred in 1812. We have no precedent for what has happened today, and the consequences of this assault will no doubt be terrible. More violence, more death, more pain for everyone.

And so the twenty-first century finally begins.

UNDERGROUND

Riding the subway at a busy time of day—morning rush hour, evening rush hour—and having the good luck to find a seat. Counting the newspapers not written in English, scanning the titles of books and watching people read (the mystery of it, the impossibility of entering another person's mind), listening in on conversations, sneaking a look at the baseball scores over someone's shoulders.

The thin men with their briefcases, the voluminous women with their Bibles and devotional pamphlets, the high school kids with their forty-pound textbooks. Trashy novels, comic books, Melville and Tolstoy, *How to Attain Inner Peace.*

Looking across the aisle at one's fellow passengers and studying their faces. Marveling at the variety of skin tones and features, floored by the singularity of each person's nose, each person's chin, exulting in the infinite shufflings of the human deck.

The panhandlers with their out-of-tune songs and tales of woe; the fractious harangues of born-again proselytizers; the deaf-mutes politely placing sign-language alphabet cards in your lap; the silent men who scuttle through the car selling umbrellas, table cloths and cheap windup toys.

The noise of the train, the speed of the train. The incomprehensible static that pours through the loudspeaker at each stop. The lurches, the sudden losses of balance, the impact of strangers crashing into one another. The delicate, altogether civilized art of minding one's own business.

And then, never for any apparent reason, the lights go out, the fans stop whirring and everyone sits in silence, waiting for the train to start moving again. Never a word from anyone. Rarely even a sigh. My fellow New Yorkers sit in the dark, waiting with the patience of angels.

10

JENNIFER BELLE

Gelato Is Gelato

Estelle stood at the front of the room in her black pants outfit with her signature brooch—a different one every week sparkling at her ample breast. "Hello I'm Estelle" was written in red magic marker on her giant pad standing on its easel. Her big square hands with their girlish diamond engagement ring were clasped together.

It was September 18, one week since the World Trade Towers had gone down.

"Are there any new members joining today?" Estelle asked in her Jewish New York accent.

No hands went up. Estelle looked very grave.

I had just come from therapy where my shrink said that the people who jumped from the towers were in an out of body state, a state of ecstasy, drugged from adrenaline, not in a regular state, not in a state that we could ever understand. As they jumped, they might have even thought they could fly. I was deeply comforted.

One by one the women in the group raised their hands and said how much weight they'd gained since September 11. Two pounds, three pounds, five pounds, eight pounds. Rounding down, I had gained three myself. Not in a regular state.

Estelle had been a leader for over thirty years. She was over seventy years old. She had maintained a "realistic goal weight" —meaning, she was fat but she thought she was thin. I loved Estelle. She was the personification of everything I wanted to be when I was her age. She was blonde. She had a good body-image. She was wildly in love with her husband. She took pride in controlling her portions.

I had never seen Estelle so serious. In all her years, she had never faced a Weight Watchers crisis like this one.

When the last person had spoken, Estelle remained silent for a few moments. Finally she spoke.

"A bagel is a bagel," she said.

Everyone sat, transfixed.

"And gelato is just gelato."

A few people started slowly nodding.

"And ice cream is just ice cream, and a cake is just a cake, and a hamburger is just a hamburger, and French fries are just French fries, and a bag of Pirate's Booty is just a bag of Pirate's Booty. . . ."

"And I ate them all," I said, without thinking. Everybody laughed causing me to flush with pleasure.

"Good!" she said. "If it makes you feel better—eat!"

We all sat there stunned.

"What's wrong with eating? If you come to my house right now you'll find every kind of ice cream and cookie there is."

I was shocked. This was too much information. She had told us what she ate for breakfast every morning—½ cup bran cereal, 1 cup skim milk, ½ cup blueberries. She had told us that she had gotten rid of all her dinner plates and replaced them with salad plates so her portions would appear bigger. She had told us that while her husband has one cup of ice cream for dessert she has 2 Sweet Sensations or ½ cup of fat free frozen yogurt. But she had never given us such a complete look into her refrigerator before. Opened her cupboards up wide. Estelle was our leader. I revered her, to the point of worship. And now she was standing naked and vulnerable before us.

"Really," Estelle insisted, "come to my house right now. I have enough kinds of ice cream so every one of you could take your pick. Does anyone here like brownies?"

There were gasps. It was anarchy. I imagined the procession. We would leave the Temple on Twelfth Street and follow Estelle, past the Fourteenth Street barricades, to her apartment in Turtle Bay. The enormous woman in the wheel chair would lead, followed by the rest of us, waving our pointsfinders, bookmarks, gold stars, and keyrings, although I personally had never earned a single star. When we got there, she would serve us enormous brownies on tiny plates.

Never had I felt more respect for Estelle. Or anyone for that matter. I knew what it must be like to enter Socrates' symposium.

"Eat!" she said. "Do whatever it takes to make yourselves feel better."

Someone laughed nervously.

"In my lifetime," she said, "I never thought we'd see another holocaust."

I stayed in bed the rest of the week eating and watching television. A week was just a week. A chip was just a chip. I couldn't wait to go back to Weight Watchers and weigh in. A pound was a pound. Two pounds were two pounds. A state of ecstasy.

But when I went back to Weight Watchers the old Estelle was back. The anarchy had ended. But we wouldn't ever be the same. Estelle had said, "Eat!" and for a moment I had known what it felt like to be completely free, to be thin, to fly.

It was like Hitler opening the camp gates. It was like my shrink telling me to just go ahead and kill my parents.

"Think of all the people who died in the towers who were on Weight Watchers, working hard to follow the plan, keeping track of their points," Estelle said. I imagined a secretary whose last meal was a Just 2 Points Bar.

"They would have wanted us to stay on the program," one woman said, wiping tears from her eyes.

"Do it for them," Estelle said.

11

JENIFER BERMAN

Prologue: The Book of John

The afternoon light is beginning to fade and when she enters the room it smells of surprise. Across the wide-plank floor he is sitting upright in bed. He is propped up against the pillows. He is bloated and blue. The stain of his skin shocks against the neatly pressed linen and as she crosses the room her steps are short and hesitant. She has never seen a dead person before. She has never seen a newborn either, but in the half-distorted light of dusk this mass of muscle, blood, and bone looks like a foal fresh from its amniotic sac.

When she reaches the bed she pokes him gently. Her finger recoils, frightened by his skin, and it seems to her that he has been dead for quite awhile. His eyes are flat and gray. They are the color of a snowstorm and they stare up at the ceiling where a watermark is causing the paint to peel. She follows his gaze. Up through the clouds where a storm is brewing and his mouth is open in a tiny question. There is mint on his breath. It is a clean, comforting smell, but other than that death has made him unfamiliar: his thick jowls and prickly ears; his fingers broad, almost webbed like a duck's; his fingernails bruised like the skin of a plum.

Her stomach rumbles. The storm is nearing. She can see it in the sky, in its shapeless clouds and the ominous still of its long inhale. This is a sky that holds all the world's suffering, holds all its splattered blood and wounded fatigue. It is a sky as open and wide as a battlefield, muddy and writhing and loud with death. And she can see the soldiers, see them clutching their souls and tearing at their bandages and moaning at their nurses to provide them some relief. And she can hear them too, the nurses, with their thin, cool voices as they slap cold skin to locate a clean vein. This is a sky that holds all the weariness of the world. It is numb, and vacant. It stares through you like an echo.

For that, she thinks, is all he is now. An empty reverberation, just a collective of molecules hovering in time. Once he was a man and now he is a congregation lost of his parishioners. There are the objects, of course: a wedding ring, a pocket watch, an assiduously cared for brush set. But in the fading mist these articles hold little weight. Once they may have defined a life, but now they merely hover without meaning. Without the backdrop of history, without a narrative, a story, this man is doomed to become merely an outline. Even she is forgetting, and without the proper documentation he is doomed to become a child's game of telephone, a birthday party amusement that without someone to decipher makes no sense at all.

12

CHARLES BERNSTEIN

Report from Liberty Street

I took a walk on Liberty Street today. Only it was not the same place as I had known before.

They thought they were going to heaven.

Large crowds surge inside the police barricades, stretching to get a glimpse of the colossal wreck. All that remains of the towers is two lattice facades standing upright amidst the rubble.

These vast and hollow trunks of steel are mocked by the impervious stare of the neighboring buildings that loom, intact, over the vacant center.

National guard troops, many no more than teenagers, stand over us, the dazzled onlookers, the voyeurs of the disaster, shouting gruffly, yet with a strange and unexpected kindness, "move on, move on, can't stop here."

We look on, perhaps not yet ready for despair, against our stronger instincts, which well up, boundless and bare.

They thought they were going to heaven.

There are so many troops that the metaphor of a war zone dissolves into an actuality.

Liberty Street is an occupied zone. We have occupied ourselves.

At Pier A on the Battery, there are two giant Apple "Think Different" ads with blown-up pictures of FDR and Eleanor Roosevelt, who preside over the scene with unflinching incomprehension.

Across the way, the sign on the almost completed "The Residences" at the Ritz-Carleton Downtown says: "Live in Legendary Luxury/Occupancy Fall 2001/Spectacular Views."

They thought they were going to heaven.

At the checkpoint at Bowery and West Street, four soldiers inspect the passes of every vehicle wanting to go north and there is an endless stream of cars, buses (filled with workers), pick-ups, dumpsters, flatbeds. Even police in uniform show their IDs to the soldiers.

Battery Park has become a military staging ground, filled with jeeps and tents and soldiers in combat fatigues.

Because the park is closed, it's impossible to get to the Museum of Jewish Heritage: A Living Memorial to the Holocaust.

They thought they were going to heaven.

If downtown seems oddly detached, out of time or frozen in it, one of the most affecting sites is at the Times Square subway station. Around the cold tile columns in the central atrium of the station, people have put up dozens of home-made signs, each with a picture of someone. They say missing, but not in the sense of "looking for" but rather—*feeling the loss*. The grief surrounding these columns is overwhelming and we look on as if hit by a wave of turbulence. Yet, despite the votive lights and candles in coffee mugs, which, remarkably, the transit authority has left undisturbed, these are secular shrines, in the most pedestrian and transient of all places in the city.

We are overwhelmed by explanations for things that, at the visceral level, can't be rationalized. Anyway not yet or not quite. Almost everyone I know is on their own particular edge, our preset worldviews snapping into place like a bulletproof shield on one of James Bond's cars. Only the presets aren't quite working, which makes for an interesting, if unhinging, shimmer at the edges of things.

We hear a lot of one song from 1918 by Irving Berlin, but not a hint of "How Deep Is the Ocean" or "Let's Face the Music and Dance" much less "You Can't Get a Man with a Gun."

They thought they were going to heaven.

The movies keep playing in my head. Not *Towering Inferno;* but, do you remember in *Fail-Safe* where the President, played by Henry Fonda, launches a nuclear attack on New York to show the Russians that the U.S. attack on Moscow was a mistake? "Mr. Chairman," Fonda tells his Russian counterpart, "My wife is in New York today on a shopping trip and I have her on the phone right now . . . Mr. Chairman, the phone has gone dead."

So it's almost no surprise to see someone with a tee-shirt that says "What Part of Hatred Don't You Understand?"

I guess when two planes filled with passengers and tanked up with more fuel than it takes to get my moped from here to Mars and back hits skyscrapers with 20,000 people in them, it doesn't take a political scientist to know there's a lot of hate there.

The scary thing is that maybe what they hated most about America is not the bad part.

They thought they were going to heaven.

I find myself walking around making up arguments in my head, but when I try to write them down they dissolve in a flood of questions and misgivings. I value these questions, these misgiving, more than my analysis of the situation.

A new sport is checking not what stores have put up flags but which ones don't. Still, there is one Afghani joint in midtown that has no flag in sight. Stu and I head over to try out the lamb kebab.

Cowards? The seeming cowardice is not in the action but in the refusal to take responsibility for the action; it's strategic rather than tactical. Not cowards. Men of principle.

They thought they were going to heaven.

"We got what we deserved" a shrill small voice inside some seems to be saying. But surely not *this* person, nor *this* one, not *this* one, nor *this* one.

Nor *this* one.

No one deserves to die this way. I think that goes without saying and yet I feel compelled to say it.

Even if "we" and "they" have felled many, too many (any is too many) in this way.

Not people willing to die for a cause (a fairly large group), nor even those willing to kill for a cause (also a fairly large group), but people willing to do *this* (a relatively small group).

They thought they were going to heaven.

Still, I don't think this form of monstrousness is only "out there." We have our own domestic product. We call it KKK or Timothy McVeigh, Lt. Calley or Dr. Strangelove.

They thought they were going to heaven.

Manhattan as transitional object: Both my parents were born and grew up in New York, their parents having found sanctuary here from places that proved . . . inhospitable. The ghosts of these transplanted souls, along with the ghosts of their many compatriots, haunt the Holy Warriors with a fury that drives them to seek refuge through the Gates of Hell.

The question isn't is art up to this but what else is art for?

They thought they were going to heaven.

"The lone and level sands stretch far away."

(September 18–October 1)

13

STAR BLACK

Perfect Weather

I

The sky was so clear, the morning beautiful,
the weather fair, neither hot nor cool, the tower
a flame far down the avenue, a white smokestack
seen at eye-level, a huge, multi-alarm fire

firefighters attend to, and then, like the descent
of chalk on a blackboard behind all that is remembered,
behind the mind, behind the apprehended,
a sight without reference, the building

ended. The next burned as a thick candle
and then there was no candle and everyone was
quiet and the traffic ended and the tunnels

closed and the trains stopped and the phones
were busy and the children showed up, finally, finally,
and there was no snow like long ago. No beautiful snow.

II

So many walked and walked and did not talk.
All dressed for the office. There were no offices.
All dressed for construction. There was no construction.
The bus drivers drove until there were no buses.

Those who talked could not say much. All talk
was no television. Nothing was rushed; midtown
was quieted by a formal mutation between what will be
and what was. What was was a café,

what was was clear water, what was
was a supermarket with so many shoppers,
the cashiers as busy as the cashiers one remembers,
and the clarity of air; that, too, was familiar,

but now it was all that was there: trapped
desks in a dark cloud rising in the clarity of air.

BREYTEN BREYTENBACH

14

New York, 12 September 2001

Then it went dark. Real dark.
Like snow.
—words of a survivor

will the hand endure moving over the paper
will any poem have enough weight
to leave a flightline over a desolate landscape
ever enough face to lift against death's dark silence
who will tell today?

the huge anthill of people remains quiet
somber and shrill, bright and obscure
as if the brown effluvium of sputtering towers
still sweeps the skyline with a filthy flag
who will tell today?

today images wail for voice behind the eyes
planes as bombs stuffed with shrapnel of soft bodies
then the fire inferno flame-flowers from skyscrapers
human flares like falling angels from the highest floor
down, down all along shimmering buildings of glass and
steel
weightless and willowy and flame-winged streamlined
reflections fleeting in the fugitive language of forgetting
the hellhound of destruction has a red tongue of laughter

who will tell?
gouged eyes do not understand that the sky is blue
through the dismal and chilly nuclear winter
people stumble people shuffle
stumble-people shuffle-people worm-white-people
where are the faces
old before their ending or their wedding
greyed in ashes from head to toe
as if clothed in the coats of the snowing knowing of ages

beneath rummage and debris rosy corpses move and
mumble
and in the East River confidential files and folders float
with shreds and feathers lacerated human meat
scorched confetti for the dog's feast

who will tell tomorrow tomorrow
where are the faces
will the tongue still think
still pulse its dark lair
with the flaming memory of bliss
will any poem some day ever carry sufficient weight
to leave the script of scraps recalling fall and forgetting
will death remain quivering in the paper

MELVIN JULES BUKIET

15

from Manhattan Rhapsody

Start at the beginning, which is to say the edge, the perimeter, the shore. That's where all but the babes of my bedrock start. And even those delivered atop my Mount Sinai like commandments, dropped in the basement of my Beth Israel like laundry, discharged from my own Columbia Presbyterian or debouched out of the fifth floor maternity ward of my Cabrini, or midwifed in tenements or, a recent trend, penthouses, those who slide between the blood-soaked thighs of mothers strapped on stirrups, squatting on three-legged oak stools, or, a more recent trend, afloat in pools of lukewarm, bio-energized fluid, all of them, they all commence their lives no more than a mile from that magic line where the water meets the land, because that's as far as I ever depart from the twin rivers and amniotic bay that surrounds me.

An island always implies a shore; sandy, stony, spanned by greasy timbers or a perforated steel grid, it's always distinct and distinctively unlike those stupid sprawling Houstons or sophisticated sprawling Parees that just dribble into their tedious suburbs. Even a tunnel that appears to crown inland—voilá!—rather like the infant's own arrival, regal or meager, depending on their bearers' circumstance and the endowment of the institution that hosts them—has actually broken through from liquid to solid substrate several blocks prior.

Less so now than four, three, two or a mere one hundred years ago, amphibians still inhabit the few remaining shallows of my banks where they have not been filled-in, built-up, buttressed and macadamized over time. Generations of hearty, semi-mutated frogs and snakes have adapted to the oil-slicked tidal pools that lap wistfully at pockets of earth that fall between the jurisdictions of my Housing and Highway authorities. Just a few feet here, nearly half a block there; it's sufficient. My amphibs are tough; they have to be. I'd like to see the Calaveras County champion try to hop across the FDR Drive. Splat!

I'll stake my toads against any torpid country pond dwellers any day. Imagine a contest in the arena of choice, my choice. "Take me to the Garden," I'll say, and I won't care if it's the original gilt-encrusted, velvet-seated wedding cake actually located on Madison Square or the cigar-scented, wooden-seated version that presided over Eighth Avenue between 50th and 51st Streets between 1925 and 1968 or the current—and, if I and Patrick Moynihan have our say, eventually former—antiseptically smokeless, plastic-seated incarnation above the antiseptically smokeless, plastic-seated Penn Station that took the place of Stanford "Take him from the Garden" White's glorious temple of the rails.

Mind you, I'm no liberal landmarker who gets weak-kneed at the sight of a cornice or egg and dart moldings. It's not the old for old's sake that interests me. I'll tear down the great as well as the humble, a twenty-story hotel along with a dumbbell tenement, but only to make room for something grander yet. Remember, the Waldorf once stood on the site of the Empire State Building, which before that was the site of my first millionaire's daughter's country house when 34th Street was the Hamptons. I'll take stature in any form, be it mock-Caracolla, chrome deco or Gehry garish, a platinum contraption that will also have its day and give way to a successor simultaneously inconceivable and inevitable. As long as the show remains the same. Mud wrestling for the masses. Bulging-throated guys and spotted dolls. If they can make it here, they can make it anywhere.

But winners as they are, it's not my frogs that are my most beloved or most successful species in ecological terms. I'll admit that the frogs of Madagascar have mine beat in population density and reproductive rate. No matter, sheer numbers don't matter to me. Once upon a time, I had those, too, but recently Sao Paulo, Mexico City, and Tokyo have surpassed me in objective categories like human population and spawn ratios. So, imminently, will a dozen other awful third-world cities, Seoul, Lagos, and Bombay and a bunch of unpronounceable Chinese metropolies. Big deal. It's other things that count. It's big deals that count. It's money and power and energy. Not energy reserves like those under Caracas or Riyadh, or manufactured energy sources like Three Rivers Dam or Chernobyl, but expended energy, human resources, the kind that's here today, gone today.

Call me impatient. Call me immature. Blame my upbringing. I spent the first couple of billion years of my existence in isolation from everything except the weather. Boiling magma, glacial ice. I didn't even know what years were. But neither did the dunes where the pyramids would rise or the flats between the twin rivers of the Fertile Crescent, or the shore of Phoenicia. They're prior, I've got to admit that. First out of the box; best yet to come. While they were weaning the species that would finally redeem, exalt and define me, I was still alone except for mitochondria. Then came bacteria and frogs as well as bears and turkeys and mosquitoes.

Speaking theologically, I spent the first twenty-three hours of the sixth day of creation alone while the creature that I hadn't yet been introduced to made his way from Olduvai Gorge to Sumer to Rome—there's an ancestor worth recognizing—to Genoa and Amsterdam and London from whence he set sail with the aim—evolutionarily thinking—of finding me, the only place where he could truly find himself. And then there was man. Woman, too, eventually, but not at first. No, at first it was man. Lenapi.

16

PETER CAREY

Union Square

That evening we are standing on the corner of Houston and 6th Avenue watching the huge earth moving equipment and heavy trucks rolling, bumper to bumper, in a never-ending parade down towards the devastation. Here is the endless might and wealth of America. Here are the drivers, like soldiers, heroes. These are not military vehicles, but huge trucks from small companies in Connecticut and New Jersey, from Bergen and Hackensack. Seeing all these individuals rise to the crisis, with their American flags stuck out windows and taped to radio aerials, I am reminded of Dunkirk. I am moved. We are all moved. The crowds come out to cheer them. I do too, without reserve.

This is the same corner where we will soon be lighting candles for the dead and missing, where my eleven-year-old Charley and I will stand for twenty silent minutes watching those photographs of lost firefighters, wives, mothers, fathers, sons. It's hard not to cry. We watch the tender way our neighbors lay flowers and arrange the candles. We do not know the people in these pictures, but we do know our firefighters. We shop with them. We wait in line at the supermarket while they buy Italian sausage and pasta for their dinner.

Pleasant hoarse-voiced Jerry from the laundromat is there on the corner. He is always on the street, but tonight he wears a stars and stripes bandana and he cannot be still. He has three grown-up sons downtown right now, working in that perilous pile of deadly pick-up sticks. Jerry and I embrace because what else is there to do. When one of his sons almost loses his hand it is miraculously sewn on by microsurgery. I am praying, says Jerry, there is just a lot of praying to do.

Everywhere people are touched by death. Our friend David across the road has lost his best friend, the father of a brand-new baby. Silvano the restaurateur has lost a fireman friend already, and as Charley and I walk out of our immediate neighborhood we are dismayed to see the huge piles of flowers outside the tiny fire station on West 3rd Street. The station was always so small, it looked like a museum. But now we stand, Charley and I, and we close our eyes and say a prayer, although I don't know who I'm praying to. There is no God for me.

I have to be outside, amongst the people. It is all that gives me any peace. I want to stand in the deli by the radio. There I can be with my neighbors. We touch, embrace, cry, are half-wild with anger. Everybody's emotions are very close to the surface.

One night—which night?—my 15-year-old Sam says he wants to walk around the city. He wants to see Union Square where there is the biggest massing of candles and memorials. We walk along Houston Street which is now a war zone, huge trucks from the New York Housing Authority stand in readiness to remove the rubble. We head east and then north. He is taller than me now, and likes to put his arm paternally around my shoulder.

As we walk he says to me, apropos of nothing, I love this city.

We walk to Union Square and I am proud of the complex, multi-faceted way Sam is talking about these events. He is concerned that local Muslims may be victimized because of our anger, cautious about retaliatory bombing, but mad too, like I am. The notion of fleeing does not cross either of our minds, not for a second.

We stand amongst the extraordinary shrine at Union Square where nuke-crazed groups stand next to pacifists, all united by their grief.

We see so many people whom we know. The sweet-faced man from our post office whose continually lowered eyes have always given him a rather bemused and almost beatific expression, comes out of the dark to embrace me.

As for my own feelings, I am more vindictive than my son. I want to strike back, pulverize, kill, obliterate anyone who has caused this harm to my city. I may be Australian to the core but I have become like the dangerous American the world has most reason to fear. This phase passes quickly enough. It has passed now. But on those first days and nights I was overcome with murderous rage.

Once, a year or so ago, I heard my son saying, "When we bombed Iraq."

"No," I said, "When THEY bombed Iraq."

"No," he said, "We."

I have joked about this moment often, but in truth it put a chill in me. I was very happy for him to be a New Yorker, but I wasn't sure I wished him to be American.

But on the second day after the attack on the World Trade Center, the day Sam turned fifteen, I bought him a large white T-shirt with an American flag on its front. Sam is a very hard guy to buy a T-shirt for, but this shirt he put on immediately, and then we went out together again, out into the dark, out amongst the people, giving ourselves some strange and rather beautiful comfort in the middle of all the horror that had fallen on our lives.

"I love this city, dad. I love it more than ever."

I did not disagree with him.

LAWRENCE CHUA

17

The Quick and the Poor

In Milan, it was hot and the streets were narrow. They turned in on themselves and meandered in unobvious patterns. He went looking for the Pinacoteca and wound up in the wrong one on the other side of the city. When he discovered his mistake, he walked rapidly to the correct museum, a painting gallery on the second floor of an art school, but it was too late. The student working at the door was a skinny boy with curly, unwashed hair and thin spectacles who told him that the museum was closed for lunch. He turned from the student and walked out onto the crooked streets, cursing the indulgence of it all, the lunch hours, the museum, the country, the world. He hated how it all went on, how people had lunch when his father was dead. His father was dead for only a week now and it was indecent how the world kept turning in his absence.

He went to a bar and drank a San Bitter Rosso with tonic water while standing up. It was a bright red drink that refreshed his eyes and it had a sober and abstinent taste. The bartender poured the drink but did not look at him. The bartender was arguing about a football game with an old man who looked like a regular customer. The old man listened quietly to the bartender's excited voice. Occasionally, the old man offered soft, quick replies that drove the bartender into irritated fits of language.

When he finished his drink, he left the bar without saying good-bye and walked around the streets killing time until the museum reopened. He looked at the old facades of the city, the well-swept bars and the restaurants with lunch-stained linens.

He wished there were some evidence there to mark his father's passing. His father had died quick and poor, leaving behind nothing but some papers and an old silver-plated watch, nothing of value and nothing of worth. A writer who once roamed these same streets had written that men do not die like men. They die like animals. But that was a long time ago and the city was different then.

He walked back to the museum, but the lunch period had not yet ended and the guards gave him a hard time about coming in. They talked to him very quickly in Italian that he did not really understand. They pointed to a counter and the line of people forming behind it. Why would he wait in line? He had waited long enough. But there is no justice in the world, and in the end he waited like all the others waited to buy a ticket to the Pinacoteca. There was a famous painting there that he wanted to see. He stood in line and watched the guards and was angry that they were keeping him from seeing this painting.

He entered the museum, finally, resenting even the young woman with quiet half-lidded eyes who took his ticket. He went searching for the famous painting. He did not have far to go. The painting pulled him into its orbit. It was the first painting he really stood in front of and looked at that day.

It was a painting of a man lying with his eyes closed and a sheet across his naked waist. His feet stuck out from under the sheet, and the soles of the feet faced the viewer. There were wounds on the man's feet. Above the knees, the man's soft penis stirred under the cloth. Lean, dull flesh curled around the man's rib cage and his face was the color of something that no longer had breath. There were wounds on the hands also, and if one looked at the holes clearly enough, one could catch a glimpse of something moving just out of reach. In the corner of the painting, three faces leaned towards the man. They appeared to be crying, but they were not really crying at all. There was something unreasonable about their sadness, its pretense.

He looked at the mourners and the man for a while, and then he saw that the man's legs were too short for the rest of his body. This is wrong, he said, and he put his fingers in front of the man's legs to measure their relationship to the rest of his body. This is totally wrong.

An alarm went off, a little bird whistle. An attendant walked over to where he was standing with his fingers splayed in the empty air before the painting. He could hear her footsteps falling on him. It was the woman with dull eyes and she said something to him that he did not understand. She motioned to the painting and the space between it and him and him and her. He looked at her and his voice was no longer impatient. Yes, he said. Yes. I know how to look at a painting.

18

IRA COHEN

Holy Smoke

Taking Tuesday back
or removing the black figure
from the constellation of Karma
would only condemn us to experience
again and again the time loop of history
as in the relentless barrage of TV sets
in a world without an audience.
"There is something in the air," you said
dreaming of a plane crashing into
the twin towers of Nostradamus,
nor was there any security when you took
your flight back across the Atlantic
a week later.
A shudder in the loins engenders there
the broken wall, the burning roof and tower
and Agamemnon dead . . .
Walking up the stairs the fire fighters
could not put out the fire from the heavens
Black smoke encircled the crowns &
the heat passed even Dante's depiction
of the Inferno's daily routine.
What is the way to true Reconciliation?
What is it that we must reconcile
to break the chain of our own making?
How to lure the Lightbringer back to
Paradise?
Don't expect answers from the man with the bullhorn.

Ask the Shambala Masters or David
Carradine, the Kung-Fu champion—
Remember Bamiyan & the blown up head of Buddha!
It will take detachment to detach.
Attachment will only take us straight
                                        into the trap,
there where all the bullion lies buried
below the 3000 dead.
P.S. The money goes through Switzerland.

September 17, 2001

19

IMRAAN COOVADIA

The Same Tune

Finding the right tone for a piece, any writer can tell you, belongs to the core of discovery which interesting writing requires. Tone, which is another name for irony as well as for confidence, measures the distance between author and subject. Even when it varies from paragraph to paragraph, it does so within given limits. The sense of tonal consistency is one of the real pleasures of reading, and, I think, writing, because it reassures us that the experience which the book encodes has been managed, and that the world it regards is basically intelligible. The planes which crashed into the World Trade Center on September 11, 2001, simultaneously crashed into our capacities for such reassurance. After the disaster, for many weeks, it was and continues to be impossible to concentrate, read, or write, or imagine as before. These abilities are only slowly being restored as we rescue all that which makes us whole as writers and citizens. This includes, above all, a sense of proportion, also finding the right tone, and a tacit faith in the infinite future.

Although I am having trouble since September 11 leaving reality for the happier but more uncertain regions of my second novel, I have little trouble writing about my son, maybe because only a part of him belongs to reality. The rest is composed of something far more interesting. I have the good fortune to be the father of a child who is all or half Jewish, half Russian, and half a New Yorker (on his mother's side) and all or half Muslim, half Indian, and half South African (on his father's side). You will see that the fractions add up to more than one hundred percent, which, I feel, is as it should be. He connects, on all six sides, people with six-sided political leanings and affiliations.

I want Zaheer Zev Ostashevsky Coovadia, with all of his beautiful syllables, to grow up in a world where religious war, jingoism, cultural conflict have gone extinct, so that his compacted name makes sense to everyone, and not only his parents. Zaheer, in Arabic, means manifestation or shining object, and—according to Jorge Luis Borges—an infinitely elusive thing that fascinates the mind and never escapes memory. Zev, in Hebrew, stands for wolf. My son is fourteen months old when I am writing this, still on his milk teeth, so there should be time to arrange this, after the present emergency, when the damage these acts have done to trust and religious harmony can begin to be mended. He, who will grow up to embody a name that embodies more than the sum of its parts, is the multi-fractional reason I cannot doubt that amazing promise made about the United States—the promise found not in the Constitution but in the words of the American poet of "love and relationship," Walt Whitman, who dedicated this country to be, now and forever, the "teeming nation of nations."

20

EDWIDGE DANTICAT

on the day of the dead

this November 2 feels like the 2nd day of the dead
the other one came too soon so we had no time to prepare
no time to call on la flaca, the lady of the dead
no time to call on le bawon, the guardian of the cemetery
no time to clean the gravesites, yank the weeds
repaint the mausoleums and cover the tombstones
with garlands of cockscomb or beds of carnations
or wreaths of marigold, the flower of four hundred lives
no time to make pan de muerto or pen patat for our deceased
or pour tequila or babancourt rum as libation on their heads
no time to set off fireworks to rouse our angelitos
or ti lezanj from their premature rest
no time to burn incense to lure them back this way
if only for a while
no time to gather up a wash basin, a towel and soap
for them to bathe if ever they should return
no time for a mariachi or rara band to think up a good song
only time for llorada—the weeping
only time for kriz—convulsions the body uses to mourn
only time for the plaintive chime of somber church bells
only time to recite the rosary under our breaths
only time to ponder our three deaths
the one that happens when our breath leaves us to rejoin the air
the one that follows when we are given back to the earth
and the most final one of all
the one that ultimately erases us
when no one remembers us at all

ALICE ELLIOT DARK

21

Senseless

TV had become all war all the time, on every channel. Even when Clara surfed past the Shopping Network or MTV, condolences crawled across the bottom of the screen. For the first few days after the attacks she'd been obsessed with it; she'd turned the TV on the moment she got home and kept it on until she left again; kept it on during meals, baths, sleep (what little there was of that), and phone calls. She turned the sound down when someone called but kept her eyes on the screen, reading the latest, watching the buildings explode into fire and collapse over and over again. She'd never much liked the architecture of the World Trade Center, but it seemed disloyal to even remember her own private opinion of it now. So much seemed disloyal, including the amount of information she wanted. She was part of a group now, the large United States. She was supposed to be resolved, live her life, not worry too much. Yet her life had become infused with the dead, and to go on living, she had to know the daily tally. She couldn't remember where she'd left her keys, or if she'd taken her vitamins, but she kept track of that number. She believed—irrationally, stubbornly, grandiosely, and holding herself in contempt for so doing—that if she watched enough television and learned enough facts, if she controlled the information, there wouldn't be another attack. It was all up to her.

She cut back on her monitoring after running into two friends in the coffee line at Starbucks. They mentioned a development Clara knew nothing about.

"Where'd you hear that?" she snapped. There was electrical activity in her chest. Her friends inched backward, away from her competitiveness.

"NPR," they said.

NPR! She'd always avoided NPR. She didn't like the monotone, the low modulated voices that reminded her of the way adults spoke reasonably to children when they knew they could be overheard. Nor could she stomach the tacit accession to a certain angle on the news that everyone took, that whole East Coast liberal posture, which she found smug, even if she mostly agreed with it. But of course NPR would provide more coverage, more experts, more variety than the networks. Why hadn't she thought of it?

"What channel is that?" she asked.

The women exchanged a look. Clara White didn't know that?

As soon as she got her latté, she rushed to her car. It took only a second to locate the channel—there it had been all along, only a few clicks away from her usual station. She leaned back and listened to the monotone. The president said this, Ariel Sharon said that, Colin Powell was going to meet with such-and-such leaders. Clara was rapt, thrilled with the intimation of nuance and the degree of control suggested by this subdued stream of information. She felt the first real relief she'd had in days, the support for which she'd been longing. She wanted to be spoken to in this quiet, reassuring voice. She supposed she'd held it in disdain for so long because it was the very thing she wanted, and she was far too discerning to automatically allow herself that.

It was all settled then. She'd accede to NPR. Her friend Beth would laugh at the development, claim it as yet another of the unintended favors Osama had done for America, and Clara would laugh along with her, at herself. Then she'd drive around town with the low burr of Leonard Lopate and Terry Gross keeping her company, keeping her on her toes. She'd dutifully send in money to the local station. It was a plan; but when Clara turned the motor off, and there was a sudden silence in the car; and she was cut off from reports of what was happening; and she knew that the people who ran the world and the people who terrorized it were going about their business without her; and she felt utterly alone, with nothing reaching her ears except the sound of her own breath; she panicked, and quickly turned the radio back on. There it was, the calm burring voice, the one that knew everything. She tried to listen, to catch up, but her heart had begun to pound uncontrollably so she couldn't pay attention. *Stop,* she thought, *please slow down, please repeat that, go back to the beginning, I've missed too much, I don't know what's going on, please start over.*

Her pleas made no difference. The voice droned on. She snapped the radio off, and began to weep.

22

ERIC DARTON

The Therm

There was once a foolish merchant who—no, that is not how to begin. The way to begin is: The first time I saw the city, it was through a break in the trees on the opposite side of the river. Its walls reared up in tremendous grandeur, and though hardly in ruins, I knew at a glance that the city lay deserted, that it had once teemed with people, all bent on living well according to their various notions, and on getting rich when they were young, so they might never work thereafter, and spend their days instead in the spa, or by the thermal springs, either curing their trifling maladies, or preventing any such from taking hold. I could imagine, from where I stood, how they held their glasses beneath the spigots of healing water then sipped, and in the instant dropped their vessels with a crash into the trough below, so overcome were they with well-being. Yet this breakage was no disaster, for everywhere vendors sold glasses for a modest sum which could be fitted back again into a little wicker basket worn about the neck like a talisman, and which, bouncing against the breastbone as one walked, did greatly stimulate and tonify the heart.

Upon the simplest glasses incised marks at regular intervals showed how much water filled the vessel, and, after taking a draught, what measure remained, while the most luxurious had lines and numbers painted in black and gold, and, reflected in the bottom, a radiant image of the drinker at the pinnacle of his health and vital powers. Those who possessed the less ornamented glasses usually drank in sips, attempting—though the water flowed abundantly from the taps—to measure out each imbibing in conformance with the intervals cut in the glass, while the rich-glassed citizens often sought to drain their vessels at a single gulp for the pleasure of more quickly recognizing themselves in miniature shimmering below.

Now how do I know these things? I only know that I know that I know. For as I gazed across the river I saw many great buildings all clustered together, yet in a pleasing picture overall: the edges and openings were all of ashlar, and the rest laid in courses of ruddy brick that, set against the pale green of the willows and the deeper hues of the plane trees and pines, and lighted by the dawn, or indeed the sunset, gave rich play to the shadows, the bold arches and vaultings; and though the whole was too massed together to discern the proportions of particular structures and I, being no architect, could in any case only hazard after their logic, yet the place looked all of a piece, and one could scarcely imagine what had caused its people to abandon it.

Even in that instant the angle of the sun shifted so that the largest archivolt now appeared as an awning above a portal, and thinking to cross over, I looked up and down the bank for a boatman, yet saw none. But not far along the path, lay a boat moored and across it a long pole, and nearby a little box for offerings, and by such signs I gathered it was the boatman's day off and I would have to shift for myself.

To my surprise, the journey over was an easy one, and the boat rode stable, so I never feared to capsize. The pole found a firm bottom and did not threaten to stick fast as it can in some treacherous lagoons, and though the river flowed vigorously, I encountered no violent currents, and so was able to steer without difficulty to a ready docking, and there 'lighted whereupon —and here I am sure I will try your belief in the veracity of my telling—the boat turned about of its own accord and poled back the way it had come. And when I yelled "hi!" and clapped my hands, it stopped and turned a jot as though to signify that it would willingly return for me at any time I desired it.

The quays I found entirely devoid of life, but passing under some vaulting, seeing everywhere writ *Water! Health! Life!*—which though it was in dialect and mighty stylized, I recognized the meaning of—I soon found myself in an arcaded square, the four sides of it identically façaded, a fountain at the center, and at every corner a tap, so that water was provided from five sources. Most pleasant of all was to see that not only did the springs run plentifully, but that at every station stood lines of people: travelers, townsfolk, pilgrims, all with cups in hand and some of them leaning upon staves which they cast away immediately upon having drunk, so fast and furious that several boys employed themselves in scurrying about gathering and removing the discarded staves to who knows where, lest they become a hazard underfoot, and girls swept up the broken glass into numerous bins, and never have you seen such charming and proper children anywhere on the face of the earth.

I glanced about and saw that no one jostled and all waited patiently, yet not long, to imbibe, then thought I would fain get me a tumbler that I might drink too. Again, the sun shifted so that I saw clearly the stalls where I might purchase one, and eyeing the merchandise, settled on a glass of middling worth, whose bottom would not show my face, but turn the color of health when I had drunk, and so to the nearest spring. This happened to be the central fountain 'round which a line wound in a spiral, so that when I arrived at the source I was dizzy from circumnavigating it. I at once dipped my glass and finding it warmed my hand not a little, drank the water down at one draught.

Like all the others before me, as though seized by a paroxysm, I instantly let go my glass and saw it shatter into a thousand pieces in the trough by the basin. I did not see the little girl sweep it up for I fell backward into the arms of the man behind me, who caught my weight 'ere I touched the cobbles and set me back upon my feet.

"It is the warmest spring," he said in a sympathetic tone, as if by way of explanation, and indeed it was. Nor can I tell you more, but that the way to find the city is to search for a break among the trees by a riverbank, and that you should not be surprised if you lose hold of your glass the first time you drink before you can see into the bottom.

Afterwards, you will be able to grasp it long enough to recognize the colors of salubrity, or perhaps your own radiant face greeting you from within.

23

LYDIA DAVIS

Grammar Questions

Now, during the time he is dying, can I say, "This is where he lives"?

If someone asks me, "Where does he live?" should I answer, "Well, right now he is not living, he is dying"?

If someone asks me, "Where does he live?" while he is dying, can I say, "He lives in Vernon Hall"? Or should I say, "He is dying in Vernon Hall"?

When he is dead, I will be able to say, in the past tense, "He lived in Vernon Hall." I will also be able to say, "He died in Vernon Hall."

When he is dead, everything to do with him will be in the past tense. Or rather, the sentence "He is dead" will be in the present tense, and also questions such as "Where are they taking him?" or "Where is he now?"

Actually, then I won't know if the words "he" and "him" are correct, in the present tense. Is he, once he is dead, still "he," and if so, for how long is he still "he"?

People may say "the body" and then call it "it." I will not be able to say "the body" in relation to him because to me he is still not something you would call "the body."

People may say "his body" but that does not seem right either. It is not "his" because he does not own it, if he is no longer active or capable of anything.

I don't know if there is a "he," even though people will say "he is dead." But I see that it feels correct to say "he is dead." It may be that this is the last time he is still "he" in the present tense. But no, I will also say, "he is lying in his coffin."

I will continue to say "my father" in relation to him, after he dies, but only in the past tense, or also in the present tense? He will be put in a box, not a coffin. Then, when he is in that box, will I say, "That is my father in that box" or "That was my father, in that box" or will I say, "That, in the box, was my father"?

I will still say "my father," but maybe I will say that only as long as he looks like my father, or approximately like my father. Then, when he is in the form of ashes, will I point to the ashes and say, "That is my father"? Or will I say, "That was my father"? Then, will I say, "my father is buried there" or will I say, "my father's ashes are buried there" and if I say that, then do those ashes really belong to my father?

In the phrase "he is dying," the words "he is" suggest that he is actively doing something. But he is not very actively dying. The only thing he is still actively doing is breathing. He looks as if he is breathing on purpose, because he is working hard at it, and frowning slightly. He is working at it, but he surely has no choice. He breathes, and he frowns. Sometimes his frown deepens for just an instant, as though something is hurting him or as though he is concentrating harder. Even though I can guess why he is frowning, he still looks as though he dislikes or disapproves of something, or is puzzled. I've seen this expression on his face hundreds and hundreds of times, or thousands, in my lifetime, though never before combined with these half-open eyes and this open mouth. To me it looks deliberate, because it was always deliberate.

"He is dying" sounds more active than "he will be dead soon." That is probably because of the word "be"—we can "be" something whether we choose to or not. Whether he likes it or not, he "will be" dead soon. He will have to be dead soon, because he is not eating.

"He is not eating" sounds a little too active, too, because it is not his choice. He is not even conscious of it. He is not conscious at all. But "is not eating" sounds more correct for him than "is dying" because of the negative. "Is not" seems correct for him, at the moment anyway, because he looks as though he is refusing something, because he is frowning.

24

SAMUEL R. DELANY

Echoes

Against the echoes of our feet in the stairwell—she was coming up; I was going down, holding the banister, step at a time, with my cane—it brought back those seventeen months of cues in which they tried to get food to the prisoners without which they would have starved, and a woman who'd learned that the one beside her was Akhmatova leaned to whisper: "Can you write this . . . ?" with all the situations' intense differences, then, now.

In our stairwell, a decade younger than my soon-to-be-sixty, Lois looked up, smiled, stopped: "Hello, Chip. How are you? Ah . . . You know my daughter, Lois. She has the same name as mine. I was going to tell you this. Really, I'm so glad I ran into you. I know you've seen her in the building here: my daughter Lois—she's twenty-two. You know, she worked in the World Trade Center. She was engaged to a fireman. David, he was twenty-five."

"Is she all *right*?" Then I thought I was being too bumptious.

"Well, sort of. They were planning to get married, just this October. Her and David. That morning, three weeks ago, you know, because she wasn't feeling well, she called in about twenty to nine to say she would be coming in late that morning—maybe she would be there by ten-thirty. So, of course five minutes after she hung up, the first plane hit. At the firehouse David heard there was trouble; he didn't know she'd stayed home. He had his whole ladder company up and running down there to offer help and see what they could do—and, of course, to get her out of there. Well, when the buildings went down, he was killed—and the other boys. They were men, but I call them boys—because, you know, I'm fifty-two."

"Oh . . ." I said, as sincerely as I could, "Lois, that's . . . awful!" How many times that month did we say or think or write, "That's *awful*! How's Lois doing . . . ?"

"How do you think?" elder Lois said too quickly, this plump Latin woman with champagne-colored hair. "She's a basket case! She's seeing a therapist—but I don't know if it's doing much good. Oh, she just cries . . ." Lois shook her head. "David was going to get her a dog for a wedding present. They'd picked it out together, but it was going to stay in the kennel until they moved into their own place—this month, in October. Well, the other boys in the ladder company, the ones who were left—they got the dog for her and gave it to her. For David. Oh, Chip—I just don't know what to do for her. You're a writer, aren't you?"

"Yes. That's right."

Lois looked at me.

"I mean, do you think there is any way you could write . . . ? I mean, write something? To tell people that story? I don't know—I just would like it if people knew, somehow. That things like that happened." Lois shook her head again.

Over the next weeks I've thought of other things I would also like to write about: About Vince's Turkish wife, Asude, going back to Istanbul to help after the earthquakes. About a piece of music that made me stop and listen to it, as it tumbled out among a dozen unmemorable songs from the speakers beside my computer. About Boyd saying, "Write your story as simply as you can for the most intelligent person in the room." About why it is so much easier to tell Lois's mother's tale (which I have, among a dozen others, certainly more than a dozen times, now) than it is to write it. About how, at Paul's party where the two artists were about to do the video and computer demonstration of their memorial laser columns, the Iranian woman interrupted to ask us for a minute's silence for those bombed in her country. About crossing Broadway at

79th and going from bright sun into the shadow of a building, where—now that the light was off my dusty glasses—I saw people coming toward me over the street, and a smoky blue afterimage pulsed over the face of a young woman stepping off the corner, lighting a cigarette: Lois (Lois's daughter) smokes —I've seen her smoking in the stair; though not for three months.

But on the steps, I said to Lois (her mother, Lois), "Lois. You know. I don't really know—really. But. I mean, well . . ." Well, but, there is some of the story.

25

MAGGIE DUBRIS

The Ruin

Skies tapped this tower. Terror broke it.
The stairwells burst . . .

Cracked walkways, pillars fallen
The work of the welders, the steelsmiths
smolders
                Grime scours the great towers
                Grime on murder

Shattered the stone glass, beams broken
Time over-took them
                                        And the traders and titans?
Towergrip holds them—one by one
clasped in death's grasp, four thousand
sons have passed.

                                        West Wall stood
South Tower, sunstruck glass, rulers fell often,
stood under snow, a hundred floors crashed;
Stands yet the ground-steel, scorched by jetfuel,
by planes fear-flown
. . . gleamed the old great plaza
. . . shrunk to blown dust

Light where the lobbies, realms where tiles shone
radiant, rich-copper, such strong noise
these boisterous bars, bankers filled
with laughter, careless: Terror changed that.

Came a morning fire-drenched; from the skies men fell dead
Death gathered in its bright garland
Where they stood to save, vast graves
And at land's end, ruins

Those who would build again
turned to dust. Thus these streets are weary;
red fire, crackling curtains
of glass, once sky high, streaming downwards . . .
Scorched steel . . .

There many a traveler
heart glad, soul bright, stood smiling
cameras clicked, the flush of men come
to feast on men's marvels: on silver, on gold,
on futures told and traded, on light-filled avenues
on this sparkling city of song and celebration.
Flashed fevered light; wild jazz spilled
hot from the source, and the towers all caught
in its heaving heart; that the nights were
lit til deep dawn, that was fitting . . .

When young dreams, loosed, streamed over old stone
unto the dream-tank . . .

. . . It was a gleaming thing

. . . this city . . .

(This poem is patterned very closely on an Old English poem called *The Ruin*, a description of a deserted Roman city, probably the city of Bath, written about 300 years after the fall of Rome. The poem was found partially burned, and is one of the earliest surviving poems written in the English language.)

September 2001

26

RINDE ECKERT

Shorebirds Atlantic

Death has become regrettably commonplace, not the grand affair it was:
no long procession of mourners, no fabulous benedictions,
no commending of spirits or flaming pyres before the monumental stone gods,
no great communal outcry of grief for the dear departed souls.

To the casual observer, nothing out of the ordinary:
the sea comes and goes, shorebirds negotiate the surf.

Two people wait for the ebb-tide: one is a good swimmer, one is not;
but in the right light they might be mistaken for each other.

They met yesterday in a bar; he told her his tragic story.
This isn't fair, she said, we only just met.
This is Atlantic city, he said, you take your chances.

The wind comes up over a low wall, east by northeast I think.
What are those shorebirds? I ask
Terns, she says

We watch a marine throwing stones at incoming waves.

I see Atlantic city as a boy might: angles at war with the beach contours,
boardwalk old soldiers gripping the rail. They look seaward:

rheumy eyes, longing,
the whole bit.

Your cynicism is what's killing you, she says;
you're becoming expertly lonely, terribly wise.

Down at the water's edge, the marine is still killing waves
with salvos of smooth stones.

You know, she says, looking over her shoulder,
somewhere in this town there's a woman seated at a kitchen
table
with a felt pen, making an outline of her hand.
She thinks it looks like a blueprint for a fortification,
a great protection for the heart of a city.

You know, you're making a law of your pain, she says.
You know, he says, you're making a virtue of your fear.

We are looking out on the wine dark sea,
a confusion of epics, or domestic tragedies, associated . . . and
aloof.
This is the Atlantic, no great mystery
all trawlers and trade lanes . . . but the wind is up

It's a cancer, I say to her, straight across the table—
Still life: a white Russian, two fingers Johnny Walker, a bingo
card.
It's a degenerative disease . . . nothing can be done.

She smiles wanly: she's automatically sad; she cares automatically;
automatically I hate her for it and love her just the same

I see her as a flock of swifts or sparrows, myself a great rude-
ness at the margins,

nipping the small slow birds.

We are powerless against the innocent, I think to myself.

This isn't fair, she says, we only just met.
This is Atlantic city, I say, you take your chances.

I remember dark hair and windows from some winter in
  Minnesota; my voice trails off.

I've told her the tragic story; A man dying of cancer walks
  out over his head
before the pain becomes unbearable. A woman he just met
  watches him go while thinking
she really ought to save him.

She'll never be the same for this, he thinks; she'll back up the
  beach . . . disappear into Atlantic city . . . but she'll never be
  the same for this.

We're all in over our heads, I say, matter of fact.
This is nothing new, you're simply watching me walk out.

Death has become regrettably commonplace, not the grand
  affair it was:
no long procession of mourners, no fabulous benedictions,
no commending of spirits or flaming pyres before the monumental stone gods,
no great communal outcry of grief for the dear departed souls.

  Still life: Atlantic city bar, two strangers, a white Russian,
      two fingers Johnny Walker,
      a bingo card, a conversation:

Here are the rules:
You walk me down to the edge. You watch me wade out

I look back once to make sure. I disappear.

Very simple, she says, graceful in fact; but I'm afraid I'll find
it all too sad.
I'm afraid I'll try and save you. I'm afraid I'll run out to pull
you in.

No! This is how it'll go:
You'll stand your ground. You'll watch me pass. You'll say to
yourself:
This is a man I met yesterday in a bar who imagines his death
at the center of a great myth, himself a great stone monkey
sinking in the breakers, his sadness unimaginable to the
innocent city girls.

Did you come here as a kid; is that the draw—a return to
innocence?

No, it's the hot dogs, the gambling, the prostitutes, head
liners at the big houses, heroin addicts looking for a fill
card or a number-queen of spades, B-15
BINGO!—a barker with no fingers on one hand:

So where'd they go, Gramps?
"Cherry bomb, fourth of July, lit it and never let go, lit it and
held on
like a dumb shit, POW!-fingers all over New Jersey and miles
out.
But hell . . . Left me a life line goes clear around the back of
my hand says I'll live forever, I'll live for goddamn ever—
BINGO! BINGO!

Trouble is, I never learned to count past five . . .
but, hey, I'm perfect for the bingo business.

(he sings a wordless lament)

Let's go; the tide is out. There will be the daily deposit of
crusts and carapaces.
We can make a killing in small shells and fiddle crabs.

What happened to our tête-à-tête, we were comparing notes?

Yes, but I thought a walk among the dead would refresh our
memories

You know, she says at the edge of New Jersey,
you hold your hand in a fist when your face is cold.

I never was the man I used to be, I tell her.

Somewhere in Atlantic city a woman contemplates a paste-
board wall of outlines—with a felt pen she made the wall
positively sing with fingers.
Somewhere in Atlantic city a marine is punishing the water
with stones, one by one.
Somewhere in Atlantic city a barker with a blitzed hand sells
magic numbers to the hopeful; he counts himself lucky on
a big scallop of a scar.

I see Atlantic city as a boy might: angles at war with the beach
contours,
boardwalk old soldiers gripping the rail.
They look seaward: rheumy eyes, longing, the whole bit.

There we stand at the edge of New Jersey.

You know, she says, I can see myself some fabulous pudgy
matron gripping her apron bellied out with exotic shells.
She wades between the splashing children and a raft of uncles.

Hey look, I say, holding up a soggy bingo card . . .
the last of the virgin timber.

Hey look, she says, showing me a large luminous agate . . .
Hope!

(he laughs)

Thank god, I say, thank god some people never learn.

What did you call those shorebirds?, I ask

Terns, she says. Terns.

An epilogue:

> I met a man yesterday in a bar.
> He imagined his death at the center of a great myth.
> He saw himself a great stone monkey sinking in the breakers,
> his sadness, unimaginable

I could have saved him . . . and ruined everything

27

JANICE EIDUS

Baby Lust

For the past few years, John and I have been agonizing over whether or not to have a child.

Our lives are full. For most of our marriage, we've been happy with our decision to be child-free. We've been oblivious to the charms of squalling infants and overly precocious toddlers; we've vastly preferred our cats. So why, about four years ago, did I begin yearning for a child?

I don't know. But I do know that I've tried very hard to talk myself out of these yearnings. They're "trite," I tell myself, and "foolishly romantic." After all, my friends with children are no happier than I; some of them are far less happy, feeling trapped in loveless marriages. One friend with two small girls, widowed young, is chronically in mourning. Another, once an up-and-coming visual artist, has put his career on hold for almost 15 years, working as a businessman to put his two boys through private schools. Another has a son who's a heroin addict.

But my yearnings won't go away: I spend many sessions discussing them with my therapist. She (a mother and grandmother herself) doesn't want to "discourage" me, but she wants me "to be realistic." "You'll have far less time to write than you do now," she says, "and you *already* complain about not having enough time. And you'll be utterly exhausted." Relentless, she continues. "It will probably be difficult for you to get pregnant. You may have to adopt." "And," she says, at last truly frightening me, "nothing puts more strain on a marriage than having children. Your relationship with John will radically change."

So we agree to put the idea of having a child to bed.

But the reality is this: I still feel "baby lust" whenever I pass a mother or nanny out with a little one. If the baby is laughing and cooing, my envy level reaches stratospheric heights. When a baby cries anywhere in my vicinity—on the bus or subway, at a nearby table in a coffee shop—I have to stifle the urge to rise and gather her up in my arms.

And then on the morning of 9-11-2001, at a little after nine o'clock, I find myself standing out on Sixth Avenue in the West Village, a few blocks from my apartment, just a couple of miles from the World Trade Center, close enough to feel that I can reach out and touch the flames. I watch as the second plane hits, watch as the buildings burn and disintegrate, crumbling like cigarettes.

From 10:30 that morning, and for the next few weeks, John and his colleagues at St. Vincent's work 24-7 administering desperately needed crisis assistance to all those who descend upon the hospital (soon to be known as the "Ground Zero hospital"): the 6,000 family members and friends seeking news of their loved ones; the shellshocked lucky ones who somehow managed to escape; firefighters and police. (And even now as I write these words four months later, he and his staff are still working overtime helping those in need: small schoolchildren who witnessed bodies falling from the sky; families now in deep mourning; residents displaced from their homes; and so many more of the psychologically wounded.)

So I spend the rest of 9-11 (and the next few days) with my friend Jaime who lives a few blocks away from me. For hours, he and I sit side by side in my living room, grasping each other's hands as we watch CNN with disbelief. Then we head outside to buy supplies, food, and clothing from the few stores in our neighborhood that are open. We walk a few blocks west to the temporary morgue that's been set up, where donations are being accepted for workers at Ground Zero.

And throughout all this, even as I stand on line at the morgue, even as I experience a kind of sorrow I never could have imagined I would feel in my lifetime, I can't stop envisioning myself with a child—with *my* child—by my side, my child whom I will nurture, comfort, mentor, love, and protect, who will inspire me to work harder to make the world a safer and better place, a world in which such a terrible thing won't happen again.

I hand over the coffee and bagels, heavy socks, flashlights, and batteries that Jaime and I have brought to the morgue, and I promise myself that when things have settled down a bit, when John and I can open our apartment windows without breathing in thick, overwhelmingly putrid smoke, when the National Guard ceases patrolling our block, when he and I can walk freely in our neighborhood without having to show I.D., when he at last has a free evening in which to begin to relax and unwind, I will tell him as gently as possible that the subject of our becoming parents hasn't been put to bed, after all. And I feel hopeful—confident, actually—as I begin to retrace my steps home from the morgue—that now he will feel the same way.

28

MASOOD FARIVAR

Man on the PATH

Early on the evening after the twin towers fell, I took the PATH to Manhattan from Jersey City where I live. It was my first trip to the city since the attacks. I had been moved by the quiet grief and surge of patriotism on display on our side of the Hudson but I was not prepared for what I saw as I came out of the 14th Street station and walked down Sixth Avenue towards Houston Street.

Smoke still lingered in the air. Most stores were closed. A few people casually walked in the middle of the street. The once-bustling street, now closed to traffic below 14th, had turned into a long stretch of make-shift shrines at bus stops, pay-phone booths covered with "Missing" fliers, couples holding hands, and small groups taking part in candlelight vigils. But what I was most moved by was the display of flags. They were everywhere. Giant flags on storefront windows, bandana flags on sidewalk vendors' foreheads, little flags sticking out of backpacks, and piles and piles of stars and stripes on the vendors' tables. As an Afghan, I'd never carried the black, red, and green flag of my own country. Suddenly, though, I wanted to feel what it was like to proudly hold a flag, wave it at passing ambulances, police cars and fire trucks. It would be a good way to show my solidarity with Americans. It was my way of saying, we're in this together. I'm with you. I share your pain. So I bought a passport-sized flag for $2, and sheepishly held it up as I walked to the East Village to meet a friend, all the while self-conscious of the incongruous spectacle of a Non-Resident Alien carrying an American flag. What am I doing, holding an American flag? I don't even have a Green Card.

But as I passed some angry-looking vendors who seemed to be studying the faces of every passer-by, I realized that the flag could serve a larger purpose than an awkward show of patriotism. It would give me a sense of security at a time when my co-religionists were drawing the violent ire of bigots around the country. It would help me blend in with the native crowd. I've always been a proud Afghan, but on this evening, walking down Avenue of the Americas in my GAP khakis and Brooks Brothers buttoned-down shirt purchased at the World Trade Center, I feared that someone might ask me where I was from, mistake me for an Arab.

"It's good protection," my friend said later, when she saw my flag. "I guess," I said, "but I didn't buy it for that reason."

When I got to the PATH station the following evening, the rush-hour crowd had thinned out. I was still carrying my flag. It was unusually bright inside. The two benches had been removed from the middle of the platform, and the "WORLD TRADE CENTER" sign had been switched off. As I walked to the far end of the platform, a 33rd Street train pulled in. I stepped into the car, sat down, and surveyed the handful of people inside. No one I should be on guard for, I concluded.

Everyone looked tired. A young, scraggly couple sat at the other end of the car in silence. Across from them, an old man under a "Drug-Free New Jersey" poster, next to them two young Asian women and a white man, and closest to the central door, a young man by himself, quietly reading a little book.

On any other day, I'd not have looked at the man twice, but something about him piqued my interest. He wore an outsize black coat and dark slacks, and sported a long, neatly trimmed beard. He was hunched over a little, leather-bound book that he held in both hands. I couldn't make out the book. But as he looked up momentarily, I could see his deep, dark eyes behind his glasses. He had a light complexion. I looked at him closely. He could have passed for an Orthodox

Jew but there was something un-Orthodox about him. The missing yarmulke. He was not wearing a yarmulke or an Orthodox hat. Still, I couldn't be sure. I couldn't tell if he looked European or Arab. He could be Egyptian, I thought, or a Ukrainian Orthodox Jew.

It was not an uncommon sight on the PATH, a bearded Muslim, and sometimes a clean-shaven one, reading the Koran on late-night rides, or an Orthodox Jew perched over his Bible. I never made much of them. But it was two days after America had come under attack, and Muslims around the country, afraid of violent reprisals, were keeping a low profile. The local falafel shop in my neighborhood had yet to reopen, the cab stand was empty of its mostly Arab drivers, and the Arab shoe repairman near my apartment had plastered an enormous American flag on his window. It would be rude, foolish, even reckless, for a Muslim to flaunt his faith in such an overt way on this particular evening, I thought.

My curiosity increased as the train neared the Christopher Street station in Manhattan, and the man continued his quiet reading without looking up. I got up from my seat to steal a glance at his book. As I walked past him, he was still hunched over his book, but I could see the distinct, black Arabic letters on its cream-colored pages. The book was bound in a zip-up black leather case. It was the Koran. I was stunned. What did he think he was doing? Wasn't he afraid? What he was doing was suicidal. The train went on to 14th Street, my stop. As I got off, I could see the man still engrossed in his reading, at peace with himself. He shifted in his seat slightly but didn't look up even though, as I thought, he was aware of my invasive eyes.

I wanted to talk to him, ask him if he was afraid, but I knew what his answer would be. Why should I be afraid? I'm not a terrorist. Why should I hide my religion? I'm a Muslim and I'm not afraid of practicing my religion. I read the Koran because I love it and because it's every Muslim's religious duty. The Prophet said reading the Koran cleanses the heart. God will protect you when you're in danger, and when the time to go comes, it comes. No one can stop it.

He had kept, on the PATH train to Manhattan, what I had also learned as a Muslim but had since lost. I have not carried the flag again.

29

CAROLYN FERRELL

"9/11 Victim's Identity Discovered Only through Investigation Led by Hairdresser"

Where was I? Where was I? Printer paper, thumbtacks, my father, my mother, last year's taxes, manila file folders, a ham sandwich no tomato, socks from sidewalk vendor. *Why didn't he agree with me, when push came to shove? A son's love never dies, as they say. Why couldn't he realize that?* He was talking to me the other night on the front porch, watching the house next door, the Pauluses'; it was burning. Forget him. Try to forget him. Envelopes: long white, security, embossed, Freda's special company letterhead—can't use that or else! If Shay were here, she would laugh. Someone like Freda with her own eternal stationery! The idca! Shay would laugh her head off, tell me to look on the bright side. Because she is someone that knows more than hair.

Sounds, sounds, sounds. People just in, now they're filing out. I'm alone. Headache tablets, water from the store downstairs, not from this lousy cooler—someone once complained to Freda about seeing roaches around it, and all she would say was,—*Whoever heard of roaches near water? They love food, you imbecile!* Just like Freda to use a word like *imbecile* and not *idiot,* like she usually does. I was standing right at the cooler at the time, reading my dictionary. Sounds, water, more sounds. On the verge of tears sometimes only who the hell cares.

Egg on a roll, coffee black, hundreds of stolen sugars from the deli since their prices seem to go up every thirty seconds and I'm going broke on these kinds of luxuries. Shay asked me why don't I make my own ham sandwich in the morning before I leave? Smart thinking, Shay. But who has the time.

Smoke, headache, number two pencils sharpened with grade school sharpener, computer screen, paperclip necklace, the kind Mother always asked for when I was a kid. *Why did he insist on cremation? Cremation is for the godless.* He had his ideas, I had mine. He tried to set things right the other day as the Paulus house was going up in flames. Too late. Plus I'd wanted her buried out in New Jersey. She always loved New Jersey. Said people gave it a bad rap because of the turnpike and all those cars, but what state doesn't have its cross to bear? Said New York was an accident waiting to happen. Said New Jersey was a place where it was country and city all at the same time, which she absolutely loved. From my window I can see the smoke stacks. I can see the winding roads. I can see the stores. I can see faces, most like mine. She would have wanted a grave over there. *Why didn't he care?*

Whenever I go to *World of Hair,* Shay tells me I should let bygones be bygones. Then she does this thing: not exactly deep color, no Grecian Formula or anything cheesy like that, but a rinse. The kind that stays in two weeks and makes the curls look delicious. Shay says women really go for this kind of thing. Wants me to be out there, but the truth is I haven't had a real woman in ages. They just don't seem to make them the way they used to. Mother was a classic—is it so wrong to hold out for more of the same? Does that mean not moving on? *He* used to call me Mama's Boy. I want him to eat those words one day.

Tie pins, coins for chocolate vending, stacks of papers from Monday, the Berger files and the Hanson files, both from the middle of last week, stacks of papers from the week before. Not always like this. In fact, voted Employee of the Week, but that was back in '93. Shay says I'm still the Best. Then applies the rinse, no harsh chemicals, no ammonia. Then cuts my hair. She's right—I am delicious. But then that is so like Shay. A heart of pure gold. I tell her, when I'm under the dryer,—*Stop messing with me! Stick to what you know!* And I laugh, so there are no hard feelings. Shay laughs, too. Doesn't know her own strength.

Smoke. Smoke. Sounds. Where are they going? It's not like the world is coming to an end. But if you asked someone like Freda, she would say, in typical fashion,—*How do you know? This could be it.*

John comes by and says something about security procedures and I tell him I have got myself one hell of a headache and he says it's all right, I can just lay my head on the desk and await further orders. Good old John. He tries to make me laugh by saying,—If push comes to shove, you'll have to leave the ham sandwich here.

Why the hell did you have to go and cremate her? Lucky we got Mr. Flittner to do the service on such short notice. And him wondering all the while why we aren't crying, why we are five whole feet from one another. Just a pile of ash—when will I see her again? A son's love. A son.

John says,—Are you talking to me?

And I get embarrassed, so glad Freda isn't around to see this, hear my mistake. She loves it when I talk in one place but my words are in another.

John says,—Maybe you'd better follow me. Things look like they're getting hard.

Computer disks, ball point pens, a small teddy someone once put on my desk on Valentine's. Who was it? Freda had said,—*Don't look at me,* but then Shay said,—*It was most likely her.*

I assure John and hold up the ham sandwich for proof. He nods and goes away, becomes part of what's happening out there. Sounds. A feeling in the air that maybe this is the end of the world (wouldn't Shay laugh at that?) but it makes my teeth hurt. My feet throb. Shoes, shirt, tie, waste paper basket, flickering exit sign. If Shay were here, she'd laugh herself silly.—*You're more boring than I imagined,* she'd joke. Post-it pads, greasy telephone, desk blotter from '93, when I was voted Employee of the Week. Me, boring? But I would laugh, because she only means well. Wants me to be out there.

A package of sugar-free mints, a book of matches from Windows, a stapler. I can remember this one time. Shay was brushing my hair and she asked me,—*If you ever get married, would you invite me?*

Silly question.

Another time it was,—*If I died first, would you come to my funeral?*

It's good to mean something like that. I mean something. *I mean something.* That's where I was. Pens, paper, stacks, files, hot carpet. Ham sandwich looks old, from yesterday. *I mean something.* The other day, on his front porch, watching the Paulus house in flames, he whispered,—*You'll always be.* And he sounded so much like Shay. Standing there in front of the engines, the sirens, feeling his life entwine with my own, like wisps of smoke curling upwards into the night sky.

Author's Note: This story is based on a *New York Times* article from 10/14/01, written by Leslie Berger, about an office clerk named Paul Lisson, who perished in the World Trade Center disaster. The photo caption read: "It's possible to live a life of unconnected anonymity in the city. A life a lot like Paul Lisson's. His hairdresser ended up reporting him missing."

This story was written in his memory.

30

RICHARD FOREMAN

CONVERSATION BETWEEN MR. X AND MR. Y

(Mr. X and Mr. Y are sitting at the edge of something bright, turbulent, and impressive. They sip drinks and smile. Other people stand around, ready to serve them more drinks, whenever they desire more drinks than they are now drinking.)

I know you will never believe this—but there is a thematic center to life which is being denied, and therefore, the real catastrophe (I mean—the real catastrophe) is just around the corner.

And what will be the form taken by that real catastrophe?

Because it will be real, it will hardly be noticeable.

Then it will be no catastrophe.

That may be correct.

Ok. Why do I feel like crying?

You tell me.

Because I am about to be unhappy?

Oh no, you will be very happy—unless, of course, really bad things start happening behind your back.

If they happen behind my back?

You'll feel their effects without knowing the true source of things.

The source of things is a mystery? That's OK because I like mysteries.

Some people are lucky. Some people figure out ways to turn unhappiness to their advantage. However, you won't be one of those people. However, then again, you may be lucky. You may—most of the time—be reasonably happy. Well, that's lucky in a certain sense of the word—

Then I am beholden to you for small moments of happiness and mystery, because the truth of the matter is—I don't really want to know what's behind this world. Do protect me from knowing such things.

Do you understand, my friend, that you have just lost part of your brain? You have been cheated, my friend. Part of your brain has been taken away from you. As a result—you are on automatic pilot.

Automatic pilot? Hmmm . . . then it follows that I myself don't know those things that are overwhelming to me. Thank God—

Here, hold onto this small morsel of emptiness—

Why?

For stability of course. All these words that go bouncing back and forth between us—isn't this just Mr. X talking to Mr. Y in search of a certain stability? Or do Mr. X and Mr. Y say things because they both know that in saying "things" they are always saying more than anybody else (—Mr. Z in particular) thinks they are saying?

(Pause)

Get it? The more I say the more you and I get de-stabilized!

But is that desirable?

Of course! That is highly desirable!

You mean—tumbling from these comfortable chairs—

Unfortunate, isn't it. But these mere pieces of furniture will have to stand in for that magic object we could easily name our revelatory encounter. But wait a minute—!

(He rises, and opens a door)

If we were to walk through this door, out into the dangerous streets, would we be even more likely to encounter something that could genuinely change a person's life?

I don't think so.

Probably not.

(Mr. Z walks through the open door. Mr. X and Y are visibly startled. Mr. Z says—don't be alarmed. I expected to enter bearing gifts, but there was a miscalculation—)

It would hardly have been appropriate, would it? Because anything you, sir, could conceptualize as a gift—would place me under unfortunate obligations.

(Pause)

Why don't you go away?

Wait a minute—maybe he should not go just yet—

Then he should sit down.

Maybe we should make some radical changes, and he should sit down and we should go.

No, I don't think we should go.

WHAT'S REALLY GOING ON HERE LADIES AND GENTLEMEN? EMPTINESS WANTED TO ENJOY ITSELF. SO IT MADE ONE SMALL AND PARTICULAR UNIVERSE IN WHICH EVERYTHING THAT HAPPENS CIRCLES BACK UPON ITSELF IN ORDER TO PROVIDE ENTERTAINMENT FOR EMPTINESS, WHICH WAS AN EMPTINESS THAT WANTED TO ENJOY ITSELF, IN THE MIDST OF ITS OWN EMPTINESS.

31

DEBORAH GARRISON

I Saw You Walking

I saw you walking through Newark Penn Station
in your shoes of white ash. At the corner
of my nervous glance your dazed passage
first forced me away, tracing the crescent
berth you'd give a drunk, a lurcher, nuzzling
all comers with ill will and his stench, but
not this one, not today: one shirt arm's sheared
clean from the shoulder, the whole bare limb
wet with muscle and shining dimly pink,
the other full-sheathed in cotton, Brooks Bros.
type, the cuff yet buttoned at the wrist, a
parody of careful dress, preparedness—
so you had not rolled up your sleeves yet this
morning when your suit jacket (here are
the pants, dark gray, with subtle stripe, as worn
by men like you on ordinary days)
and briefcase (you've none, reverse commuter
come from the pit with nothing to carry
but your life) were torn from you, as your life
was not. Your face itself seemed to be walking,
leading your body north, though the age
of the face, blank and ashen, passing forth
and away from me, was unclear, the sandy
crown of hair powdered white like your feet, but
underneath not yet gray—forty-seven?
forty-eight? The age of someone's father—
and I trembled for your luck, for your broad,

dusted back, half shirted, walking away;
I should have dropped to my knees to thank God
you were alive, o my God, in whom I don't believe.

32

AMITAV GHOSH

Neighbors

In 1999, soon after moving to Fort Greene, in Brooklyn, my wife and I were befriended by Frank and Nicole De Martini, two architects. As construction manager of the World Trade Center, Frank worked in an office on the eighty-eighth floor of the north tower. Nicole is an employee of the engineering firm that built the World Trade Center, Leslie E. Robertson Associates. Hired as a "surveillance engineer," she was a member of a team that conducted year-round structural-integrity inspections of the Twin Towers. Her offices were on the thirty-fifth floor of the south tower.

Frank is forty-nine, sturdily built, with wavy salt-and-pepper hair and deeply etched laugh lines around his eyes. His manner is expansively avuncular. The Twin Towers were both a livelihood and a passion for him: he would speak of them with the absorbed fascination with which poets sometimes speak of Dante's canzones. Nicole is forty-two, blond and blue-eyed, with a gaze that is at once brisk and friendly. She was born in Basel, Switzerland, and met Frank while studying design in New York. They have two children—Sabrina, ten, and Dominic, eight. It was through our children that we first met.

Shortly after the basement bomb explosion of 1993, Frank was hired to do bomb-damage assessment at the World Trade Center. An assignment that he thought would last only a few months quickly turned into a consuming passion. "He fell in love with the buildings," Nicole told me. "For him, they represented an incredible human feat. He was awed by their scale and magnitude, by their design, and by the efficiency of the use of materials. One of his most repeated sayings about the towers is that they were built to take the impact of a light airplane."

On Tuesday morning, Frank and Nicole dropped their children off at school in Brooklyn Heights and then drove on to the World Trade Center. Traffic was light, and they arrived unexpectedly early, so Nicole decided to go up to Frank's office for a cup of coffee. It was about a quarter past eight when they got upstairs. A half hour later, she stood up to go. She was on her way out when the walls and the floor suddenly heaved under the shock of a massive impact. Through the window, she saw a wave of flame bursting out overhead, like a torrent spewing from the floodgates of a dam. The blast was clearly centered on the floor directly above; she assumed that it was a bomb. Neither she nor Frank was unduly alarmed: few people knew the building's strength and resilience better than they. They assumed that the worst was over and that the structure had absorbed the impact. Sure enough, within seconds of the initial tumult, a sense of calm descended on their floor. Frank herded Nicole and a group of some two dozen other people into a room that was relatively free of smoke. Then he went off to scout the escape routes and stairways. Minutes later, he returned to announce that he had found a stairway that was intact. They could reach it fairly easily, by climbing over a pile of rubble.

The bank of rubble that barred the entrance to the fire escape was almost knee-high. Just as Nicole was about to clamber over, she noticed that Frank was hanging back. She begged him to come with her. He shook his head and told her to go on without him. There were people on their floor who had been hurt by the blast, he said; he would follow her down as soon as he had helped the injured.

Frank must have gone back to his office shortly afterward, because he made a call from his desk at about nine o'clock. He called his sister Nina, on West Ninety-third Street in Manhattan, and said, "Nicole and I are fine. Don't worry."

Nicole remembers the descent as quiet and orderly. The evacuees went down in single file, leaving room for the firemen who were running in the opposite direction. On many floors, there were people to direct the evacuees, and in the lower reaches of the building there was even electricity. The descent took about half an hour, and, on reaching the plaza, Nicole began to walk in the direction of the Brooklyn Bridge. She was within a few hundred feet of the bridge when the first tower collapsed. "It was like the onset of a nuclear winter," she said. "Suddenly, everything went absolutely quiet and you were in the middle of a fog that was as blindingly bright as a snowstorm on a sunny day."

It was early evening by the time Nicole reached Fort Greene. She had received calls from several people who had seen Frank on their way down the fire escape, but he had not been heard from directly. Their children stayed with us that night while Nicole sat up with Frank's sister Nina, waiting by the telephone.

The next morning, Nicole decided that her children had to be told that there was no word of their father. Both she and Nina were calm when they arrived at our door, even though they had not slept all night. Nicole's voice was grave but unwavering as she spoke to her children about what had happened the day before.

The children listened with wide-eyed interest, but soon afterward they went back to their interrupted games. A little later, my son came to me and whispered, "Guess what Dominic's doing?"

"What?" I said, steeling myself.

"He's learning to wiggle his ears."

This was, I realized, how my children—or any children, for that matter—would have responded: turning their attention elsewhere before the news could begin to gain purchase in their minds.

At about noon, we took the children to the park. It was a bright, sunny day, and they were soon absorbed in riding their bicycles. My wife, Deborah, and I sat on a shaded bench and spoke with Nicole. "Frank could easily have got out in the time that passed between the blast and the fall of the building," Nicole said. "The only thing I can think of is that he stayed back to help with the evacuation. Nobody knew the building like he did, and he must have thought he had to."

Nicole paused. "I think it was only because Frank saw me leave that he decided he could stay," she said. "He knew that I would be safe and the kids would be looked after. That was why he felt he could go back to help the others. He loved the towers and had complete faith in them. Whatever happens, I know that what he did was his own choice."

33

JAMES GIBBONS

The Death of a Painter

You felt like you were in a spaceship. The morning after the catastrophe, Anne walked along Atlantic Avenue. The police clustered in groups, talking, pointing, watching. Most of the Arab shops were open for business. As if subject to a new reflex, Anne found herself looking for splintered glass and wet graffiti. Drifts of poisoned wind seeped into the lungs.

The stunned walkers who crowded the avenue were wary and fatigued. Even the bland September weather seemed suspicious. But there was also a kind of shared electricity among the people on the street, an almost festive unease. They moved toward the river to meet with their own eyes the new, unimaginable skyline. For Anne it would be a first glimpse, displacing, she hoped, the images she'd seen on television.

She remembered her residency in the Trade Center three years before. She had done some of her best painting there. For weeks she'd kept the hours of an overworked bond trader, painting late into the night in the unreal hush of the 91st floor. The other suites on the floor were vacant, and the walls had been stripped down to their flame-retardant coating; there weren't even carpets on the floor. Such a raw space, she'd thought while setting up her studio there. She loved it. There was something so unruly about it, something that made the Towers' massive order less imposing. *It was like working in an enormous cave.*

Most of the artists felt privileged to work there, to take meals in the cafeteria at Windows on the World, to crack jokes with the guards who inspected their strange bundles by the elevators in the lobby. *Sometimes you felt sick. Remember how the towers would sway in the wind? Your ears would pop in the elevator.* One of the residents, a Ghanaian, couldn't shake his giddiness, even by the end of his stay: we're in New York's New York, he told Anne. *We're at the center of the center.*

Then there was Gilles, the Belgian who advertised his disdain for all things American with unflappable hauteur. "This cannot last," he proclaimed at the window, gazing north toward midtown. "All civilizations die. Of course," he said, his black eyes smiling at Anne, "This is hardly a civilization." When asked why he had applied for the residency in the first place, he replied, "Art is a business. I am learning how to be a businessman." He might have been joking; it was always impossible to tell. He spoke glibly about fast food, globalization, and an assortment of American evils that had poisoned the world.

But Gilles's abilities as a painter were enviable, and everyone in the residency, not least of all Gilles himself, knew it. One night, when they had both been working very late, he told Anne that he didn't really care about his ideas, which were, after all, the predictable outcome of his education and background. A sort of script, he said. "And politics is endless tedium," he went on. "If a painting is done well, it should put any idea to shame." They kept talking, sitting cross-legged near the air ducts by the windows, and shortly after midnight Gilles asked Anne to come back to his room. A few others were working on the floor but no one could see them. Anne made no answer, but they left together and walked to the hotel. In the hallway, outside his door, she decided she would not go in. "I'm engaged," she said, which was true at the time—but this was an excuse. Furious, Gilles railed against her "Puritan culture" and insulted her work, reversing the flattery of the past few hours. They stopped speaking to each other.

It was like a city unto itself. And now there was no 91st floor, no 92nd floor, no more residencies. Distracted by her thoughts, Anne made her way through the Brooklyn streets until she reached the Promenade, where she joined a crowd of dazed and curious spectators. She leaned against the rail and stared at the dirty white plume rising into the sky. Helicopters churned overhead and landed on the opposite shore. *You felt, perhaps for the first time, that you were a member of the workforce, part of the great throb of people making a living, day in day out. Wouldn't have expected that to mean anything, but it did.* Gazing at the skyscrapers across the river, Anne thought of their vacant floors and the city's mundane frenzy, now suspended and imperiled. The stillness of noon hung in the air like an unspoken word.

The following evening, pacing her apartment, unable to turn the television off, Anne could not control her anger. She felt mastered by events. Already there were directives to return to routine, especially if you lived in the outer boroughs: work, shop, see a movie, eat at your favorite restaurant, let's get things back to normal as best we can. The officials and broadcasters were right, of course, but even they didn't believe it would be easy. Could she really just drive to her studio in Red Hook and begin painting as if nothing had happened? What was there to express; her shock was inarticulate, and her sense of grief—she knew none of the missing—was vague, though no less real for that. She felt speechless even in her thoughts. She feared there was no way she could respond to the televised images with pictures of her own. Painting had always been the way she had met the world, and now the world was demanding her stunned attention, her submission, her silence.

She thought of Gilles. Their quarrel had made it impossible to banish him from memory. She had refused him, mysteriously and not for lack of desire. She wondered what he was thinking now. He liked to mock Americans, but how deep were those feelings? They had regarded the city from the same unearthly perspective. They had worked side by side as artists. He'd said that ideas and politics were nothing next to painting. That was what she believed, she told herself. But she felt paralyzed. Gilles might help her. She wanted to talk to him.

Anne had heard from so many in the hours since the attacks, among them estranged friends and ex-lovers. They wanted to know if she was safe; the old grudges made no difference. She'd had long, draining conversations with many of the artists she knew from the Trade Center. Gilles's name had not been mentioned. She would have to call his closest friend among the residents, an English sculptor who lived in Los Angeles. She found his number and dialed it.

The news was sharp and sudden. There had been an accident last spring in the south of France, near Vence. His motorcycle. A wet road. "I thought you knew," said the voice on the phone.

That night, Anne dreamed that she was walking hand in hand with Gilles in New York. It was an ordinary block of brownstone buildings, in Park Slope perhaps, or on the Upper West Side. The street was crowded. Everyone stared as they walked slowly, deliberately, with the somber air of a procession. Anne was veiled in a white *burqa*. A heavy fabric covered her mouth. She felt suffocated and helpless. Then Gilles squeezed her hand and her fear subsided. She was not alone.

The next day it rained. Anne drove to her studio and began to paint.

The 91st and 92nd floors of Tower 1 of the World Trade Center were used as studio space for artists. The Jamaican-born sculptor Michael Richards, one of the artists-in-residence in the Lower Manhattan Cultural Council's World Views program, was among the thousands killed on September 11.

34

CAROL GILLIGAN

If I Forget Thee

In the floor-bar class at the Green Street studio, I take a balloon, a pinwheel, and a tennis ball and find a space on the floor. It is 8:30 in the morning, and the class begins with breathing.

"Take a deep breath in through your nose and let it out through your mouth," Marcus says. The air, sucked into the assembled lungs, comes back out into the room in a loud hiss. Marcus gets up from his folding chair and walks among the dancers, placing a finger on the points where energy is held. "Cool," he says, as the energy releases; "now you're cooking." My legs lengthen out of my hips, and the air coming in reveals a space that has opened inside my body.

"Take your balloons and place them between your knees; take your pinwheels, arms in fifth position." The rhythm of the class picks up; lying on the floor, we raise our hips, pinwheels spinning as we breathe out on the count of three, and then lower ourselves, vertebra by vertebra, back onto the floor. "Now take your tennie," Marcus says, "and place it just at the top of your collar bone. Lift from the back of your neck, letting your head rotate forward, your chin following the curve of the ball." He comes over as my tennis ball wobbles and then rolls onto the floor. Settling himself behind me and cradling my head in his hands, he guides the lift which suddenly feels easy, my neck lengthening, the tension evaporating as he says "soften," and then, "very cool."

I settle into the morning leg work, wrapping my soul in its familiar language—*couper, passer, dégager, battement*—each move named, following a pattern, like china, like the willow pattern, like an old story, like this story.

When my mother died in April, suddenly after not dying year after year, defying expectation, despite prediction, refusing medical intervention, driving the staff at the hospice crazy because they were prepared to help her in dying but not to provide services for life—I was in shock. Suddenly there was nothing between me and the horizon. I hadn't realized that it was my mother, standing there, providing shade. One morning I looked at myself in the wide mirror spanning the front wall of the Green Street studio, my face flushed, my hair wild —and I realized that I was seeing myself with only two eyes, not the four eyes of me and my mother, she saying "your hair," and then, "darling," and then "brush the hair away from your face."

I take the four-thirty Delta shuttle to New York and then a cab to the apartment. I stand in the silent room with my tall son, his face pale, like my father's, his eyes guarding, like two watchmen. We find her passport in a high drawer of my father's dresser. Alone now in the apartment, in that freeze time after a death—like the moment between breaths, the pause between life ending and then resuming, we take her with us. "Come," we say, "you can come with us. We will stay with you, sort it out." We sweep through the apartment like ravens, cleaning. At the end of the afternoon, we come to the desk at the far end of the living room. Next to the window with the best view of the bridge. It is my mother's desk, an antique she treasured, left to her in a friend's will. We roll back the scrolled wooden sides. The center compartment is locked. When we open it, we find the last volume of her diary.

Most of the pages are blank. She had given up her meticulous recording of the tides of my father's depression. I turn the empty pages, the new year progressing relentlessly through nothingness until I come to April 28. "Bill died," she wrote, the handwriting familiar from all of the letters, the lists, the small slips of white paper labeling what was in each of the boxes that she placed on the high closet shelf. Ben is standing next to me. Tall, patient, loving. "Bill died." I read the words and start to cry.

On Monday morning in the floor-bar class, Marcus begins with healing sounds. He is going to acupuncture school, studying Chinese medicine, ancient wisdom of the body. We sit cross-legged on the floor; Marcus folds his arms over the back of his chair. "The color of the kidney is white, the season is winter, the strength is gentleness, the sound is 'whooo'—like the wind in the forest." "Whooo—" the sound sweeps through the room, the whiteness of winter, the cold of the wind, the gentleness of snow. Next is the liver, we lean to the right; the color is green, the strength is kindness, the season is spring.

I go to Israel to choreograph with Batsheva. My son Jake is working on a kibbutz, pruning grapefruit trees. We speak in Hebrew; he is almost fluent. I remember more words each day. It is June. Golden light stretched to the breaking point, holding the impossible hope. Shalom, salaam.

The color of the heart is red. The season is summer.

35

THEA GOODMAN

True Stories

Two truths and one lie: I love to eat fruit in the winter. Once, I almost drowned. On September 11th two planes punctured the World Trade Center and thousands of people died.

The first is fiction. My teeth are set and chilled on cold mornings, ready for bread, the predictable tannic warmth of coffee. Hairy kiwis hold no allure; the aging pear is too bruised. I always make the coffee the same way, packing the fine grounds into the metal disc, sliding it into the grooves until it clicks into place, waiting for the lit button to fade to black and depressing it once more. The espresso gathers inside a turquoise cup in slow dark drops. I heat milk in a small pot and add it to the cup. The mixture is surprisingly sweet. One morning the machine exploded. Black plastic, the clever German filters, and coffee scattered everywhere. No. Such violence has not taken place, though this break in the quotidian would make a good story. With words I'd try to make it believable, to bring the bitter grinds back together again. Marshaling all senses, there'd be the scent of the burnt bean, the brown stain on the wall, the ghostly chugging sound of the possessed machine as it rested in the aftermath.

I did almost drown when I was ten. A luxury brush with death. Para-sailing: the tug of the motor boat, wobbling, then straightening my limbs as I rose. My dream of flying enacted. Weightless, in a bandage-colored harness in the Caribbean sky. A plummet so quick it was imperceptible. As in dream logic, my senses skipped a beat. Next thing I knew, people say, and it is true. Next thing I knew I was deep under water, eyes wide open despite the salt, staring up through tangled ropes, the edges of the billowing red sail, the blue-green water and beyond that, in moving prisms, the paler blue of sky, the white space of clouds. Physical strength, my—heretofore—unknown swimmer's prowess and I worked my way through the color web to the surface of the water. I used to like to tell this story often. It harnessed all my fantasies together: flying, the perverse thrill of falling, underwater vision and the power to rise and resurface. The details shifted with each rendition. The trauma made me a storyteller.

Why do we make things up? Violence is everywhere. Narrative is connection. September 11th is impressionistic. Here is my rough order: First Guernica. Picasso's bombed Spanish town. Running and distorted faces. Shattered eyeballs, profile, then frontal faces with noses left on sideways. Seconds. One woman in particular. Chubby, features flying off in terror, "Oh my god!" Rushing to a payphone on Sixth Avenue she collided with a serene cyclist. Perfumed and dressed for work the biker was riding east on Tenth Street. Like me, she had not looked up yet, behind us, at the cause of the breaking street. Guernica: an apt prescient vision. Cohesion born out of shattering.

Simulacra, versions, are the only solace. I did turn around of course. Later I made strange comparisons. O's. The hole I saw in the first tower was black and round. I was incapable of making the connection at that moment that it was not just a dark circle within a rectangle, but that it meant loss. The mouths of my students hung open in similar O's when I told them. They were freshmen and prompt and had missed seeing what I had. The next thing they'd see was worse. In that dense history of minutes, we all saw and understood the meaning of our vision. From Arizona, from Maine, from the Redwood Forest, their early life stories were broken. I moved to New York City to go to college and on the second day of class—I mourned their interrupted lives. Not only the ones from pastoral sounding places. The young woman who was once a little girl in Newark, New Jersey. The boy who grew up closer, lived on Ludlow

Street since birth. They, too, like to make up stories, yet for a moment, terror petrified us.

Our motions are cautious now. Visions are crystal. Comparisons abound. Pull the pieces back together again in the worst poem you ever wrote, and countless attempts at capturing this day. Anthrax and its invisibility, its undetectability through any human sense is a challenge to all writers, to our marriage with sensory perception. Disguised murderers thrilled with invisibility, flying and falling, try to steal our incandescent dreams.

There was no milk and there were no newspapers in the delis below Fourteenth Street for three days after the attacks. Those normally teeming glass refrigerators seemed to hum louder when I opened them. Their black rubber edges gleamed like canine gums. The coffee I drank was bitter without milk and the television showed the news of an unbelievable repeated image. I thought of Don DeLillo's video-taped highway killer and the mystery image of Kennedy's assassination. One was a fictional construction, the other was "true" yet both were equally mysterious. Massive fracture calls for synthesis. In December students wrote their first short story: A southern Baptist virgin loses her virginity to a football player who then dies in a cocaine-fueled drag race, a gay teenager dreams of living on a tropical island with James Baldwin. Unsolicited, they were love stories. All deeply relevant to the living. This is only the beginning. Another Yeats, another Picasso is coming.

36

VIVIAN GORNICK

How I Read since September 11th

On September 11th, at 9:30 in the morning, I stood across the street from my apartment house in Greenwich Village, in a silent crowd, watching the tallest buildings in Manhattan burn and then fall. No one spoke, no one cried out. I think everyone in that crowd knew, then and there, that our world had changed and that New York would never be the same. In the months since that horrifying day, an atmosphere difficult to define—somewhat stunned, somewhat disoriented, strangely thoughtful—has enveloped the city and not yet abated. The town often feels vacant, confused, unrooted. And everything oddly muffled: the traffic, the noise, the crowd; restaurants, theaters, museums, sometimes half empty, sometimes even deserted.

And all the while some elusive element in our life seems to be draining steadily away. A man sits home on Saturday afternoons when every Saturday for thirty years he has gone to a jazz concert. "I don't know," he shrugs; "there's no entertainment in entertainment any more." A woman who loves New York movies turns off the television set when one comes on. "I don't know," she says vaguely, "they don't seem to apply." Another finds herself flinching at the sight of photographs with New York in the background. Everything, she says, feels like "before," and nothing "before" gives comfort.

I know what they mean. All my life, in every sort of crisis, I've turned to novels and essays set in New York to revitalize a flagging spirit; but since September 11th, I can't even open a book with a New York background. I find myself reaching for the Europeans, postwar preferably. "No danger here," I think with grim satisfaction. It was sentimentality I thought I was avoiding; but that turned out to be not exactly the right word.

One soft clear night in January, I was crossing Broadway, somewhere in the Seventies, and halfway across, the light changed. I stopped on the island that divides the avenue and did what everyone does: looked down the street for a break in the traffic so that I could safely run the light. To my amazement, there was no traffic. Not a car in sight. I stood there hypnotized by the grand and vivid emptiness. I couldn't recall the time—except for a blizzard, perhaps—when Broadway had ever, even for a moment, been free of oncoming traffic. It looked like a scene from another time. "Just like a Berenice Abb . . ." I started thinking, and instantly the thought cut itself short. In fact, I wrenched myself from it. I saw that it was frightening me to even consider "a scene from another time." As though some fatal break had occurred between me and the right to yearn over that long-ago New York alive in a Berenice Abbott photograph. The light changed, and I remained standing on the island; unable to step off the sidewalk into a thought whose origin was rooted in an equanimity that now seemed lost forever: the one I used to think was my birthright.

That night I realized what had been draining away throughout this sad, stunned, season: it was nostalgia. And then I realized that it was this that was at the heart of the European novels I'd been reading. It wasn't sentiment that was missing from them, it was nostalgia. That cold pure silence at the heart of modern European prose is the absence of nostalgia: made available only to those who stand at the end of history staring, without longing or regret, into the is-ness of what is. The moment is so stark that for writers, comfort comes only from a stripped-down prose that honors the starkness with a fully present attention. This, it occurred to me, is the great difference between what Americans mean by "postwar literature" and what the rest of the world has meant. A difference, it also occurred to me, that one could perhaps register only at the moment that it was about to evaporate.

37

TIM GRIFFIN

I Think I Understand the Various Theories of Rain

[*Any line on these pages may be spoken. Any line may be repeated. Any number of actors may be used, male or female. Line breaks may denote lines spoken by different actors.*]

I think I understand the various theories of rain.

[Mylar flows over the stage backdrop in long unrolling carpets; this may be repeated. One by one, the various members of the play step before a Polaroid camera to be photographed against the white background. Then they are given the developing photograph. The photographs may be laid out in a series, growing across the expanse of the floor. Or they may be passed back to the audience's upper reaches, so they are actually falling, in a sense, like the rain.]

I always lose track of time when listening to the rain.
Or looking at it. It exists as a gray sheet
Looking at it. It exists like the rain.

[A photocopier is opened onstage so shocking white light emanates from it, repeatedly copying *ad infinitum*.]

I forget what the sound is. Where
The sound is, what it is. All around
Me is the sound, or outside

The window

As I am beside the window
Looking out.

[A chair hanging from a loud metal track or wire is moved back and forth across the entirety of the stage.]

The day is almost not a day
In the rain. There is no difference
From night,

Except night.

It's the light
I think. Neither day nor night
Has shadows.

But I'm no longer thinking

Of what I was. I wonder who has
The time to watch it. I never do. Then suddenly

I was thinking of something else. It's the rain
That shows this to me. But then there is
Only the rain. And I am in the rain.

[Five heavy blocks of lead are set up in a row on stage, like dominoes. There is a long pause. Total silence. Then someone lightly kicks the dominoes over. All action begins again.]

There was time there, and no time. Inside the . . .

Awake, when you remember a dream but
Then forget it. At that moment,
When you almost had it. If you had had

[A solitary bowling ball crosses the stage diagonally as all other action stops. Someone has dramatically, elegantly rolled it in classical bowling style. This happens a number of times.]

It how could you have kept it? Could it
Appear in your mind again?

[Someone tosses a light bulb to another person in the midst of this action, once. Similarly, a costume rack is rolled only once through the background. Individuals wearing white fall slowly from the ceiling like rain.]

▪

Echoes of actors:

Rain. Rain. Rain. Rain. Rain. Rain. Rain. Rain. Rain. Rain.
Rain. Rain. Rain. Rain. Rain.
Rain. Rain. Rain. Rain. Rain. Rain. Rain. Rain. Rain. Rain.
Rain. Rain. Rain. Rain. Rain. Rain. Rain. Rain. Rain. Rain.
Rain. Rain. Rain. Rain. Rain. Rain. Rain. Rain. Rain. Rain.
Rain. Rain. Rain. Rain. Rain. Rain. Rain. Rain. Rain. Rain.
Rain. Rain. Rain. Rain. Rain. Rain. Rain. Rain. Rain. Rain.
Rain. Rain. Rain. Rain. Rain. Rain. Rain. Rain. Rain. Rain.
Rain. Rain. Rain. Rain. Rain. Rain. Rain. Rain. Rain. Rain.
Rain. Rain. Rain. Rain. Rain. Rain. Rain. Rain. Rain. Rain.
Rain. Rain. Rain. Rain. Rain. Rain. Rain. Rain. Rain. Rain.

The image of the rain. Coinciding
With the falling of the rain

Is what the rain is saying
When saying nothing, that moment

When there is nothing inside of the nothing
Said, the sound

It makes me think of "Guatemala": GUATEMALA

Guatemala the rain is falling.

Idiosyncrasy the rain is falling.

Introspection the rain is falling.

Adjudicate the rain is falling.

Pyramidal the rain is falling.

The rain is falling in a pseudonym.

[The dominoes fall again, exclusively.]

And somewhat silently I forget what I am thinking. *Guatemala.*

And sometimes there are voices inside the rain.

My sky's brainwash, the endearing entropy
Silencing the brainwaves, negating

The centricity of a word, the need
Arriving when suddenly unable to imagine

The rain. And that is only there
When there is the sudden lack of rain.

Passing in their grammar above us are the clouds

The End that Happened in a Sequence, exact
As a dance. Plasma is a kind of high temperature gas.

A passing inscription, never done,
Never begun, passing in numbers

What depth is there in a daydream?
A further proof of weightless houses

Is not limited to facts

38

LEV GROSSMAN

Pitching September 11th

1. Over the course of a decade a fraudulent bond trader (Robert Downey, Jr.) leverages himself outrageously, losing hundreds of millions without the knowledge of his supervisors in a futile attempt to meet the demands of his emotionally distant father (Robert Duvall) and his unhappy shrew of a wife (Molly Ringwald). But a whistleblower in accounting (David Duchovny) is on to him, and he goes to work knowing that today will be his last day as a free man. We watch him in the elevator. As the floor numbers rise into the eighties, then the nineties, we gradually realize that he is in the World Trade Center, and today is September 11th.

Miraculously, he survives the attack. Afterward he stumbles into a bar, covered with ash, and looks up on a TV screen. He is stunned to see his name there, numbered among those killed. His identity has been erased. Torn between ecstatic relief and crushing survivor's guilt, he changes his name and flees to Belize to start life anew as a simple fisherman.

2. Voiceover à la Discovery Channel nature documentary.

"Spring comes late to the Pamir Mountains" etc. Closeup on a small cumin plant, a green shrub with white flowers nestled in the rocky soil of northern Afghanistan. We follow its progress as the cumin plant is harvested, dried, packaged, shipped to America, and sold to a buyer who retails it to a chef who uses it to season a prosciutto, muenster and arugula omelet. The omelet is then served for breakfast at Windows on the World. *Irony.*

3. Events of September 11th are depicted in reverse, à la Martin Amis's *Time's Arrow.* Special effects extravaganza. Men and women in business attire make superhuman leaps from the prone position, launching themselves upwards and backwards into broken windows on upper floors of the World Trade Center. The windows inhale vast clouds of black smoke from the surrounding air, then spontaneously self-assemble into smooth sheets of glass.

4. Lengthy "day-in-the-life" account of one man's (Paul Bettany?) experiences on September 11th—with a twist. He boards the Q train on Monday morning, riding it across the Manhattan Bridge at approximately 9:15 A.M., while both towers are burning but before either one has collapsed. He assumes, as do his fellow "straphangers," that some kind of electrical fire is in progress. None of them has seen the news. They laugh callously at the misfortune of the Wall Street "fat cats."

He arrives at work—he's an insurance adjuster—to find his co-workers clustered around a TV set turned to CNN, but he spends the morning at his desk. He remains unconvinced that anything serious has happened. He is somehow unable to perceive or assimilate what has occurred. He eats lunch in Bryant Park, consternated by the pervasive smell of burning insulation, which ruins his turkey sub from Blimpie's. Gazing downtown toward the base of Park Avenue, he sees the mile-high pillar of dark smoke that hangs there. "Storm coming on," he remarks—to no one, as his office is deserted.

Unable to secure a dinner reservation—the phone at his favorite Soho bistro rings unanswered—he heads for home. The Q train is free for all passengers today, but his surprise turns to annoyance when it emerges that no trains are running across the Manhattan Bridge. He detrains at Canal and continues on foot, accepting a paper cup of water from a Red Cross worker. FDR Drive is inexplicably empty of traffic. Through the smoke he watches a steady stream of ambulances cross the Brooklyn

Bridge bound for Long Island. He frowns. The bridge is crowded with gawkers and amateur photographers, snapping the Financial District's new skyline, but he passes by without stopping. (Where is this going?)

5. Filmed performance piece. Lone figure (Spalding Gray? Eric Bogosian?) on stage describes the events of September 11th in the form of a cycle of limericks—a "limerepic," if you will. The idea would be to self-consciously "cheapen" the piece formally, to foreground its inadequacy and unimportance in the face of an inassimilable "reality" by deliberately choosing a literary form incapable of expressing any "meaning," e.g.:

> *As smoke billowed into the air*
> *The onlookers tore at their hair*
> *etc.*

6. Sci-fi thriller. Moments before the first tower collapses, mysterious figures in dazzling white clean suits materialize throughout the building. They are time travelers from the far future, come to save the victims from certain death. Each time traveler clasps the hand of a firefighter, policeman, or office worker, and together they vanish.

Only to reappear in a strange, rugged future landscape devoid of life. The time travelers have run afoul of the infamous Grandfather Paradox: by monkeying with the past, they have irrevocably altered their own present. Their utopian, technologically advanced civilization has vanished. They live out their lives in a primitive, unforgiving environment—trapped in a world they never made.

7. Shot-for-shot remake of 1986 Harrison Ford/Melanie Griffith starrer *Working Girl*, à la Gus Van Sant's remake of *Psycho* —with a twist. In the climactic boardroom scene, as the plucky secretary cements her triumph over the corporate raiders and

her scheming boss, American Airlines Flight 11 appears in the window. Muffled shouts from the hallway. The triumphant couple (Owen Wilson/Sarah Michelle Gellar?) embrace, then turn as one to face the oncoming tragedy. Fade to black.

8. (*X-Men III?*) Lonely, misunderstood Dominican elevator repairman (John Leguizamo?) finds himself trapped by fire after the second plane hits. In agony from the heat and smoke, near death from asphyxiation he jumps from the 83rd Floor.

Instead of falling he hovers in midair, then rockets upward. The trauma of the attack, and of his impending certain death, has awakened latent superpowers he never knew he had. A handful of others have undergone similar transformations—they hover in a cluster over the collapsing buildings, like so many swimmers treading water. As the roof sinks away below them into nothingness, they choose colorful pseudonyms and soar away together in formation to take vengeance on evil everywhere.

9. A man's life is narrated in excruciating detail, moment by moment, in near-real-time, starting from birth. This is a massive film project on the order of Jutzi's *Berlin Alexanderplatz,* or Lanzmann's *Shoah*. The life recorded is a stereotypically, nauseatingly idyllic American success story. Chuckling baby grows into fresh-faced adolescent. Captain of football team. Prom king. Ivy league scholarship. Recruited to bond-trading firm. Breaks all sales records. Youngest vice-president ever. Chairman of the board.

Pull back to see old man (Ian McKellen?) falling in slow motion. He has jumped from the roof of one of the towers, and the preceding thirteen hours of film have been a record of his life as it "flashes before his eyes."

Cut to young man snapping awake in bed. Sweaty sheets. Classic "waking from nightmare" take. It was all a dream. He is a condemned serial killer being shaken awake by a prison guard. Or no, he's the son of a World Trade Center victim, reliving his father's tragedy for the *nth* time. Or—yes!—he is an Al Qaeda hijacker (Naveen Andrews?) waking in a hotel room early on the morning of September 11th, having dreamed the death of one of his victims in advance. Fade to black. *Irony.*

39

JOHN GUARE

from A Few Stout Individuals

On 9/11, I saw the catastrophe from my window. I ran out in the street. The second plane hit. I ran back home to turn on the TV in hopes of deciphering this nightmare. I sat like stone, watching. I called my wife in her office uptown. She would bring people from her office home. I went out to buy food and water. I saw men in business suits who had fled the horror, caked in white ash, stumbling along the streets. I came home. I couldn't turn on the TV. I couldn't sit there. I started work on a play that had been banging around in my head for a while. I finished the play 3 weeks later. It's called A Few Stout Individuals *and will be presented in May 2002 at the Signature Theater. It takes place in New York in 1885 on the 20th anniversary of the end of the Civil War on the first Memorial Day. A veteran remembers the battle of Cold Harbor.*

HARRISON

I still hear the officers at Cold Harbor yelling, Charge! Charge! Our men lunge forward. Charge! Our men fall dead. Charge! Over and over. The new men cannot get on the battlefield. They climb up the pile of corpses and are shot dead. Charge! The newest soldiers stop. We cry out: We can't get into the battle. The entries to the field are clogged by bodies. The officers respond: Then climb up the bodies! Charge!

Days and days—the heat—the poisoned water. Charge! The bodies fall. We can't get out on the field to clear the wounded, much less the dead. Thousands of men dying. Charge! Charge! The men fall. A mountain of flesh. The shooting won't stop. Who's running this battle? Ulysses S. Grant. Unconditional Surrender Grant. Men climb up the wall of bodies. Charge! Grant is wasting his men. We are killing our own men!

I pick up a white flag and run up that mountain. Cease fire! In the name of everything good, cease fire!

Me at Cold Harbor waving that flag. That's as close to God as I ever came. Or as close as God ever came to me.

I only waved my flag for a few moments. I was shot. In India they put their dead in the rivers. I didn't have to go to India to see that!

There was darkness. There must have been a cease fire because the nurses and soldiers who lived threw us thousands of corpses into wagons to take us and burn us . . .

Well, one of those corpses came to and crawled out from under a stack of corpses—a corpse called me. My eyes and ears and nose opened all at once and I thought I was in a butcher's abattoir from the stink of flesh, the taste of blood, not my blood, but other people's blood that had seeped into my mouth. I feel the weight of the flesh, corpses twitch in rigor mortis over me, under me. I hear the groaning of the dead all over me, beside me. I thought dead would be quiet but we were bumping over stones on the way to the fire. Air moving out of corpses. I moved my fingers. I was not dead. The man over me. Under me. The right of me. The left of me. They were dead. Was I one of them? How had I stayed alive? I must have eaten the flesh around me. Drunk the blood around me for water. I can smell smoke. Flesh. They were burning corpses. They had to. Not enough earth on this earth to bury all this dead. Scoop up all the sand in the Sahara, collect all the dirt of the steppes of Russia— not enough earth to cover all these Cold Harbor dead. But I am not one of them! Don't put me in fire! I pushed my way up through the weight of stinking flesh. Was dying like being born?

My hand reaches out of the dead wagon and grabs a soldier by the arm. He sees my eyes open and he screams loud—Stop the wagon! The moving wagon stops. Don't put me in fire. Not fire! I am not dead. I swear. Soldiers prod me with a bayonet. Do you think the black one's telling the truth? My lips move. I'm telling the truth. They pull me out of the flesh the way you'd rescue a drowning swimmer out of the sea.

How many more alive men were in those wagons headed to the flames? We have to live for them. Are we still in that death wagon struggling to get out from under that ton of corpses?

SEAN GULLETTE

40

Mile High

A wintry Boston afternoon in the late seventies, and I'm lying on the living room floor, ten years old, digging through a Cutty Sark box of coffeetable books. Inside one called "A Testament" I find an inscription—"love from Parmella. Graduation 1958" —and a gatefold which opens four pages wide . . .

Whoa. The drawing, in detailed charcoal pencil, looks like a slab of slate fell out of the sky and shattered to form a jagged spike. First I realize that it's a skyscraper. Then the scale hits me: it is 528 stories tall.

As an American boy I am primed to fall in love with this building instantly. I read with satisfaction as Frank Lloyd Wright explains that his "Mile-High Illinois" is a tensile tripod and houses forty-five thousand people, fifteen thousand cars, a hundred helicopters, a system of glass-walled, atomic-powered elevators, and a tap-root foundation drilled into the bedrock. The Mile-High is a vertical city: offices, stores, restaurants, apartments, a hospital.

He begins to calculate usable square footage and my imagination takes off. I envision black tile swimming pools with underwater windows; ledges where migrating hawks flap to rest, tricking the eyes of an elderly millionaire in his grand lonely apartment staring out at the sky, hoping to see an angel. And there had to be a small bedroom up near the tip, where you see clouds moving safely behind tan drapes and silent inch-thick glass, as you drift gently away into sleep . . .

You wake up from a deep thin-air nap and it is very clear outside, the big sky over thousands of acres of Illinois farmland and prairie, patchworked corn, winter wheat, oats and sorghum crosshatched by the fast highways leading out of Chicago. Each distant farmer can see the sharp peak of this building and this window. The tip raking across the sky at over 1000 miles an hour as the earth spins, slicing the high winds over the city in half. The people of the earth and the people of the sky, looking at each other.

"A rapier, with a handle the breadth of the hand, set firmly into the ground, blade upright," 90-year-old Wright preached to a dubious architecture community, in his cranky-egoist style. "No one can afford to build it now," he assured, "but in the future no one can afford not to build it."

Ten years later the Port Authority broke ground for Minoru Yamasaki's World Trade Center. Centralization was the grand theme. By the 80s people looked at the twin towers and saw either the free market's efficient corporate mainframe or the slablike dominance of Big Brother. There wasn't much talk of the towers' transcendental meaning.

But for me, there they were, too good to be true. Again and again through a decade living downtown, I would turn a corner walking on Spring Street, or on my bike down East Broadway or the West Side, and bump into the jolly giant twins, pinstriped and proud, their beveled edges flinging off the western light. I'd stop and feel that kidlike joy return: they were awesome, incredible, dreamlike.

Being in the streets close to the base, or in the windy plaza beneath them, was a little daunting. The exterior columns racing upwards were designed by Yamasaki to be just as wide as your shoulders—so that standing near the windows wouldn't be too scary—and the temptation to stand right between two of them and look straight up was considerable. I loved riding the big fast elevator up to get loaded at Windows on the World, the haute–Holiday Inn decor quivering subliminally in the air streams of the Atlantic and the Hudson. One time clouds surrounded the bar, and it was pretty empty, but I liked facing the blank grey windows. Altitude is mostly in your head, anyway.

One clear evening, I scribbled on a Windows bar napkin an idea for a short movie, set in the bright canyon between the towers. The characters would be window-washers and angels; sitting on the rooftops, dangling their feet over the edge, flirting, a couple of them falling in love. The towers' very existence married New York City to that sky, elevated us above the earth and our mortality.

It was pretty to think so. On the bright clear day the towers fell, all of that became an indulgence for little children. Among giant twisted steel vertebrae and the evil smell and smoke, thousands of people worked ceaselessly, quietly, with a harmony of purpose that can only be called love. When they paused in exhaustion you could see their minds beginning to engage with the bad reality of it. That drove them back to work.

By the third night, civilian workers were being replaced by the professionals, and I caught a ride out from our improvised supply operation on Vesey Street, on the back of a Parks Department golf cart. As we got to the West Side Highway a torrential soaking rain began to fall. It would be a terrible night for the workers on the heaps, but I wouldn't be there. For me the rain was a balm. Looking back at the columns of light and smoke rising into the black emptiness above, I knew that by disappearing, and then passing into imagination and memory, the towers had become as real as a thing can be. I knew moreover that the people whose bodies had vanished into the dust and smoke had moved on, leaving the city with a hard-to-unwrap spiritual gift. Above in those dark clouds, a host of angels circled the airspace, broadcasting with a steady signal the necessity of both simple and grand human dreams and the burning urgency of love.

41

JESSICA HAGEDORN

Notes from a New York Diary

9:20 A.M., SEPTEMBER 11, 2001:

Fear, the rush of adrenaline, mounting hysteria. I open my door to an eerie sight: hundreds of people are standing in the middle of Washington Street, looking worried and lost. My neighbors, my friends, the maintenance workers who take care of my building, total strangers—all staring at the huge, ugly black clouds engulfing what once was the World Trade Center. There are those poised with their camcorders and cameras, ever ready to document any catastrophic event. I, too, stare at the smoke and flames, mesmerized by the awesome beauty of destruction. The sky is a hard, brilliant blue. It is the end of the world, yet the sun is blazing and it is a crisp, gorgeous morning. We are very much alive. All around me, eyewitness accounts are repeated like some gruesome mantra: *Not one plane, but two. Not two, but four. Not accidentally, but on purpose. I saw the whole thing go down, bodies falling from the sky.*

I think of the troubled Mindanao region of the Philippines, where I have just been. Where the surreal and the real are one and the same. Where the sunsets are the most glorious on earth and acts of violence are a daily occurrence. Where an equally vicious sense of humor seems the only sane and logical response. Chaos reigns, life is cheap and everything is possible in the country where I was born. The people adapt, the people survive, the people retain their grace and sense of irony and humor. But thirty years in New York has made me soft—I am cocooned by arrogance and privilege, prone to First World delusions. I thought I lived in the toughest city in the world and was therefore safe.

Nine-one-one-zero-one: sinister perfection. The numbers are high; the numbers signify creativity, pride, ambition and power. A numerologist's nightmare, perhaps—or source of infinite satisfaction?

11:15 A.M.:

In a state of siege, what does one truly need? At the supermarket, the bananas are gone. Bottles of water fly off the shelves. There are no more "C" and "D" batteries, but plenty of double "A's." I ponder the meaning of this, feeling a bit crazy. An adrenaline high, the thrill of fear. At last, it's our turn at the checkout stand. I have managed to purchase four measly bags of groceries for the Apocalypse, while the people in line ahead and behind me have stocked up on at least a year's worth of non-perishable goods. On our way home, my ten-year-old daughter reveals in a soft voice that she is afraid. It is a heartbreaking moment. All around us, a city in shock. We walk home. The persistent wail of sirens is grating and continuous.

FIVE WEEKS LATER:

I eat without appetite. Rent movies I don't watch. Channel-surf from soundbyte to soundbyte, unable to sleep. Concerned relatives who live far away call to ask when am I moving out of New York. "You're just sitting ducks," goes one of the more insensitive remarks. Fuck you, I want to say, but don't. Should I quote Yogi Berra? *The future ain't what it used to be. . . .* Or: *It ain't over til it's over.* Instead, I stop answering the phone altogether. I thank God, Allah, Buddha, the Virgin Mary, Krishna, my own mother and of course, Saint Sebastian and Jesus Christ for the invention of "caller I.D."

Shall I tell you about the smell? The sweet, nauseating smell of burning rubber, melting plastic and dead bodies? Yesterday was another beautiful day in Manhattan. Warm, sunny, breezy. But the warmer and windier it is, the worse it gets. The smells are everywhere downtown, carried by the wind. Time to summon the shamans. To exorcize the angry spirits, and bless the living and the dead. You can feel it, most days. Bad energy buried in the rubble.

GROUND ZERO

You ask me to write something about war, peace and race, but I cannot. Words fail me. "The Big Picture"—what it all means, who's really behind it, civil wars, unholy wars, crusades vs. fatwas vs. jihads vs. ethnic cleansing vs. doves vs. hawks—the complications and mess of history are a blur to me at the moment. But here's one thing maybe I can share with you, one small thing that recently came to mind. One Sunday morning, I finally got up the courage to take a walk as far down Greenwich Street as I could. I wanted to see it for myself. Not on a TV screen or in a photograph, but the actual World Trade Center ruins in all their devastating, physical reality.

Ground zero. An apt name, stark and poetic. Here was, *is* a vast, smoldering graveyard of blackened, twisted steel and rubble, right in the middle of my city. The twin towers—once derided and admired as potent symbols of global commerce and architectural arrogance—had, in a matter of minutes, been reduced to a horrific heap of trash. I was immediately reminded of Smokey Mountain, the legendary garbage dump in the Philippines. Another awesome, burning landscape etched in my memory. So cruel yet accommodating, Manila's poorest of the poor figured out a way to live there. But our New York version of the ugly mountain is so much more gargantuan in scale, it literally takes your breath away. The hauntingly familiar, acrid smells of death and decay waft through an open window in my apartment. Ground zero. Days of anxiety, days of mourning, days without sleep.

42

KIMIKO HAHN

Boerum Hill Tanka

1
Overtaking the crisp air, from across the Bay blow pages of documents and ashes of terror.

3
A neighbor hoses down her small front garden: snap peas, zinnias, morning glory vines, grief. So much grief.

5
Trying to make a daughter's lunch. Trying to find the other's transit pass. Trying to find a moment to collapse.

6
At a midnight clap of lightning I sit bolt upright—more terror? This time across the street?

8
From the Promenade—where my daughter and I saw Tower Two collapse—we look for something more than disbelief.

43

NATHALIE HANDAL

The Lives of Rain

The old Chinese man
in the health food shop
at 98th and Broadway, tells me
that the rain has many lives.
I don't understand what he means
but like the way it sounds.
I wonder if he tells everyone the
same thing or if this is something between
us, wonder if he fought any wars, killed
anyone, wonder if he ever fell in love,
lost a house, lost his accent, lost a wife or
a child in the rain, wonder if he calls for
the rain when he stirs his daily soup,
wonder what hides in his silk cloth—
rice, pictures, maybe memories of rain.
Rain he tells me, carries rumors of the dead,
of those with suitcases and epidemics.
Rain carries the memory of droughts,
of houses gone, rain like lovers
comes and goes, like soldiers go
and sometimes return, return to a life
no longer standing.
The Chinese man waits for me to ask
for more. I stand, outside is the rain—
who really knows how many lives to come.

44

CAREY HARRISON

America everything has changed

America everything has changed
The enemy is inside the gates
Can you recognize him?

The enemy eats pizza, drives an SUV
Spends his dollars on liquor and lapdancing
Can you recognize him?

The enemy is indifferent to the deaths of men women and
children
Of races other than his own
America can you recognize him?

Knowing he will die a hero, the enemy stands ready to
sacrifice his life
Without question, when his leaders require it
Can you recognize him?

The enemy might as well be living in a cave
For all he knows of the rest of the world
America can you recognize him?

He can barely spell, he can barely read
But don't call him uncivilized
(he's got email)

Nine eleven can you hear the shrilling bells
Brave men are dying for you America
America nothing has changed

45

JOSHUA HENKIN

Dog Walking

On one of his morning walks Julian found a stray dog, a beagle who took a liking to him and followed him on the footpath back to campus, staying patiently outside his dormitory and bleating occasionally until Julian didn't have the heart to leave him outside, so he let him in and fed him some milk. There was a tag around the dog's collar, and when Julian called Mr. Quincy to pick the dog up, Mr. Quincy was so grateful he thrust a fifty-dollar bill into Julian's hand and refused to take it back.

A few mornings a week Julian began to walk Mr. Quincy's beagle, and then other dogs too, and soon he could be seen walking through town with eight or nine dogs at his feet, retrievers, collies, shepherds, a Saint Bernard, and Mary, his favorite, a huge, aging Newfoundland who trailed the rest of the pack like a den mother and who, like Julian, seemed filled with the spirit of discovery, turning her head this way and that like someone perched on a parade float. Mary was so big a few of the local children thought she was a bear until Julian assured them she wasn't, she was a dog, and he allowed them to feed Mary her scraps of meat which he carried in a cellophane baggie inside his knapsack.

Sometimes late at night on the way back from a movie or simply walking through town, alone and sentimental, at once taken with the sense that his life was romantic, that the life of a young man at college was the only life to have, and filled at the same time with a sadness whose roots he couldn't unearth, feeling unappreciated, turned down by some girl, drunk and disconsolate and walking through the streets, Julian would stop at Mr. Kang's grocery where he would find Mr. Kang tending to his fruits and vegetables. Mr. Kang used a hose that sprayed a mist so fine Julian could see the individual particles of water.

Inside, Mrs. Kang was at the cash register examining a bulb of fennel. Julian felt a wave of fondness for Mrs. Kang, and for the affection she lavished upon that bulb of fennel, and he thought he would like nothing better than to own a grocery someday, he and some future Mrs. Wainwright, the two of them tending the fruits and vegetables, late-nights in the store room in back punching the keys on their matching calculators.

Other times, though, there was nothing he would have liked less than to be tending to the produce in the growing cold, and he would comfort Mr. Kang, though Mr. Kang didn't ask for comforting, with the fact that Mr. Kang would be closing at midnight while the Korean grocers in New York City were open twenty-four hours.

"New York is too busy," Mr. Kang said.

"It's the domino effect," said Julian. "One place stays open, so another place has to stay open too. It's competition, Mr. Kang. Capitalism."

"They should make an agreement to close," Mr. Kang said. "That's what I'd do if I was in New York. I'd talk to all the Korean grocers. I'd get them together in a big room and we'd decide to close."

Julian tossed a papaya from hand to hand. "New York's the city that never sleeps," he said. He started to sing for Mr. Kang —New York, New York, it's a hell of a town—and Mr. Kang smiled at him, and Mrs. Kang came outside and she smiled at him too. As Julian sang, he got to thinking about the Korean grocers in New York City, the one in his own neighborhood next to the pizza place on Second Avenue, and how everyone ended up in their own niche, the Korean grocers and the Israeli taxi drivers and the old mustachioed Italian men selling cherry and lemon ices in Central Park, as if the whole thing had been ordained by some invisible force.

He thought about the Irish girl who served him coffee milkshakes at the diner at three in the morning, the construction men perched high above midtown, and Carlos, the elevator man in his parents' building who, when he got off at midnight, took the subway back to Queens. Walking along the streets of New York, Julian liked to stare into the windows of people's apartments and contemplate the lives that were going on inside, the way he liked to contemplate Mr. Kang's life, his life outside the grocery store, his life with Mrs. Kang.

"I have to go home and study," he said now.

"It's too late to study," said Mr. Kang.

"That's the problem. I've only just started."

He shook Mr. Kang's hand, and waved at Mrs. Kang inside the store. He wound his way back to campus, holding a bag of Granny Smith apples that Mr. Kang had given him for free ("Extra," Mr. Kang had said), and as he walked toward the college gates he ate one of the apples down to the core and then he ate another one.

TONY HISS

46

Finding the Center

The World Trade Center towers were not instantly lovable or easily cherished buildings. At least, that was the reaction a generation ago of many New Yorkers, people who, like me, had their first jobs in the city in the 1960s or the early 70s and whose memories stretched back into pre-twin towers days.

It had to do, we would have said, with their design and layout; with what they had replaced; with how they had come into being. The river-edging outer fringes of the old Lower West Side, as it was still then called (the upscale rebranding of the area as TriBeCa was a later campaign), were an odd, distinctive, long-settled and little-known part of town that had already been through several centuries of wrenching changes and challenges, interspersed with long, slow metamorphoses that led to the storing up of flavor, meaning and value. In 1788, only a few years after America gained its independence, New York Hospital, whose original home was a few blocks north of the trade center, was the scene of what became known as the "Doctors' Riot." Five thousand people stormed the hospital, inflamed by the notion that medical students were dissecting the cadavers of "respectable people." Troops summoned by the governor and the mayor fired on the crowd, killing three and wounding many.

In 1866, three generations later and a few blocks north, St. John's Park, "a spot of Eden loveliness and exclusiveness," it was called in the 1840s, the anchor of a neighborhood that looked as if it would last as long as the city itself, disappeared almost overnight, when Cornelius Vanderbilt chopped down the park's famous trees to build a huge freight warehouse. Vanderbilt's idea, one which permanently changed New York, was to run freight trains entering the city down the West Side and passenger trains down the East Side. In 1913, as a direct but delayed result, Vanderbilt's railroad built Grand Central Terminal, an instantly beloved building, the most beautiful train station the country has ever seen. *Lost New York*, a startling book by Nathan Silver that came out in 1967, had a haunting, grainy, early photograph of St. John's and its trees, gaunt in the wintertime. Because of Vanderbilt's ruthlessness, New Yorkers achieved Grand Central. But if Vanderbilt had never lived, we might still have St. John's.

In Jack Finney's novel, *Time and Again*, the classic book about not letting go of an old city, you could, by concentrating enough, will yourself back into an earlier New York. I used to think—as if the choice existed—of forgoing Grand Central and reclaiming St. John's. But then I began to see a new way of understanding historic preservation: it was, at heart, a forward-looking activity, putting enough care into things already here, so they can survive to be a part of the "here" of a generation that hasn't yet arrived.

By the early 1960s, just before the World Trade Center, the Lower West Side had both old drawbacks and old strengths: You could hardly see, and had little hope of getting down to, the Hudson River for miles on end, because of a great, high, 70-year-old wall of docks that took the river for their own purposes.

But just east of the docks, night after night and for almost a mile, you could, from midnight to dawn, walk past and into the long succession of sheds and buildings that constituted the 100-year-old Washington Market, the largest fruit and produce market in the world. "One wall of a warehouse is pearled with garlic buds," wrote Kate Simon, who scoured the city for her 1959 guidebook *New York, Places and Pleasures*, "and a wall of carrots blazes from the other side."

The wholesale produce men, she reported, "are polite, quiet

and unhurried, moving softly in the sleeping city." These days the Hudson River can be seen, strolled past, bicycled along, almost uninterruptedly. The market men and their wares, however, are invisible, having been removed to Hunts Point in the South Bronx in 1967, as part of urban renewal's post–World War II idea for transforming the area and adding the World Trade Center.

The twin towers, when they arrived in the early 1970's, seemed oversized and inhumane, "pretentious and arrogant," Paul Goldberger wrote with emotion in 1979, buildings that "should never have happened." Equally disturbingly, they seemed marooned in a much-avoided, wind-swept plaza.

But—politely, quietly, unhurriedly—a new round of slow, soft changes took hold. In a generation, the north tower got a tall white television transmission tower. Now the buildings were nonidentical twins. Philippe Petit daringly walked between the tops of the two towers on a tightrope. The dirt excavated from the towers' cellars became the ground on which Battery Park City could be built. A few blocks to the north, the small Washington Market Park is an addition to the city almost as lovely as St. John's. The New York region had found a centering point: spires equally visible from Midtown, from Jamaica Bay, from the Hackensack Meadowlands. To my lasting astonishment, a friend showed me how these towers could extend our awareness further: squinting up the aluminum corner walls felt like looking skyward along a short, one-lane road, a reminder that all life on our broad earth is nestled within the biosphere, a narrow, precious, vulnerable band.

These thoughts came back as I stood in the street and watched the wounded towers try to stay standing. Then they fell, and the city had lost too many, too much, too quickly. The smile of the skyline had missing teeth.

47

DAVID HOLLANDER

The Price of Light and Air

He stands outside a brick building in Brooklyn, braised by the sick yellow light of a nearby streetlamp. It's freezing cold, and his breath fans out in a thick cloud, like fine spores of white flour. He is at eye level with a window. The window is closed, but the shade is not drawn, and he is witness to what the room's occupant—a bald woman without eyebrows or, for that matter, any tertiary evidence of body hair, a woman whom he assumes has been stricken by some brushfire variety of cancer—is witness to. That is, he can see this woman, who is no older than himself, perhaps thirty, with a thin pretty face that is all points and angles, a woman who has probably spent her life inadvertently stabbing friends and acquaintances with her face, he can see her in profile and he can see the television newscast unfold and he can see the flickering colors of that glass box wash over her like sin and redemption, and he is feeling a pang of strange remorse as she stares, wrapped in some sort of afghan, into this conveyor of pre-digested information. He is smoking a cigarette, outside of her window, and she is not privy to his presence there, not yet. He is afforded that rare sanctity of invisibility. His breath mingles with the light. He watches.

The woman shifts, and he turns his own attention to the television newscast. Soon, he will return to his basement room in a building two blocks away, where he is writing a story. He may or may not be a writer someday, but he is writing a story, and his heart is filled with the desire for this story to be important and worthy and full of light and air, and he is smoking this cigarette in front of her window because this is what validates and defines him, walking and smoking between periods of internment in his damp basement room, where a space heater glows red hot and buzzes into the night, threatening to immolate while he sleeps, lending to his subterranean existence that very sense of danger which makes it bearable. Really, he only wants to be loved.

The television newscast is desultory, a challenge to follow without sound. There are images of a car wreck's smoldering jungle gym. The face of a police officer framed in a box. The anchor woman's own deadpan smile, the pink glow of her skin, the ersatz mannequin smile. There's the image of somebody's cat, with the word "Jingles" beneath. Then there is the image of the woman herself, the woman he is watching through this window, she is also there on the television screen, hairless and smiling and talking to a dispatched reporter. He forgets, for a moment, to exhale the smoke he has swallowed up, and chokes a little. It seems to be Brooklyn, judging by the brownstones behind her in the newscast. In fact it seems to be this very street, he can see this building in the background, and because the human mind has never truly adapted to the mystery of preserved images, he cannot figure out why he himself does not appear in the newscast. The woman behind the window, the real woman that is, shifts in the afghan, runs long fingers over her hairless scalp, and he can tell that it's warm, that denuded flesh. She points at the image of herself on the screen, as if to make the connection for him, although she hasn't seen him, he's sure of that. She points and then lowers her hand, tucks it back beneath the afghan, and begins to cry.

He exhales stale smoke into the night dome of this poisonous cityscape. The streetlamp casts its green-yellow sheen. In the air, the atomized death of the World Trade Center's demise still hangs like a malediction, and his own breath mingles with these traces of dust and ash and metal, of human life and its registry of components, white bone and muscle meat. He watches the screen. He watches the woman. He needs to hold her, that's all. The cigarette's molten ash cartwheels through the darkness, his hand is on the sill, and he pulls at it but it's locked or stuck or both, and he wonders if he should knock or just shatter it with his elbow, and then he wonders if anything he ever does will be filled with light and air, and he wonders why she won't look at him, and why he's stuck here behind the glass, on the wrong side, why he can't budge things, why she is crying harder now, and what sort of irradiated potion can singe and suffocate hair follicles without killing everything else. *Over his dead body*, he decides. That's how they'll pry her away from this life, the filthy bastards. Over his dead body. He draws back his arm and lets fly. And his heart balloons with a sadness he has never known, and never will again.

A.M. HOMES

48

We All Saw It, or The View from Home

I begin the days quietly, preferring to see no one, speak to no one, to get to my desk early, before the "real world" intrudes, seeking to preserve for as long as possible that fertile creative zone which exists somewhere between sleep and waking.

The events of September 11 ripped me from that zone, putting me on full alert. The ever-unfolding implications loom so large that for the time my imagination remains—stilled.

It starts with a call from a friend, telling me there has been an accident, "Go to the window," she says.

I stand looking south, witness to Tower One in flames. And then I see the second plane; the instant it is in view it's clear this is not an accident.

The plane is moving towards the second tower counter-intuitively, rather than avoiding the tower, it is determinedly bearing down, picking up speed. I see the plane and I see the plane crash into the building. I see the buildings burn and I see the buildings fall down.

I see imagery that until now did not exist in reality, only in the fiction of film. Seeing it with your own eye, in real time, not on a screen, not protected by the frame of the television set, not set up and narrated by an anchor man, not in the communal darkness of a movie theater, seeing it like this is irreconcilable, like a hallucination, a psychotic break.

In the seconds after the second plane hit Tower Two, I did two things, filled the bath tub with water and pulled out my camera. When I don't know what else to do I document. I have always taken pictures as though storing what I am seeing, saving it for later when I am myself again. I take dozens of pictures, clicking faster, more frantically, as I feel myself pushing away.

When I go to re-wind the film, the camera is empty, the pictures are only in my head.

I spend the afternoon moving back and forth from the window to the television. By late in the day I have the sense that my own imagery, my memory, is all too quickly being replaced by the fresh footage, the other angle, the unrelenting loop.

I become fearful of my mind's liquidity, my ability to retain my own images and feelings rather than surrendering to what is almost instantly becoming the collective narrative. There is no place to put this experience, no folder in the mental hard drive that says, catastrophe. It is not something you want to remember, not something you want to forget.

In an act of the imagination, I begin thinking about the buildings, about the people inside, the passengers on the planes. I am trying on each of the possibilities, what it might be like to be huddled in the back of a plane, to be in an office and catch a half-millisecond glimpse of the plane coming towards you, in a stairwell in one of those towers struggling to get down, to be on the ground showered with debris, to be home waiting for someone to return.

There is the sound of a plane overhead. No longer innocent, everything is suspect. The plane has become a weapon, a manned missile, a human bomb. I duck. It is a United States war plane, circling.

The phone rings, people call from around the world. Attendance is being taken and some of us are absent, missing.

I am on the phone when the first building collapses. A quarter mile high, the elevators take you up one-hundred-ten stories in fifty-eight seconds. It crumbles in less than a minute as though made of sugar cubes. The tower drops from the skyline, a sudden amputation. My eye struggles to replace the building, to paint it in, to fill in the blank.

When the second building goes, when there is just a cloud of smoke, I can no longer stand the strange isolation of being near and so incredibly far—I go outside.

The city is stilled, mute. There are no cars moving, no horns blowing, and for the most part not even any sirens. Everyone is talking—this is something to be shared, to be gone over, a story to be repeated, endlessly, until we are empty.

Coming up the West Side Highway is a post-apocalyptic exodus, men and women wandering north, walking up the center of the road, following the white lines, one foot in front of the other, mechanized. They come north gray with dust, with a coating of pulverized cement. They come in suits, clutching briefcases, walking singly or in small groups. People stand on the side lines, offering them water, cell phones, applauding them like marathon runners. They are few and far between.

Wind carries smoke uptown as if to keep the disaster fresh in people's minds, somehow begging you to breathe deeper, to be a part of it.

Those twin towers were my landscape, my navigational points, my night lights. I write staring out the window, depending on the fixedness of the landscape to give me the security to allow my thoughts to wander, my imagination to unfold. Now, I am afraid to look out the window, afraid of what I might see.

I've been sent somewhere else in time, to a different New York, a different America. Today we are all war correspondents.

49

RICHARD HOWARD

Fallacies of Wonder

September 11, 2001

Most of mind is memory—it is
memory which grants the means of thought.

From modern masters we have learned a lot—
from Freud

We remember what we want to remember,
forget what we find no longer important.

and antithetically from Proust—

The only true memory is involuntary.

but we have yet to learn that memory
is a fallacious mirror, rich but wrong,

useless as record of experience,
for memory IS experience. In the end,

nothing remembered can be true, although
only what is remembered can be real.

Confusion now hath made his masterpiece
And stolen thence the life o' the building

Often, still, I turn to look downtown
from where I live on Waverly. I trust

the evidence, by daylight or by dark,
of variations in the versions of

those hundred-story towers, so neighborly
I scarcely need to look. I know that I can count

on seeing them where I remember them,
no different yet never quite the same.

I do look, though, and, where they were,
replace their being by their absences.

Memory can only be artificially improved by the operation of fantasy towards ideas in the Round Art, which uses magical images, effigies of the stars, statues of gods and goddesses, or through images of corporeal things in the Square Art, using buildings as places.

Such is the way of wonders: no longer seen
because, being there, remembered merely;

and, no longer there, remembered because
no longer seen. Did they have to be beautiful?

(Was that what the ancient wonders were,
beautiful?) All are gone but the Pyramids—

Though palaces and pyramids do slope
Their heads to their foundations, though the treasure
Of Nature's germens tumble all together
Even till destruction sicken, answer me
To what I ask . . .

merely remembered: gardens, temples, tombs,
a lighthouse and the statues of two gods.

Did some two thousand die for us to call
Remembered towers, wonders, beautiful?

The reaction has commenced, the human has made its reflex upon the fiendish; the pulses of life begin to beat again; and the re-establishment of the goings-on of the world we live in make us profoundly sensible of the awful parenthesis that had suspended them.

50

LAIRD HUNT

Still Life with Snow and Hammer

The emotions he experienced seemed to have taken hold of the deepest roots and subtlest fibers of his being. And so much the more that it was so subterranean in him, so much the more did he feel its weird inscrutableness.
—Herman Melville, *Pierre; or, The Ambiguities*

One snowy night in my earlier days, I was out playing on the street with a large green-handled hammer. My game was to stand in the middle of the quiet street and throw the hammer up into the dark, snow-filled air and to let it fall with a pleasantly muffled thunk onto the ground. Before long, I was joined by another, equally young individual, one I was in the habit of exchanging blows with, and, after wrestling around a little, by whatever mysterious alchemy of adrenaline and alliance that can still take place at that age, we took to standing at opposite ends of the street and flinging the hammer back and forth. To the peculiarly delicious pleasure to be had in launching a hard and heavy object up into the air and waiting for it to fall were consequently added the elements of targeting, trajectory and return. And it is of the latter aspect that I think especially these strange, grim days. This is because it wasn't very long before, like the lovely knuckleheads we were, we took to standing directly under the point of the hammer's projected descent and to leaping out of its way at the last second, with the idea that points were to be awarded for the nearest misses and that the game would be over when one or the other of us was hit. A car door slammed, someone's mother rapped meaningfully on a window, I'm not sure—my attention wavered and I got hit, smacked hard on the arm. Pride demanded that I sue for another round. He then, having been winged on the calf, said it could only be settled by going best out of three. We stood there a moment before the final exchange started, sizing each other up, breathing hard. Then he yelled something and I yelled back and threw. Minutes elapsed as the hammer flew back and forth between us. I believe it had begun to snow harder. We had both achieved the kind of high-pitched frenzy that is not always but can be accompanied by a great deal of shrieking and hopping around. So it was that at the end of the longest and final round, I stood under the looping falling hammer, looking up into the dark, snowy air with a mixture of terror and exaltation, as well as a sense of irreality, as if it wasn't me about to be hit on the head by a carpenter's hammer, as if there were no snow, as if it wasn't night. Stupid boy, poor child, my mother said. Suddenly, years and years have passed.

51

SIRI HUSTVEDT

The World Trade Center

As citizens of the world, not one of us is a stranger to horror. The century that is now over racked up a long list of crimes against human beings—sometimes dozens of people, sometimes hundreds, sometimes thousands, sometimes millions. There are times when an ideological term serves as shorthand for terror—as in "Collectivization," and "The Cultural Revolution." In Argentina the words "The Disappeared" came to signify countless murders, but many of these catastrophes are designated simply by place names. The place becomes the sign of the event, or as in "Auschwitz," the figure for a larger and more sweeping monstrousness. We all recognize crimes in the names: The Belgian Congo. Cambodia. My Lai. Sarajevo. Rwanda. They are words engulfed by the unspeakable. Now we have the World Trade Center. All that once happened there, the people who came and went, worked, joked, ate lunch, and telephoned home are subsumed in a name that will always mean devastation and mass murder. For us who live in New York, the difference between the other names and this one is that on September 11, it happened down the street. This time, no matter where we live in the city, all we had to do was turn our heads toward the smoke.

It may be easy to say, "Burning bodies fell from the windows of the World Trade Center," but it isn't easy to embrace the reality of that sentence. On September 11, my sister, Asti, ran uptown with my niece, Juliette, in her arms, away from P.S. 234 as the towers burned behind them. Juliette's classroom faced north so she didn't see people jumping or the burned corpses falling from the building, but other second-graders, whose rooms faced south, did. They rushed to the window and looked up. A panicked child began to scream, "Is my mommy dead?" One of Juliette's friends won't leave her mother for an instant. When the mother sits on the toilet she has her daughter on her lap. At any mention of the World Trade Center, the little girl puts her hands over her ears. A boy in the north-facing classroom has taken to bragging about carnage he didn't see. Another swears that there were skeletons walking in the streets. A kindergarten boy won't go outside because he doesn't want his feet to touch the ground. He says he's afraid of falling sticks. A third-grader wets his bed every night. Other children wake up screaming, and many have taken to sharing a bed with their parents. These are the translations of horror when it enters the mind and the body, and they seem to speak more directly to the truth than the elegant phrases we have been hearing lately, both political and literary. We have to talk, but we should be careful with our words.

52

JOHN KEENE

The Orders (from Pariah)

Pardon me, but I was thinking?
You don't have to if you're not yet ready.
Pardon me?
Set your bags down there but be careful not to break the tape.
Am I the first one?
It must have taken hours.
There is the rutted highway that muscles along the river, and the narrow airbridge between the hills that rim the valley, and the descent down the ladder of suburbs that stand where the forest once fanned.
Down there.
It must have taken hours.
Only if you work alone, but much of it is still sitting on the trucks behind the barricades.
Am I the first one?
I remember. There was a time when even I explored these possibilities, routines, the adamantine rigor of submission, this station and its alternating frequencies?
Not yet.
How when you pass through one side you can almost brush the limit, but at the other end there is only the hard distance and the flood lights blaring, and you return or follow.
Follow.
Or beyond.
You had to.
Do you remember?
I was thinking—

It's gossamer.
I can hear it.
That is the kind they assign us, the sole one, which takes some getting used to, but once you roll it out a few times you start to notice how light it is and don't think twice.
Am I the only one and are there others?
Was it difficult?
The role. Like all of them I receive regular relief on these shifts. As you can tell tonight I'm working a double. Was it difficult? It must have taken me hours to assign everything to its proper place. I set aside a small contingent from each category, for there was only so much space. I had already mapped the route and calibrated the distance here, so it was only a matter of final messages, markers, not forgetting to pocket the ticket.
It must have taken hours to burn everything you couldn't carry with you.
Can you taste the smoke?
Usually.
Who are the others and how can I tell them?
It must have taken hours to fold each corner, making sure to utilize the necessary seals. The moon scything on the ceiling, which is when I rose as always. The dial buzzed and then I had to burn everything I couldn't carry with me.
Which is required.
Which is required, as you know, by the most recent statute.
How sorry.

▪

What did the other ones say, and do you remember them?
I realized that under the circumstances the memory of flight and flaming plastic might be fragrant.
Takes some getting used to?
Not really, I tried to savor all the little things: velleities, shadows, the low din or limbo of my absence, which provides a reflection.
Difficult?
I came to fathom the edges?

Or beyond?
Of the soul?
You must not.
How am I to know if you remember?
But there are densities and surfaces that can be achieved through only a concerted exertion, whether inside or outside the workshop, and I began, I tried.
Expectation?
I was succeeding?
Be careful.
I was.
Sorry.
Twice last week I received the order, first as a message, which was lost.
Usually.
And then in a small white envelope. On its flap.
Sterilized?
My eyelids burnt at the touch.
Embers.

▪

How many will arrive after me, and what will you do to make them tell you?
Action. It would have been foolhardy of me to imagine the possibilities without the repercussions. Moon scything on the mirror, the mind turned towards its utter definition, the grid I had not seen but imaged, each one written down, displayed.
The message.
Visible from all sides.
The envelope.
Anyone could.
The ticket.
See it.
What will you do to make them tell you?
Do you have one?
Ken.

I thought so.
It must have taken me hours to replace everything, find the proper names, contain them. I sat aside from each category a sample, for there was no place left once I began the journey. Still I brought them with me, and they wait here, and not only I?
Which is difficult.
But others, eventually?
What will you do?
Will.
Now, at the end, only the memory of the flight, and this vastness, white and flooded with longing, and this waiting, here at the gate, under these conditions, the ticket, seals, the tape.
Will.
Hear it.
Will.
It's gossamer.
What will you do to make me tell you?
Usually, there is the entire hierarchy to consider.
Ken.
Will I tell you?
And there is the role.
Ken.
The routine, responsibility.
Ken.
Rule, the order.
Make me tell you?
I was thinking.
You don't have to if you're not yet ready.
Tomorrow?
Anyone could.
Set them down here.
Tomorrow?
We can talk about this more?
Tell you?
Tomorrow.
Tomorrow.

53

JOHN KELLY

TRAVEL LOG

Who thought it was a movie
Who put such hatred in their hearts
Who went to work early
Who put the sun in our heads
Who told us we were the universe
Whose bubble has burst
Who looked up in horror
Who ran for cover
Whose kindness came through
Who missed it by 10 hours
Who heard from abroad
Who's got a cell phone
Who's in a different time zone
Who wanted to be home
Who felt cheated
Who's a troubled tourist
Who's gray in the face
Whose papers rained down
Who fans the flames
Who feels the victim
Who tasted the vengeance
Who sang new anthems
Whose ideals are in power
Who loves the flag
Who saw an "angel"
Who lived to tell
Whose dog is this
Who was ushered on a raft
Who crossed deep river
Who crowned this ruler
Who measured the space
Who planned the event
Who grinned
Who sobbed
Who reached the other side of the river
Who watched with wary eyes
Who fears not, and this, and this
Who grieved from afar
Who terror sparked
Who stores bottled water
Who bunkers their mentality
Who's got the tools
Who picked up the pieces
Who bumpers their sticker
Who sees white and black
Who knee jerked their shit
Who played the songs
Who lights a candle
Who was *Tribune* weary
Who wanted to come home
Who bonded with tour mates
Who saw sobs in Berlin
Who couldn't find comfort in Dublin
Who suspects too many
Whose feelings are crystal clear
Who's sick of the spin
Who's searching for remains
Who's writing a screenplay

Who stole the watches
Who's hosing it down
Whose turf is kinder
Whose god blesses more
Whose cheek is turned
Whose track record is cleaner
Who's numbing with sex
Who's drinking too much
Who had a birthday
Who's dreaming strange
Who saves the papers
Who's just blown away
Who scans the walls
Who will savor their life
Who's returning calls
Who's checking in
Who scans a map
Who can't take a nap
Whose child is this
Whose spirit is failing
Who's learning
Who's stewing
Who's brewing
Who's scheming
Who's healing
Who's loud
Who's pissed
Who haunted the payphone
Who played songs to distract
Who counted his days
Who's not really here
Who's not yet there
Who was not afraid to fly
Who counted the day
Who flew the Atlantic
Who knows what's next
Who's present
Who's angry
Who is just sad
Who can say
Whose fortunes are fallen
Whose priorities are shifted
Whose time is precious
Who's leaving
Who's falling behind
Whose eyes
Whose arm
Who knows
Who's moving away
Who's dancing
Who's reeling
Whose world I rocked
Who came from afar
Who scans the horizon
Who didn't come home
Who's calling
Who's watchful
Who's flying
Whose one night
Whose night
Who's mourning
Who made such a space
Who leads
Who wears fatigues
Who was watching from afar
Who longed to fly
Who watched it from the sky
Who isn't afraid
Who walks the streets
Whose home

9/28/01

54

WAYNE KOESTENBAUM

Super 8

Liszt blended ersatz Hungarian experience
  and French hotel sensibility
(stale seminal linen)
  to fashion transcendental études I may
one day play if I can figure out
  how to relax my wrist
and make the page an unbordered
  Super 8 adventure starring Parker Tyler as fisherman
of souls and Greta Garbo as Simone Weil
  staying alone at Hotel Sacher
where cathexis and analysis
  interminable were invented
and my favorite sleeping pill
  Trazadone
which an American baroque poet agrees
  impedes cognition
and gives an Emersonian transparent-eyeball
  morning-after headache
this description courtesy of a prof named Porte
  who lectured me on manure
in the work of Henry David Thoreau
  what a detour this poem has become!
not the usual odyssey
  through the modern unconscious
with music by Elmer Bernstein
  a Ross Hunter production starring Susan Kohner

reprising her *Imitation of Life* role
as "passing" showgirl daughter
I dreamt of a 'fifties chanteuse
à la Peggy Lee or Julie London
her name was Clea Vage
Clea owned a beachhouse
in Queens and published a book of poems
called *Liner Notes*
why is someone outside mowing his lawn
at twelve midnight in December
why isn't that fool in bed
reading new interpretations
of the Bay of Pigs?
I feel guilty fleeing the city
to spend the night in the country
far from terrorism fears
to write a poem I linger outside time
perhaps in an elevator
a mambo club
east 51st or Gotham Book Mart
a back room
Tower Records Bed Bath and Beyond
the subway, Q or N or L
the lines I never take
because I don't know where they go
or why and when they stop
in my dream the M5 bus
took me from Rockaway to a beachhouse
not Clea Vage's but Marianne Moore's
and her tetchy Mom's
they discussed rhinos and pedophiles
at their last seance
which I attended dressed as Valentino
my *Son of the Sheik*
costume bought at a Santa Monica yard sale in 1955
before I was born

Steve's potential client the French wine importer
    first name pronounced "Yvonne"
wants to build an escapist modernismo
    maisonette on 23 acres
Steve likes butter more than I do
    I prefer confiture
served in polished silver bowls with espresso spoons
    we ate perfect jam
near a Dordogne watermill
    an ill lady slept on a sofa
while we consumed confiture
    this hotel famous for fruit jam
though a reputation founded on jam
    is perforce a limited renown
at night I can speak freely
    authority no longer a distant colonized isle
toward which I veer with broken sail
    days I sleepwalk
like Liz in *Boom!* demanding
    "Injection!" or the tranquillizer
shot in *Suddenly, Last Summer*
    after she accidentally wanders
into the lobotomy rec room
    where the mad-beyond-repair
rock and suckle stuffed animals
    forgive these fetishes
in my childhood's living room
    hung a reproduction Soyer painting
three female dancers
    I mistook for three lunatics
on coffee break
    lounging in a mental asylum corridor
I feared their splayed skinny torpid limbs
    when my father
first used the word "schizophrenia"
    in my presence he defined it

as a grown woman afraid to get
  off the toilet
because outside her bathroom
  enemies lie in wait
as a youth I made two dramatic movies
  with my Super 8 camera
The American Time Bomb
  premiered at our avant-garde seder
and *What Men Live By*
  based on a Tolstoy fairy tale
my other films were realistic reportage
  older brother on a horsie
closeup of my baby brother crying
  as he flees two taunting kids
why didn't I protect him?
  closeup of my baby sister crying
topless in our backyard's plastic wading pool
  the provocation unclear

55

RICHARD KOSTELANETZ

Unimaginable

Deposited mostly
In attractive Florida beach towns
Favored by retirees,
Where they could have defected
In favor of honest jobs
And comfortable lives,
If not lifetime rewards
From American intelligence agencies,
These provocateurs instead chose
Immediate death
And eternal ignominy
As mass murderers.
Fools,
Most of us would agree,
They certainly were.
Not twenty-year-olds,
Like most suicide bombers,
These were older gents,
Some of them educated;
A few reportedly had families
How it is possible
That so many
So superficially fortunate
Could be so psychopathic?
Behind them,
How could any manipulator(s)
Trust so many

To be so crazy?
(This is stuff for novelists.)
Nonetheless,
Nineteen kamikazes
Plus backup folk
Do not a critique of America make
not six decades ago during WWII
And not now.

56

GUY LESSER

24 September 2001, or Manhattan Seen in a New Light

For thirteen nights the cluster of dark office buildings across the river
has been graced by a pale nimbus of dazzling sodium.
Another evening is haunted by the portents of "if only . . ."
If only how-it-looks could be severed from what-it-means,
then this illuminated view of local haze and ghostly smoke
would be lovely.

But tonight the televisions speak.
Before Nine-One-One.
After Nine-One-One.
The toll that's rising,
as rescue fades into "recovery."
The sputtering candles versus the baritone commentators.
The Kodacolor snapshots of the lost on every street corner.
The newsreel files of daily life in Kabul.
A new Crusade (despite all disclaimers),
winged in matte black armor.
The "new" us (with little flags gaily waving from every antennae).
An all too venerable "them."
A cloud filled future imminent with lukewarm war.

If only that which happened,
could be severed from where it leads.
Then the abracadabra of bright white sodium would be
returned to
glass and steel and flesh,
the world would walk to the gray flourescent hum of normal
life,
and we could regain our happy indifference to the words of
government.

57

JONATHAN LETHEM

Entry of Buildings

They caught him at the door of the American Tract Society Building, on Nassau. He was entering the building and they caught him at the door, two private security guards from the Park Row Building around the corner. Someone there had called security when they saw him in the lobby, peering around corners, examining elevators. The guards had followed as he exited. They'd stayed at a distance, watching, as the man stuck his head inside the Potter Building on the corner of Beekman. An ordinary looking older man in a transparent raincoat over a dull brown suit, a hat with a withered peacock feather, and carrying a thick book under one arm, glancing at it periodically for—what? Inspiration? Information? It was worrying.

Finally, at the doorway of the Tract Building, they pounced.

"Looking for something?"

"What's the game, man?"

The man seemed shocked to be confronted. He held the book in two hands at his chest.

"Visiting," he said.

"That supposed to mean?"

"Whatcha got there—a *Koran*?"

"Visiting—buildings," the man said. "Entering buildings. I beg your pardon."

"Visiting for what purpose?"

"I would be embarrassed to say."

"Lemme see that."

It was an odd tall paperback the thickness of a Yellow Pages.

The *AIA Guide*, by White and Willensky. Subtitled *The Classic Guide to New York's Architecture.*

"What are you planning? A bomb, maybe?"

"Never." The man trembled.

"Explain yourself."

"I couldn't. I'm only visiting. Entering, then leaving. Give me the book."

"This is no time for random visiting and entry, guy."

"I'm sorry to differ but it's in no way random."

"You know someone? Got business?"

"Nothing to do with business."

"You're talking in circles, man."

"Believe me, my mind is lately *going* in circles. I'm telling what I can tell."

"It's suspicious behavior. We have to call the cops."

"You're not police yourselves?"

"We're uniformed citizens and we're holding you for the cops."

"Here?"

"Back at our building." The security guard struggled, lacking a precedent. A problem lately everywhere. "Where we took the complaint. We'll wait and you'll explain to the authorities."

"Make him walk ahead of us. I don't want him behind. He could be booby-trapped."

"He's not booby-trapped."

"Make him walk ahead."

They turned the corner, walking in formation, back to Park Row. "The book, please," said the captured man.

"What are you, mister, hung up on buildings?" The book was returned.

"In a way. I'd prefer to say nothing."

"Just entering and leaving, huh? That's your game?"

"I felt an urge to visit."

"Gotta control those urges."

The man shrugged. They came to the entrance of the Park Row Building. "Inside," they commanded.

"This is yours? You work here?"

"Sure."

"I envy you. This structure has a major significance."

"How's that?"

The man puffed up with what he had to tell them. "Listen, the buildings, the vanished ones, they were the tallest, yes?"

"Sure."

"Now it's the Empire, correct?"

"Get to the point."

"Yours, the Park Row, it was—" He flipped the book's pages, searching. "Between 1899 and 1908, it was the *world's* tallest. The city's, therefore. 386 feet, it says here."

"Don't shit me."

"I wouldn't. Look."

"Don't touch his book!"

The one guard frowned at the second for the panic, then looked at the page. After a moment his partner joined him. They read together, standing on the sidewalk.

For a moment they all saw it, the city's history unfurling backwards, tallest by tallest, to when some church spire, perhaps, towered over the whole enterprise. The island where they stood, once green.

"Nine years it held that status," said the man, gently.

"Dang," said one guard to the other.

"Yes," said the man. He closed his book.

"This is all you're doing?" said the other guard after a minute. "Just, what did you call it—*entering*?"

"A moment inside, then out. No time for more."

"You doin' that *whole book*?"

"It seemed—it seemed to need doing. Before anything—"

Again the man fell silent. They all did.

"All right, listen," said one of the guards. "Just go."

"No police?"

"Not today. They're too busy to waste their time."

"He's lettin' you go, man, so go."

"I can't promise to stop."

"Listen, you have our *blessing*."

The man only nodded his thanks. He tightened his raincoat, tucked his book, and moved uptown again as though he'd never been intercepted.

The two watched him go, then glanced up at the Park Row's two ornate turrets.

Nine years, a fair run.

It was a hell of a job to guard a building, but at least they were drawing a check.

58

JOCELYN LIEU

Shopping (3:58 P.M. September 11)

Not all of the lights are on inside. The cosmetic counter—the first thing they see on entering the K-mart on Astor Place—is covered with white sheets. The sheets take the contours of the standing mirrors and displays concealed beneath. In the dim light, the department store looks like an abandoned ancestral home.

They have come here because the baby was restless from being kept in all day under the constant eye of the TV. But once outside, the air gently stung their cheeks and throats. She didn't want to think of what it was they breathed. The park was out of the question.

Almost mindlessly, they walked west. Except for the occasional emergency vehicle, the streets were empty. The afternoon light fell golden on the windows and walls. Crossing Lafayette, she saw the thick plume of smoke rising in the south. It didn't flow straight up into the sky, but twisted like the dark cone of a silent tornado.

People filled the sidewalks. Almost all were walking north. Many wore business suits. They walked singly or in pairs or groups of three or four, some talking, some quiet. One man in green surgical scrubs was bleeding from a butterfly-bandaged wound on his temple.

They ended up in the ghostly K-mart because the bookstore that was their vague destination was closed. Most of the stores they passed were closed, as if for a national holiday.

Past the cosmetic counter stand six-foot-high stacks of cartons of Halloween candy. Miniature Milky Ways. Three Musketeers.

"Do you think it's open?" her husband asks.

"Wouldn't they have locked the door?"

None of the usual rules hold, however. Reality has been broken. Pushing the stroller, she walks deeper inside the cavern, not knowing what they will find.

The air conditioning doesn't seem to be on. Past the stacks of black-and-orange cartons, a middle-aged woman with several brightly colored garments draped over her arm appears to be the only other customer. But the escalator is running, its metal teeth rising into the semi-gloom above.

She gets Gracie out of the stroller. Her husband takes the baby's hand, and solemnly they step onto the moving stairway. Watching them ascend, she feels a stab of panic. She doesn't want to be separated from them even for a moment.

Folding the stroller, she follows. At the top of the escalator stand two white-sheeted ghosts, one with a jack-o'-lantern face. Still holding her father's hand, Gracie jumps happily up and down before the two mannequins.

"What now?" her husband asks.

"We let her play, I guess."

Gracie breaks away from the ghosts and runs down an empty aisle. Hundreds of shoes lie on the floor. The metal racks that usually hold the shoes and boots and slippers are almost bare.

Hugging a black rubber boot to her chest, Gracie staggers around a corner, out of sight. Her father strides after her.

When Jocelyn finds them again, the baby has abandoned the boot for a kitchen broom, its pink straw brush still wrapped in a plastic sheath.

"Clean!" she yells.

Leaving the stroller behind, Jocelyn steps over a pile of work boots and kneels before her daughter.

"Give Mommy a hug," she says.

It is beginning to dawn why the shoes are strewn around as if by a violent storm. The walkers—those thousands of people who survived the destruction and fire—had been in need of them.

"Let's go," her husband says.

Gracie shakes her head no. She clasps the broom tighter.

TAN LIN

59

Various Slo-Moving Clouds Are Damaged

10:45 Two planes, American Airlines planes, reluctant, going down, gleaming with fuel, abort their flight paths. They cast soft, misused, or unintended shadows in the lower arenas of the atmosphere—over pedestrians, public school clocks, figure-eight shaped gardens of the hospital, a blue-grey river criss-crossed by ferries. One of the planes is falling through a cloud when the telephone rings. I am the President's courier and I know nothing.

Floor 106: Report 2, on the President's ottoman, near the hot desk. In the armature: resin clouds and dislodged newspapers visible and flaring for miles through the vertical ceiling of this highly sensitive and plastic airspace suck through the wind pipe and affix to our 106th floor windows, which we cannot see. I hand over Report 2 from Ground Zero, which I ratcheted out of Wisniski's burnt hands. In the high-floor suite filled with briefs, graphs, take-out Chinese food, the President of Eastern United States (EUS) worships or believes he has the power to turn on airplanes. He watches them like swans, engravings, mistakes in the sky. In the meantime, the secretary of Vanished Homelands hands him his favorite catalog of framed fighter pilots. The President has a photographic memory, which means he is jaded by what he has engraved, which he sees subsequently, thrashing the reflections of his panorama. He has poor word retention skills, he is a hard ass but he draws with placid tension the 12 spokes of the horoscope or the mortal outlines of dead things. For this reason he is beloved. But not, however, because he is from Texas, cow country, flag and rattler land—as is his mother, his brother but not his father.

10:46 Two or three black projectiles, vacuous or unscented, spill gauze-like from the fax. They are sporadic, or they are granular, or they are mechanical, Lazarus-like, grid-like. Or they are typed long-hand and combine many slo-moving things at once. They show the spectrum of the imponderable, human mistakes, ignored time signatures, zeros, they show us how neatly cross-sectioned the B and K rows are laid out like typewriter keys by someone with obvious talent. And a number of the superannuated grids are quite improbably suggestive. They suggest that they were magnetized, like load-bearing curtains, and that *that* has made all this veering likely, made some imponderable noise halfway between calculation and multiplied crinkling of a windshield, grinding water and short whistling. The fanning and whistling noises combine into a spectacle, a broken piece of armature.

10:53 One of the towers in snow.

10:54 The son dabs his needle between his lips and draws a photograph on stone. The son, the President writes plainly, arrogantly, with stiff upper and lower case letters resembling a caption. "The fuselages gleam and are too tough to puncture with a fork."

104: I put down the cell phone because I am still in love with her and because of other things on the floor. I am still capable of all these things and Sandy touches the spider plant. A shadow appears, on the plant, outside, on one of the engravings. The President does not fail to take notice and says plainly that there are planes outside, gleaming like shadows. "There are planes outside. They are gleaming like shadows." He adds: "They remind us of us. They are American Airlines planes. We commissioned those planes to fly us wherever we wanted them to take us. They are larger than we thought they would be. We thought they were parallel to the buildings at first but they are not. Some of us are annoyed and we cannot do anything about it because our anger knows that it built this inside of something else." That night, we were at a bar, in Lower Manhattan, thinking of each other's President, and yes, drinking lukewarm vodka tonics and week-old beer, and I am falling in love again and again and again.

76: (code) Of course: I am slo-moving courier of snow and ibis and I want to get married.
(code) I am Amy.
(code) I am Amy, the ex-wife of the former president of the technical operations and the engineering feedback. I like to work for clear blue water. The parking lot is full of emergency vehicles. I hold my eyeglass case, which is red. On my way out, I see two or three bodies parachuting from the upper floors. One of them is smoking.

102: Analog buttons? Chipsets? Carjacking? Open detection systems?

32: Of course, some of our members were caught at various moments making love to the sales people, fucking the sales people and the sailors. And the braid of my hair is too long. The following is black information and therefore encrypted: Fake alternate firewell. The man stitches wallets with his hands. I am his lover. I saw him on Monday, on Church Street, running from work. By July, we have moved in together into his apartment and we want to get married in June.

27: On this floor, news is keyed to each sender. For this reason, the news is variable. Other families with children have just moved here to run hoses through the windows. The new girl likes to touch the red speaker wires too often.

PAGE 14: (each bearing a time-stamp)

Suppose an image is outlined by a flower or a word for flower. Suppose the catalog is missing a page. Or two. Suppose one of the flowers blooms or fails to. Each spring I am alive in, which is in correspondence with a number. On the table, what looks like an artist's book, a manila folder. I examine the grey paintings of aeroplanes. They appear to be the shadows cast by a candle's flames. These are the symptoms a courier has to dispose.

11:43 I change jobs. I am not Amy. One of my new jobs is to paint photographs of what I see. Every painted photograph must be done in an interval of time, corresponding to 3 minutes. One of the photos I draw creates a bomb inside it. It airbrushes in a crater in the building's southwest foundations. Pedestrians run furiously past a jagged edge that looks like a foreign language, something that happened in another country. This is figure 1A. I have never seen a bomb like this before, with a head made from poured concrete and a tail section from street signs soldered to its unbuttoned side. I have never seen a concrete bomb before.

On the second page of photographs, and next to the manila folder, a hand. The hand is writing some of this down. Alternately, some of the people in the crater are already dead.

Details: ?

110: Sandy runs to the 110th floor to fetch my gold-lined courier bag but we

SAM LIPSYTE

60

The Grief Technician

It took him forever to find the place, even with his company map. He'd ridden out on the elevated train and walked a good way towards the river. The house was a brick affair on a quiet block, flagstones, flowers, some plastic gnomes. One of the gnomes had been crushed and the driveway was really just a spit of sick grass between strips of concrete, but all in all it was a nice spread. The welcome mat on the stoop said "The O'Reillys."

Lewis felt eyes on him from behind the lace curtains in the window, wondered if you could really feel somebody else's eyes, knocked.

He was fairly new to this work.

The man at the door was tall and unshaven. His eyes, now that Lewis could see them, looked swollen and runny.

"Yeah."

"I'm looking for James O'Reilly," said Lewis.

"Yeah."

"Can I come in?"

"Why? What are you selling?"

"Nothing."

"Then why do you want to come in?"

"I need to talk to you."

"Is this about Jesus? Are you going to give me the good news? I just can't handle that right now, okay?"

"It's not the good news," said Lewis.

"Then what?"

"Your wife is dead."

The man stared at Lewis for a while.

"You came here to tell me that? I know that. It's been months. One day she went to work and that was the last . . . oh, shit."

The man began to sob a bit. Lewis put his hand on his shoulder, stroked it in the manner he'd been instructed.

"Let's go inside and talk for a while."

Booze was bad for the process but Lewis accepted a beer from the man. They sat at the dining room table and drank. The table was scattered with snapshots of a woman about the man's age, sometimes posing with him, or with a little girl. A child's drawing of the house they were sitting in was tacked to the wall. The pale crayon sun in the corner of the picture had a photo of the woman pasted to it.

"Our daughter did that," the man said. "I told her that her mother lives inside the sun now."

"That's a beautiful thought," said Lewis.

"Couldn't think of what else to tell her. Who the hell are you, anyway?"

"I'm a grief technician," said Lewis.

"Come again?"

"My firm's been hired by the city. We've been working with the victims' families."

"I've talked to some counselors."

"I'm not a counselor."

Lewis reached into his satchel and put the O'Reilly file on the table. Photographs, e-mail transcripts, bank slips, hotel receipts. All of it was forged, but Lewis had to admit that lately the quality had vastly improved.

"What's all this?" said the man.

"It's a story I'm going to tell you."

"What kind of story?"

"A story that will make you feel very bad for a while. But later, you will feel much better than if I hadn't told it to you."

This was right out of the manual and Lewis was proud he'd remembered it verbatim.

"I feel pretty bad as it is."

"Then you won't mind if I begin. Basically, the deal is this. Your wife was having an affair. She had quite a few over the years, but recently she'd gotten very serious with a man at work named Wilkinson."

"Wilkinson? That fat bastard? She was always bitching about him."

"I wouldn't know about that," said Lewis. "But you can look for yourself."

He slid some photographs across the table. Most of them showed the woman in bed with a fat, young man. A few showed them at a sidewalk cafe. One showed them shopping for bathroom fixtures.

"Oh, my fucking lord," said the man, and began to sob again. "I'll kill that prick."

"Wilkinson died with your wife," said Lewis. "He had no family."

Now Lewis slid the financial statements over.

"What's that?"

"She was trying to steal money from you. Wilkinson was helping her hide it."

"Oh, Christ! What else! What else!"

"That's it," said Lewis, sat back in his chair with his satchel in his lap. "You can keep those materials."

The man let his head drop into the crook of his arm.

"Why in God's name did you tell me this?"

"It's a city service," said Lewis.

"But why?"

"Sometimes a terrible truth can cleanse the mourner of seemingly unconquerable suffering," said Lewis. This was from an older, discontinued manual Lewis had found snooping around the office one day. He'd liked the ornate phrasings and had secretly adopted some of them for his sessions.

"You mean like closure?" said the man.

"Exactly," said Lewis.

Riding back to the office Lewis looked out the smeared

windows at the rows of houses. They were all identical but for some reason he thought he could make out the O'Reilly residence. That man would be in bad shape once the shock wore off. But he was relatively young and eventually he'd come to see his marriage as an unfortunate episode which had nonetheless provided him with a loving daughter. He might dream of his wife on occasion, but it would be about her betrayal with fat Wilkinson, not her fiery death. Otherwise he might mourn forever and never find happiness again. It wasn't perfect, the service, but it was just about all they had in the war against grief.

61

PHILLIP LOPATE

Altering the World We Thought Would Outlast Us

My first inkling of an attack on the Twin Towers came from the FedEx man. He rang the doorbell around 9:15 A.M., and when I signed for the package, he said, shaken: "Did you hear what happened? A plane crashed into the World Trade Center. You can see the smoke from here." My first response was, "So what? Planes do crash." Inside, the phone rang and it was my mother-in-law, telling me to turn on the television. I had been looking forward to writing all day, and so I said rather testily that I couldn't turn the television on and hung up. But something urgent in her voice disturbed me, and so, against my practice, I put on the television and saw the second plane crashing into the World Trade Center.

Now I was queasy, realizing that something unprecedented was happening. I tried to type a few sentences. My concentration was poor, but I resisted giving myself up entirely to this (so it yet seemed) public event. At around 10:30 my wife called and said she was sticking around my daughter's school, in case they decided to close it. I replied—the resolve had suddenly formed—that I was going for a walk, to see what I could. "Why don't you stop by the school afterward, and look in on us?" she asked. I said I doubted I would, not adding that suddenly I felt a sharp urge to be alone. The tragedy had registered on me, exactly as after my mother had died: a pain in the gut, the urge to walk, and a don't-touch-me reflex. The closer

I got to the waterfront, the harder it was to breathe. The smoke was blowing across the river, into Brooklyn. Cinders and poisonous-smelling smoke thickened the air, and ash fell like snowflakes on cars and one's clothing. When I turned away from the water, I encountered hordes of office workers. Not all seemed upset; there was a sort of holiday mood, in patches, of unexpected free time. Some younger people were even laughing. The middle-aged and elderly, on the other hand, seemed profoundly disturbed. The natural order of things seems wronged when the elderly, braced for their own diminishment, must absorb the knowledge of how vulnerable and perishable their society is—the world they had expected to outlast them. I myself felt, at only 58, that the attack was a personal affront to one's proper autobiographical arc, as though a dire subplot had been introduced too late in the narrative.

All at once, I wanted to be with my family. My shirt was flecked with ash when I turned into the school. The lobby was crowded with parents, many picking up their children. Cheryl was standing by the door of the multi-purpose room, waiting for Lily. Lily seemed happily surprised to see me mid-day; I hugged her. She trooped off; school seemed as safe a place for Lily as our house. Cheryl milled around with the parents who had returned from the financial district; they were engaging in that compulsively repetitious dialogue by which an enormity is made real.

A few days later, my wife reproached me for having shown up with ash-laden clothing; she said I could have frightened the children. I said I did not think anyone had noticed me. But her reproach was justified: I was indulging the fantasy that I was invisible, not a team player. Some sort of communal bonding was taking place, foreign to me, beautiful in many respects, scary in others. My wife and I both felt anguished all week, but it was an anguish we could not share. The fault was mine: Selfishly, I wanted to nurse my grief at what had been done to my city. I mistrusted any attempt to co-opt me into group-think, even conjugal-think.

When I got home, my wife was glued to the television. Uneasy about joining her in this electronic vigil, yet feeling I had no choice, I joined her. Our daughter said, "Why do you keep watching that? They keep saying the same things. We know that already. Two planes crashed into the building." She was right: There was something punitive about the same information, the same pictures, over and over. This has become our modern therapy in catastrophes, the hope that by immersing ourselves in the media, by the numbing effect of repetition we will work through our grief. It doesn't work for me: I get a kind of sugar buzz and feel nauseous afterward.

I feel so identified with my native city that it took a mental wrenching to understand that all of America considered itself a target. I knew the Pentagon had been hit, but the attack on a suburban military complex did not seem as significant, as humanly interesting. The American flags that started appearing everywhere seemed fitting, especially if taken to honor firemen and police who died trying to rescue victims. But if they were a nationalistic statement about America as the greatest nation, then I could not join that sentiment. The only banner I wanted to fly was the orange, green and white flag of New York City, with its clumsy Dutchman and beaver.

I expect that this dreadful experience will add to the scar tissue left by other atrocities of life, like the death of one's parents, the illness of one's children or the shame of one's nation (My Lai), sorrows over which one has no control but that cause the deepest regrets.

62

KAREN MALPEDE

The Dumpster

Kate is about to fall completely apart when she hears the man right above her raging, a primal force, a large, big-headed man standing in a dumpster, bellowing, a lion-chested man, thundering, as he yanks at the garbage, sniffs disgusted at the insides of plastic bags, spent television tubes crusted with coffee grounds, a rusted car radiator, a bent ironing board, chalky sections of sheet rock, throws the pieces of used up things to the ground in the alleyway near the Quiet Cafe, where they bounce, crack and moan on the cement. Kate leans against a brick wall, transfixed by the brute force, the rage manifest in the muscled arms causing the crash of metal and glass. Kate wonders what has got into him, the man in the dumpster crying out, enraged infant shouts spurting from his throat sounding alien even to Max who has never dared make such sounds before. Max had been warned to keep quiet. A body. Max wants a body. A body to slip into the earth in a simple wood casket. Something solid, made of flesh, to mourn for. A body from which Max could see the spirit had fled, up to the sky on a Beanie Baby. He needs that. Simple, clear death. Because, long ago, Max had been left and no one came back.

Kate, in a stupor, exhausted, watches the very strange sight of the man in the seer sucker suit tossing refuse, when he suddenly throws a primitive green velvet shoulder bag, the kind Ana would sew from scraps, did sew, in fact, it has often dangled from Ana's shoulder, bulging with walkman, hair brush, spare rhinestone studs for her nose. Like a god on a garbage heap he picks the precious thing up out of the muck and flings it to the ground at Kate's feet. Ana's green velvet bag soggy and wet, lies limp on the cement. Kate hurls herself from the wall where she's been stuck. She kneels on the hard ground, grabs for Ana's torn green velvet bag, clutches it to her chest, begins to rock back and forth, a woman in grief for a daughter lost. Here on Avenue B in the late September heat, Kate moans and shrieks for the loss of girl-flesh.

This is an odd sight for the policeman on the beat, or for anyone else who might stop, the lion man on the dumpster up above about to fling a broken chair, the metal sort whose cane seat has caved in, perilously close to Kate's bent head, her arms locked around the velvet bag, rocking back and forth on her knees. Max, chair raised high, stops and sees. His folly begins to come clear. No body pieces have been discovered, no little girl in her party dress, bobbing to the top of this dumpster. Instead, there's a living woman beneath him who has lost something precious. Max stands quiet on his garbage perch, looking down. He would not have recognized the face on the body he searched for, would not have remembered the eyes or the soft roundness of calves, roughness of elbows of little girls. Hitting the sky on her own pink pony, galloping away, she left Max alone in this dumpster today. What Max sees, looking down, is the grief-stricken mother he longed for at Rikers, the mother shrieking for Max, her skin olive toned. The mother, inconsolable, who has lost her child. This is the comfort he sought.

He leaps down from the hard metal container, jolted by aging knees he's forgotten are his, so young did he seem a moment ago, in an instant he stands over Kate, a man to the rescue, his hands on her shoulders, lifts her up. Her tear-stained face is lit by a streetlight. Max softly asks questions. He needed exactly this late-night encounter to give him back control of himself. Kate gulping, saliva and snot choking her, Max offers his real, old-fashioned linen handkerchief. Kate, blowing hard, says in a whisper, afraid of her own words, "this is Ana's bag." Max holds her tight. He needs to hold someone, something, close to his chest. He wants to be near this woman who weeps for the child she lost. He needs to hear how terrible that sound is. Kate rests herself against the beat of his breast, so long since she'd been held by a man, his heart thudding loud in her ear, for a moment she lets herself float in the big-chested male womb, thinking she's rescued. "Only let Ana be safe," shocked at this comfort she's found for herself, Kate pulls herself off. At the same time, Max, embarrassed by his own voyeuristic need of her grief, gently removes her to arm's length. The woman looks down at the wet velvet bag she holds. Kate is slowly remembering that Ana's bag is actually dark forest green while this one now in the street light looks lime, but who could tell from the height at which it was flung and wet, it looked darker than it is. She holds the bag under the light, away from herself, its strap falling down. There is some sort of silly appliqué on it she has never seen before. It is no longer a living thing. She lets it fall to the cement.

(Excerpted from The Hyperion.*)*

CHARLES MCNULTY

63

A Rat's Life

Is that muscle hanging off my hind leg? Just keep moving old boy—there's no telling when a new abode will appear. Crazy humans! They can bring the whole house down on our heads, but they'll never get us all. A few always escape. Next thing you know we're back in full numbers. A glorious infestation. But I have to admit I've never seen anything as bad as this before. (And believe me, I've encountered a sadistic array of exterminating measures in my four fugitive years.) Still, I can't possibly be the lone survivor. My line is Houdini-like when it comes to escape. Somewhere, a twitching sensation tells me, a son of mine is shimmying down a sewer pipe to safety.

Fell asleep around dawn under my usual garbage bin behind (I don't like to brag but . . .) one of the posher corporate hotels in the area, and woke up in the middle of a smoldering junkyard. Sad to say but not even I can glean some benefit from the downward turn of things. The debris is deadlier than any subway track. Twisted metal that slices into your flesh from every angle. Glass and concrete vaporized into a smell that could kill something fifty times my weight. Fortunately, I've always been adept at holding my breath. I remember a particularly vicious janitor once closing the lid of a public toilet on me and flushing repeatedly. Let's just put it this way: Universally loathed as I am, I've learned to expect the unexpected.

A voice inside me keeps shouting, "Water, water!" I'm going, I'm going! But first I have to find a clear path out of this inferno. Meanwhile, the noise alone is enough to split your skull. The endless sirens! It was like waking up to the Apocalypse, which, as a devoutly irreligious rodent, is not the kind of thought I'm given to entertain. At least most of the screaming has stopped. Now it's just the yell of orders. If only darkness would fall and the humans would go away. I mean real darkness, not this choking cloud of soot. "The unpeopled night," as one of our lyric poets called it. Funny how the memory of those words make me almost forget my burning claw!

Did they blast the entire city? Dark thoughts are beginning to (forgive the pun) plague me. Though I am, by nature, a nervous optimist, I can't help wondering if the jig is finally up. Constant vigilance takes its toll on a body. Ear pressed to the ground for footsteps. Every shadow a potentially lethal menace. The stress is relentless—and for what? When disaster strikes, who can be prepared? Trust an old rat when he says that we exist merely at the sufferance of chance.

It was never an easy life. Not to say that there weren't the occasional half-filled pizza-box days. One miserably cold winter's night I even found an untouched bag of Krispy Kremes, the discarded treasure of a fat person's qualm. Diving headlong into that windfall, I emerged a few minutes later covered in a white dust that left the sweetest taste in my mouth. But even with a bloated belly of glazed sour cream, you can only keep the hunger at bay for so long. And the worry never goes away. Is that blood pooling at the end of my nose? Looks like I may have to bite off part of my ruined foot after all. Perhaps I'll rest a little first in the crook of this rubble heap—alone, abandoned even by fleas—and dream of the old trails and tunnels. The freedom of yesterday! Gobbled as quickly as a sparrow's fallen crumb.

64

PABLO MEDINA

Ode: The Day After

Prepara tu esqueleto para el aire.
—Federico García Lorca

Let go of me stone sleep,
let go of me night waning
in Brooklyn, hammer of reason,

red light, green light,
socket where the eye should be.
Let go of me washed out clouds,

pocked walls, pocked cars,
war wish and metal mouth,
let go of me asp of smoke,

plaster and dust storm,
what I am, what I shall become.
Let go of me five million pages

that float in air like birds, that land,
that peck the ground, that bathe in ash.
Let go graveyard,

church where God is sitting
in darkness wondering
what to do, what promises to keep,

where to pile the bones. Let go
of me transit of money, pulverized dreams of the children of plenty.

Let go photoland and video
land and newspaper land and slogan land.
Let go of me feast of delusions.

▪

There are people leaning out of windows
falling like wingless sparrows;
there is a man calling his wife,

a wife calling her daughter,
no one answering. There are staircases
leading down into a peeling husk,

a billowing flame, the belly of earth.
There are empty streets, the flyers
of the missing, the flags, the call to arms.

There is restlessness, loss
of words, closed doors, blank pages,
there once was a city of hope,

there once was money like summer.
Where is Whitman's voice, his beard
like milk, his heart like a fist on fire?

There is a woman waving goodbye
from the boat of her death, the wing,
the blade, the cut, again, again.

▪

Let go of me sun blood, moon milk,
let go ground zero, frozen zone,
abattoir, meat grinder, calamity

of begging dogs, here, here, don't hide
from sorrow, here, here, mark
our foreheads with Tuesday's ashes.

There is a flange, there is a capsule,
there is a wire on which we hang.
There is a form for the sky

growing tense and thick,
a shape for the ocean askance,
there is an absence, a presence,

a purpose. All of this in my dream,
all of this in the shadows. Deus
absconditus, show me your face,

Deus indifferent, kiss my lips.
Let go hope of no hope.
Let go tear, let go fist in the throat,

let go morning with its blandishments.
On this Golgotha we will plant our cross,
roots deep in the rubble,

and feed on our fellows and drink
of our city so time can bloom,
winter come, river flow.

65

ELLEN MILLER

His Friendship with Fear

If I couldn't have another Dad it was only fair that he couldn't have another girl, that I retain my queenly rank as the only girl allowed to stand on his heavy boots, smell his smell, as he moved through our life, relieving me of the burden of putting one foot in front of another, of having always to choose, choose, choose the best possible direction, all the while knowing that even a slight misstep could send me falling: from a bridge into a river; from a scaffold into a burning, chemical vat. It takes one mistake, one quick, imperceptible loss of balance, and, as he'd say, *You're toast, kid. You're toast. The second you stop being afraid, you're finished. Dollars to doughnuts, you get cocky, you get dead-nuts dead. Get on friendly terms, a real special first name basis, with fear.*

From fourteen to forty-one, every workday of his life, Dad was scared. Everywhere in the world were exactly two kinds of jobs: the safe and the dangerous. Experience never made Dad unafraid. He simply, without fanfare, accepted fear and the likelihood of grave injury as a standard work-day inevitability, like lunch with the crew or alone on a scaffold, like fatigue, like fumes. His morning routine: rise, get into uniform, shave, shower, shit, brush teeth, drink pot of coffee, put on boots and cap, get to site, feel crushingly, heart-stoppingly, acutely panicked about dying within the next eight hours. To earn his wage, Dad did frightening things that other people didn't want to do but had to get done by somebody. He tolerated daily terror (and exposure to chemicals that killed him), as beggars earn their wages by enduring cold, rain, viruses, fungi, phlebitis, humiliation, varicose veins.

At his first job, an old-timer, who called everyone under the age of 40 *Jimmy* and everyone over 40 *Mack*, took him up with a rope, showed him how to hook up to the bridge over a muddy ravine, to fold his body over itself into asymmetrical halves, torso pressed to thighs, to turn his face and his roller or brush skyward when painting the underside of the bridge's arches. There, after that virgin ascent, the boy who became the man who became the only Dad I'd ever get watched a painter fall from the bridge. "When you're fourteen, everybody over eighteen's old, so I dunno if he was Jimmy or Mack," Dad said, "But that guy went straight down, like an arrow, headfirst, and stuck there." His boots were a study in verticality, pointing stiff and straight up from the mud, two knives stabbed parallel into peanut butter. Dad watched two guys from the crew trudge through the mud to remove the dead guy's boots, where he kept his money, and wade back out, counting the dead man's cash, dividing it equally among the crew—"Because that's how Jimmy (or Mack) works"—and resume painting the bridge.

Dad liked that job; the old-timer, whose name was *Old-Timer*, drove Dad, who was too young to drive, both ways, every day, taking slower, greener routes. Driving home that first day, Old-Timer explained Jimmy's fall. Or Mack's. "He wasn't leaning back enough."

Dad had said, "I'm looking at this old bastard, like, you're fuckin' kidding me or something? And he says—get this—'When you're hooked up, hanging from one rope and one hook, 900 feet above water or concrete, there's nothing at that moment, nothing on God's green earth, that you want to do less than the one thing you hafta do, You hafta lean back. If you don't want to die like that poor sonuvabitch—lean the fuck back. I'm telling you, the only way to survive this job is to hold that fear like you'd bear-hug your best old drinking buddy. Relax into it. Lean right back into it—that thing that scares the most shit outta you.'"

Dad's experience stood contrary to the erroneous but commonly held idea that repeated successes conduced to increased confidence. The more bridges he painted, the more afraid he felt every morning when he awoke knowing he had a bridge to paint. Every triumphant negotiation with gravity made him more likely to lose the next negotiation. Every day Dad didn't fall off a bridge or water tower—or breathe in the critical mass of toxin, already building up in his blood, nudging him toward a slower death—made it more likely that the next day's hazards would do him in. A postcard pasted to my desk today serves as a reminder. It says: *Gravity: It's not just a good idea. It's the law!*

You never get used to fear. You only get used to not being used to it.

It's like a piece of dry steak. The more you chew it, the bigger it gets.

▪

When we buried him, it was the opposite of him going up to work. He descended toward the world's bottom, supine in the cheapest coffin my mother's money could buy, instead of climbing, rising above it, standing at its top.

The good news that day was that as his dead body went lower and lower, groundward, down, down, down, he felt no fear at all. Not that day.

PAUL D. MILLER
A.K.A. DJ SPOOKY
THAT SUBLIMINAL KID

66

Rio/Iguassu/São Paolo

This piece is dedicated to those who seek to build understanding amongst the world's diverse cultures. We owe it to the victims of 9/11 to learn from the disaster and create a world where it will not happen again.

The towers of the city stretch away in every direction, and its basic metaphor is unending omnidirectional urban compression. Endless favela, endless humanity. It takes several hours to drive across the city, but it's worth it. The sights are almost too much: the parrot that says "mother" ad infinitum on one corner. In Iguassu, a homeless child comes up to the car to ask not for money, but where I'm from, where my face belongs. Another corner has kids listening to *baile* music from the "funk balls" that are choreographed gang fights between rival favela gangs (the young men all dye their hair like Goldie—bleached blonde super close-cropped, platinum blonde skin head look, the girls rock low cut skirts made of plastic and synthetic materials, an update of Miles Davis's 70s album covers). The kids have boom boxes, it's summer, and the rainy season has kicked in.

This city sprang from the trade winds and found itself at the crossroads of the north and south—it's a place where worlds collide and the sounds all come from outside—dubbed versions of NYC hip-hop and electro, reggae infused with afro beat for the Axe sound systems, live MC's who do not understand the words they say—over rhythms like Dr. Dre's "Guess Who's Back?" glossalalia—many tongues, the language of hip-hop momentarily reduced to pure enunciation. All of this flows through the streets like water, or rather, information—a "knowledge game" of the unconscious. The music, its eddies and currents reconfiguring ethnicity and identity. This is a city that never had a Baron Haussman like Paris or a Robert Moses like New York. The circuit board patterns of the Northern American urban landscape are confronted with the idea of the city as a generative syntax: each block regenerates another pattern, and alters the proportions of the surrounding buildings. The roads are almost labyrinthine—not in the Old European sense of places like Lisbon or Porto in Portugal (places that gave Brazil its early identity), but more like Lagos: urban planning at the whim of the IMF and World Bank, streets that have meaning as long as currency supports the project. After that, the money vanishes, the project stops, the road ends. The favela begins.

After the New Year, which Europe began as "E-Day"—the largest consolidation of currencies in history—the favela becomes another kind of temporary autonomous zone. Oscar Niermayer on one hand, Greg Lynn's Deleuzean "hyper-surface" on the other. The utopian dreams translate into compression and unplanned growth: that's the architecture of hyper-modern involution—think of it as a world "upside down" architecture—a comedy of values, a carnival of all souls where identity is like a poker deck. Pick a card any card, it's the dealer's game . . . you can't win. In South America the economics of consolidation bear a different completely hybrid face that, because of the dominance of the U.S., will confront the extremes of 21st-century economic upheaval—Argentina as the reflection of E-Day—three currencies, all useless. The reflection of E-Day is one of seamlessness—the surface finally absorbing the nation states that gave birth to "modernity"—we face the world after the fall of the twin towers.

The question for art now is how to build new narratives with the material at hand. The shards of modernity cut deeply, and they leave wounds that will have to heal in new ways. If

Mary Shelley's *Frankenstein* was the archetypal parable of early modernity, then we need new forms. Recombinant form is pretty much now the basic way we look at the world. Combine, split, reform . . . the dj method of synthesis has taken hold of almost all aspects of the creative act. "E Pluribus Unum"—out of many, one. . . . The operating system of hypermodernity asks for a lot more.

As I type, I can see the distant favelas. The children dance to *baile* music . . . how can I tell? It's a style with a certain cadence, it's a theater of gesture where everyone knows the moves. . . . *Baile* music is considered controversial—people gather to dance and fight. It's a modern update on how capoeira evolved out of the culture of slavery in Brazil but less coherent. People die, and are hurt by the dance moves because that's what they go to clubs for: their social rituals of identity formation are from the dance "funk balls." At the balls in Europe, social values were reflected in the precision of dance moves. The same is going on here. Costumes, preparation, and intensity of performance make it happen, and violence is part of the basic syntax. People carry razors and use them to stab and carve their dance opponents. A misplaced glance, a "wrong" gesture can set off a battle. All for social dominance in a realm of theater, and the soundtrack made from fragments of dj mixes from around the world. The sounds are networks for these kids, and their body language telegraphs a theater that is all too close.

The Brazilian playwright Augusto Boal describes the impact of carnival on Brazilian culture as "legislative theater" because he saw people interact through texts that are both distant and intimate. *Baile* music, for him, is a paradox that only carnival can resolve. So for the rest of the world.

One can only hope that Brazil's lesson in multiplicity can be shared. The loops close in and become the groundwork for 21st-century culture and aesthetics.

67

MARK JAY MIRSKY

Time and King David

When I began these travels I was somewhere past fifty, still under the illusions of a man in the midst of his strength, able after a week of diet and exercise to assume the form that a handsome woman in her twenties could *assume* was only forty two or so; the mature figure of a knight like Launcelot. Now time has carried me ten, twenty years forward, into a desperate terrain where like that stalwart timber of Arthur's court, I bleed too freely and rise to contests I should have long ago resigned from, taking my place in the hermit's cell that the tale prepared for me. I am lost in the corridors of the world I imagined but it will do me no good to come out of them.

▪

In this chamber of Upper Manhattan whose ground still bears the name of a Dutch village, I come out of the door under the eaves to discover like a latter-day Rip Van Winkle that I have bowled on a strange green while the world beyond or behind has spun on. In the cycles of a game I have dreamed and slept, losing the best years of my wife and children to hours that can only be found (or have been lost) in the chambers I emerged from.

Free of all time, I have no time. It is a nightmare that Aristotle could not abide and must have made him insist—one world, one time! Our dreams, however, give entry to it every night as the planet spins away from the face of its sun.

▪

Who am I? One of the last of the House of David, the family to whom the promise of election still lingers in the daily prayers. David, a king from whom the Holy One is said to have withheld the honor of building His House. David, tarred as the sinner, an adulterer, the man who wandered as a *meshuggeh*, is excused only because he was in love with God. How well I know the tale. "Shine your face on me!" his cry. Ah, if he had danced like his father-in-law the Benjamite, Saul—a prophet, raging naked in a band of naked men with flutes and drums! No, David was already cursed by the customs of that funeral site, Hebron, binding on a loin cloth as he pranced before and after the old wooden ark, lumbering up the mountain of a foreign city on a clumsy ox cart. Still, David was faithful. He left no stones, no imposing structures that can be traced in the outlines of their broken roots, the ideas of priests and scribes, bent on raising an image of their logic. Only stories, some landmarks that they touched (a pool hollowed from the limestone cellars in the hills of Benjamin, the Gihon's spring under Jerusalem) survived him.

David, the father of our house, understood the Holy One. To pin that mystery into narrow, urine-stinking walls? The unhappy family of priests who scrambled after him would insist on that. Solomon, the son whose fame rests on his bedchambers, was the child who would abet them. Our poor house is scattered across the world because of the lightning their temple attracted. Dust is holy. Dust and round fieldstone. Take up the boulders among the flowers of the field, chink them with the wet earth, and pour out your tears upon that altar as a sacrifice.

68

TOVA MIRVIS

Potato Stories

I. My great grandmother Gertrude lived at the edge of Grudnow, which, depending on the wars, was sometimes in Poland and sometimes in Russia. Outside the town was a field where people dug for potatoes. One time she and her brother Shale went out to dig. Before starting, she took off her shoes, and they bent down and began. When they had taken all the potatoes they could find, they stood up to leave. But her shoes were gone, stolen by two Polish boys.

II. She just loved those shoes. They were soft black leather with silver buckles, and when she dug for potatoes, she searched for a plot of grass to hide them. Keeping a watchful eye on her shoes, Gertrude dug and sang and thought about one day when she might own a beautiful dress to match. She thought that one day she would fall in love and get married.

Once, when she had gathered enough potatoes, Gertrude went to put her shoes back on. But they were gone and in their place stood two Polish boys. Come get your shoes, they taunted. Gertrude and Shale knew about the things that could happen. They dropped their sacks of potatoes and ran. Somehow they made it home safely, and when they emptied their pockets, they had a few potatoes left. Their mother made a thick soup and they ate well that night.

But still, this got them thinking. Poland was no place for Jews. Gertrude was sixteen when she and her family left. As the ship sailed, she looked over the railing and watched the city grow smaller. Breathing in the ocean air she dreamed of America where nothing bad could happen. When she arrived in New York, she thanked her lucky stars that God had delivered her with His outstretched arm. Back then, she was beautiful and it was America that made her so. She rolled her long hair on top of her head and wore new stylish clothes. Men took one look at her and were in love. She met a nice young man who gave her perfume bottles and silk ribbons and the most beautiful pair of light blue satin shoes. When she held those shoes in her hand, she knew she would marry him.

III. It was a good day for potatoes. They found potatoes the size of eggplants, round and smooth and ready for boiling. Gertrude knew this was no ordinary harvest. She remembered the night before when she, unable to sleep, had looked out her window. In the stars, she had seen the faces of ancestors who came before her and the generations who would come after. As the sun rose and the stars shut themselves off, she saw in their place the fields that lay at the edge of her village, filled with potatoes as numerous as stars. Stomachs rumbled in every room of her house, and she understood that the stars were telling her that she could be the one to save her family.

Now, with bags bursting with brown potatoes, she turned her eyes upward to offer a prayer of thanks to the sleeping stars. But one star wasn't sleeping that day just as she hadn't slept the previous night. It flashed and twinkled and made her look up and out, where she saw two trolls coming towards them. Nothing Gertrude and Shale had heard of trolls prepared them for how terrible they were. They had gray fur and they looked half human, half animal. Gertrude and Shale were of course afraid. But they were also brave and smart. Gertrude tossed the potatoes into the air, until the sky was raining brown potatoes. The trolls were so busy staring at this falling bounty that they didn't notice two children running past. And as they ran, Gertrude's black shoes sprung to life, flying behind them, escorting them home.

IV. The boys holding the shoes at first were just boys, and Gertrude wasn't afraid. She didn't believe anything bad could happen. She thought that because her family was close by, she would be saved. She thought that because it was a sunny day, nothing could go wrong.

As the boys drew closer, she saw that they were older and she started to feel afraid. She tried to hold onto her brother, but the boys started running after them and she let go of Shale's hand and ran. She thought only of her long red hair whipping out behind her, of wanting to run faster, so her feet would leave the ground and she would fly.

But she couldn't fly and she couldn't go any faster and they weren't interested in Shale. She heard their footsteps keeping time with her own, theirs and then hers, until she only heard theirs. But she was almost home, where her family was warm and safe and waiting for potatoes. She felt their arms on her shoulders, their breath on her neck, and as they pushed her down, she thought if she closed her eyes, they would go away. But soon she saw Shale catching up and running past, hiding under the steps that led to her family's door. And not thinking of him before, now all she thought of was Shale under the steps, his mouth a frozen circle. Watching. Holding his breath. Waiting for it to end.

69

ALBERT MOBILIO

Some Place, No Place

This is where. This is where it happens. Pace it off, toe to heel, heel to toe. Five feet. Fifty yards. A quarter mile, this way or that. The width of your palm, the length of your outstretched arm. This where it can be measured, sifted down to acres, pounds, and miles of wire. Something impossibly large, now hidden under the sofa; something irresistibly hard, now lodged under the lid of your eye. This is a roof under which the sky can be made small; this is a door which swings wide but through which no one passes. There is a spark. A spark as long as a day, as sharp as that day's edge where it cuts against night.

That was where. Where it happened to me. Or where it happened to you. Where we were standing, or nodding, or maybe where I watched myself walk by, my face reflected in the windows of a parked car. You were walking. You were sleeping in. We were meeting at the coffee place. I was reading alone; she had gone into the city. She was home turning on the radio. You were where you were, and waiting there. You were thinking how this was another one of those places where you find yourself lately. You didn't have change; you would have to break a bill and go through the morning with coins jangling in your pocket. You hated that. It was early. I was getting things done. It was as if we knew where we should be and we'd finally gotten there. Or almost there. Just across the street from there. But then again, you were thinking, maybe not.

This is when we learned. Where we found ourselves inside, or found ourselves in conversation. I was on a roof. They were all over the roofs and they had no idea about when they would not feel what they were feeling. You thought about me in Michigan. Or was it Fourteenth Street? There was some shouting between buildings. We were like Apaches on the high ridge looking out across the plateau for the approaching wagons. I was in a cab going across, going under, heading to the West Side and I was listening so hard I wouldn't let myself swallow. This was when we learned something factual. An irrefutable thing with its own place amid the jostle: a field of cut grass or broken glass, either way some place clear. The day had only started yet we were already tired. This is when the hours pressed past you so slowly. You could feel them shoulder their way into air that waited, undisturbed, inches ahead of their arrival.

This is where I met. This is where I meant to meet you. Miles apart, we hurried in the direction of bridges. I paused to watch the footage. Ceaseless repetition, though once was enough, but not really. Fond worldlings, we watched, everyone watching. We are the size of a place that's big enough to make us small. Our arms and legs are intersecting streets; we fit within a geometry whose corners you somehow learn to see around. A line of Hart Crane's I've always loved, *The City's fiery parcels all undone*, harshly bent to fresh sense. When would it mean again what it meant before. I was telling you where I had gone, about my face in some car's windows as I walked. This was then a marked-off place of barricades and klieg lights. A town made out of paper, its spires built by the gaze of unshaded, too attentive eyes. This is where we happened. Where we were living as if, and as if, and *as if*. This was when we mattered. Where it mattered. Where it happens still.

70

ALEX MOLOT

Earlier Winter

When I say Canada, people always ask about the winter. How cold does it get up there? Very cold. Much colder than here. So cold that you can feel your cheekbones beneath your skin. How much snow do you get? So much that you can still see it come May or even June, at least in some places. But when it snows, I continue voluntarily, the streets are always cleared overnight. Only once, maybe, did I miss school. And everyone is used to the cold. So tightly have I packed down my memories that they almost crunch under the telling.

But it's only a typical winter scene. I am clearing the snow from our driveway. This business of clearing snow can be strangely satisfying. Splitting the snowy seas one sweep after another, I liberate the driveway. A gradual stretch of pavement rises, growing longer and longer. But a layer of ice remains overtop, the ice of snow melted and re-frozen. It is ugly ice, dark and rough. The thin sections give way quickly, the thicker after several hard pounds, and the thickest not at all.

By now I do not feel the cold; I am warmed by my exertions. I look up and see my father approaching. Perhaps he is returning from work. Or maybe just out for a walk. As he nears, I wave. When he reaches the driveway, he looks down and says, "That's good enough. Remember, the ice protects the pavement."

Words burdened by so much. Of the wisdom that passes from fathers to sons. How we must hide and shelter our true selves beneath icy overlays. That we trap or are ourselves trapped by this art of remembrance. What strikes me hard, though, is how simple the telling is and that I cannot. It forces on me all that has since happened. Loss and disillusion. Sadness and regret. The gap between what I feel and what I know.

The ice protects the pavement. How well the pavement controls its fear. For pavement, that is. And what of the boy clinging to the firm and faithful feel of his shovel? Often sleepless with fear, I wonder.

MARY MORRIS

71

The Night Marchers

On the day I was supposed to be in hula school, I found myself in Bronxville, teaching a class. That September I was going to Hawaii on an assignment and my editor told me to enroll. I'd learned a few things about the hula before leaving. That it is not just a dance, but a ritual that requires long preparation. To do it right you must grow your own orchids, weave your own skirt. The dance is the end of a long preparation. My editor told me she wanted me to go to attend classes. Watch a performance.

I began looking into all things Hawaiian. Shirts, surf warnings, the best luaus on the Big Island, my destination. On September 8, I had dinner with friends who were thinking of buying a shack in Hawaii, but they had been warned by islanders. The shack they wanted was in the migratory path of the night marchers. These are the spirits of the dead who walk at night, searching for home. My friends told me that I had to be careful about driving in the dark and not intrude upon their journey.

I was at my desk on the morning of September ll, completing arrangements for my trip when my mother-in-law called. She asked if Larry had left for work yet and when I told her he had, she said, her voice trembling, "Where exactly is his office?" Larry's office was at 1 World Financial Center. The first building standing behind Ground Zero with all the windows blown out. Larry would never return to his office after that day. But from nine that morning until mid-afternoon I didn't care if Larry would be returning to any office twenty minutes from home. I cared if he would ever return.

▪

I canceled my trip. Very reluctantly I told the *Times* I could not leave my family at that time. And the day after I was to arrive on the Big Island, the day when I would have been weaving grass and learning to move my hands and hips, I was waiting for students in my office. More than anything I thought how I did not want to be there. One after the other as they came in, going over their assignments, asking me what they should write about, I found my spirits sinking. One student in particular annoyed me. She came in and said she didn't know what to write about. She had no ideas. Nothing seemed to matter to her. I told her we all had to begin again. That it would take time to figure it out. I held back my own tears as I gave her a pep talk, trying to make her feel better when I could barely make it through the day.

An hour later she did not show up for class. We waited, then I began the workshop, reading from Faulkner's Nobel address. Trying to give them all meaning when I could find none for myself. But what was bothering me, what was at the back of my mind was the student I had tried to cheer up that morning who had decided to skip out on class that afternoon. Did the student know all I had given up to be there that day? Didn't she know what my family had been through and how hard it was for me to attend? Why wasn't she there? Had I said the wrong thing? Or perhaps, and this plagued me most, she just didn't care.

After class I continued with my office hours. At about four o'clock while I had another student with me, I saw the student who hadn't appeared in class. She was fluttering outside my door, anxious to talk to me. "What happened?" I asked her when I was free. "Why weren't you in class?"

"They found my cousin's body just after I talked to you. I had to call my relatives. . . . We had to make arrangements."

I sank back into my chair. "I'm sorry . . . I didn't know."

"We were lucky," she said, "Most families haven't recovered theirs. But now we can bury him."

When she left my office, I found myself trembling. Thoughts of hula school and cowboy parades, luaus and seaweed wraps were fading. It was almost dusk as I took the train home. Crossing the Harlem River, I gazed at the empty skyline, the void before me. All that remained were thoughts of the night marchers, migrating, moving in darkness, trying to get home.

72

TRACIE MORRIS

Steeple-Peeple

Sirena was a minor magician. In this day and time, everyone was. I mean, you had to have some protection. When all the buildings left, all the big ones, lots of things went with them. Like: luck. "How quaint," anybody outta Philly said, looking at the 12A's on the push-button dash. Cute. Like the lions on libraries. An effect.

But after the burning, the white soot, the sand in everyone's eyes, the ones with the brown edges, they offered their services. "See, see, see, They said? You were being silly. Notice how they were the only ones around without 'In God We Trust' on 'em. Forget papal dispensation, we have the Sirius shit. Think Dogon's a fluke all you want, we got the pointy tip deelio."

The Freemasons finally got really free and put the Prince Hall members in the mix. They wasn't stupid, finally got the real-descendants to thicken the blood of them Euro-ethnic peasantry of questionable stock. (Hey, don't act like . . . in these days and times: Italians, Black Irish, the Hebraic—and where you think the S-l-a-v in slavic is from, anyway, but a variation of some old school melation?)

The lingo flowed from that consensus. The point was, or should I say the tip, was they all fell in. The super secret construction workers made a plan to help on the d.l. One line coming, the other going, doing the handshake to the firefighters, breathing gear in tow. "We'll hook your boys up," they said to the concrete-streaked men. Made funereal signs in the dust, crosses, triangles and such. With their friends' ring-fingers, their own toes.

This time, the bedecked medallers were let in on the plans: "Nothing happened to the courts, Wall Street's still ringing—up or down. Shouldn't that tell you somethin'? First, the design was off. No curlicues, pinnacles or gargoyles, even, for goodness sake. A big ol' square. Now, if the 60s and Nixon told you anything about squares . . . Jeez!"

▪

Arguments like that went on for days. It was like the Aristide ultimatum at Governor's Island. All the people who coulda helped out, been on the lookout, were cordoned off. Same effect. Making a ruinous situation worse. Well, while the big boys played Trump with spades, Sirena was out of earshot. "Clip, clop" went the tentative ram. "Temple's down the block," she said. Always assuming it was her. "Look, man, how many times I gotta tell y'all. Levitation, tarot, runes, chackras, and astral projection is my Euro staple. No Wicca or Kabballah. One's four blocks up on 19th, the other's four more on 23rd." She doesn't even get into the older-school colored stuff. I mean, what isn't? It's all variation on a watered-down theme: Egyptian-Kongo, with Mamma coming after the baby, like the Yoruba say twins do. South Central up East. Blooming in India, up and over. Central to West: Fon fun, Egun, stools. Permutating everyplace. Hey, even GMO's had to start from some sort of real seed.

Sirena's wondering about her period this week. Bloodletting is still her preferred method. They got them pills now, those estrogen disrupters, but are they any better than tampons? Men always finding a way to get up in the 'nanni. You know? Well, anyway. This means, no drumming circle for her. Brothers always get feelings about that. How, when it gets down to it, Aña is all about the g-force, ain't it? Even the tones forget all that man-handling and go over to the women's side. Start decrescendoing right there on the spot. Papito been practicing for days on his Okonkolo flow, so she's not going to have the brother fall off just by standing there.

"Ah-ight," she says. So now, I've got other things to do with my day. Cool. Wish I could go meditate like the sisters used to do before them penises started bursting everybody's bubble with their unidirectional minds. "Oops. Sounding like super-cynic," she says to the invisible forces around. Thank goodness her third eye stays shut, with a bit of crust in the corners. If she had that Haley Joel Osmet joint, she'd be even more distracted. Bad enough her perfect hearing gets all that paper rustling and door slamming when the windows are all closed. Why they gotta be see-threw and rowdy? Sometimes she wants to say: "Okay. Hi, already. Now just go on to Heaven, re-incarnate or something." "Oh, and stop tripping out my cats."

▪

Not one to be rude to guests, though. She just mumbles their way, omni-directionally, every once in a while. If it were just the dearly departed, well, that'd be one thing. But the "all of the above" category of beings was just too much to sort out. 'Specially with all the stuff she's got from all her journeys, astral and lower-grade physical.

"Oh, yeah. Hungry." Wondering what kind of signal her intuition is giving her grumbling around inside and making her feel lightheaded. "Mom, check. Bro, check. Cats, check. Business, check. Home, check." After going down her psychic list, she realizes it ain't that deep. No nether world bell ringin', she hasn't eaten, really, since yesterday afternoon. Blood sugar levels may have metaphysical allusions, but she betta find some grub for her mug, pronto or it's all about the migraine tinitis in about 2 minutes.

"God, I've got to go shopping." She chuckles. Some people, not knowing what she knows, would assume groceries would simply appear at the door at this point. Even the grandest of spell-casters know to clip coupons. Plus, why waste the effort? The energy it would take to levitate a baked potato could be used to slather on some soya sour cream and organic chives. Even toss some "salit" with that jammie.

The cats always peep at her when she's talking aloud to see if Sirena means them, herself or all them other beings they see. Relatively speaking, they know she's comparatively of poor vision, but it's hard for them when they's vision's perfect to remember they hanging out with Mrs. Magoo, God/desses loopy dawtah, particularly when she's so good at feeding you.

"Don't look at me with those soulful eyes, you cutie." She says picking up the smallest one of the pair, kissing her on the head and rubbing her tummy. "No early eats for you. You've got another couple hours." Her best gauges of trouble are these two mewlings under foot. All's well when they're looking around mildly interested in play but not energetic. One thing Sirena hadn't had time to look into was lyncanthropy. "I'd love to see through your eyes for a minute, Shona. You must be having a good time in that other realm." This wasn't her "spider sense" talking. It's deduction. There has to be a reason why they sleep so much. "I wonder what's so interesting in their dream dimension."

A lot more going on than in hers. Even her sex-fi fantasy life is boring. Reading tarot cards doesn't get you a date, it just tells you, specifically, that you don't have one. Creative visualization doesn't extend to that arena, to be sure. "No wonder I'm single. I can't even imagine anything interesting to do." Not that I haven't had a chance to find out, that's for sure. Freaks of the week always look for the naïve P to turn out. "Hmm. That's a whole other kind of hunger. For now, to the health food sto'." "Uh!" The dust. The flittering souls around like fireflies. "If y'all don't git offa me. Go into the light, already." she said disdainfully. "Okay, no disrespect. But dang, I just got outside. I'm yearning to breathe free fo' a minit, damit!" Black chippies know that's some irony for a second. "God Bless," she says sincerely this time. Thinks: I've got to get them off this plane. There's got to be a wholesale way to do it.

Wholesale. Right. Off to the health food coop. All the organic collards I can muster. The old school ones that take a couple hours to cook instead of the GMO variation of "quick grits" they've got in those Parmalat canisters at the commercial store. "Collards, tofurkey, soya cheese, free range eye shadow and . . . glucose-free candied yams." (She could still see her mother rolling her eyes.) While Sirena was rolling hers unconsciously (sympathetic magic training makes you have weird recollected facial expressions sometimes), she goes "Blam!" right into another cart. "Damn, hope he's not a Warlock," she says thinking involuntarily of Samantha Stevens. What a contrast—in hair styles to start with.

Then she looks up again—tmtps—she goes: too many thoughts per second. "Sorry," she's about to pull off. "Damn, and fine, too." Another thought. In the diaphragm bands this time. Uhm, hungry. And she pulls the thin tape away from the jalapeño style air-popped soy chips nearby. Waited too late to get some complex sugars in my system. She feels the rough bubble of pain around the base of her neck.

"No problem." She almost forgot someone was around her. The fine guy. Assuming this will be another fleeting thought, she smiles, briefly nods and is about to continue on. Those damn little hooks in the front of the cart are locked with his little hooks. Sirena bends down to hook them off and can tell the guy is checking out her chest in the tightish tee. "Whatever" first fleeting thought. "Straighten your shoulders" the second. Not that it'll get her anywhere. As usual. Secondary sexual attraction doesn't mean anything to men. They think with their missing foreskins about 300 times a day. It's like rubbing your eyes when you're tired. Habitual and uninteresting. Sirena looked into his eyes, briefly again, she wasn't interested in scanning him, even for a minute, then lumbered down the aisle, in search of "non-lactose" frozen treats.

ANNA MOSCHOVAKIS 73

Thought Experiments

THOUGHT EXPERIMENT: THE RING OF GYGES*

Someone is probably reading over somebody's shoulder. The train is probably running late; the content leaves something to be desired, but nobody knows what it is. Instead, they all know each blade of grass, how a criminal's made, what constitutes grief and how it's removed. In addition, they (kind of) know Kung Fu, Swahili, and the waltz.

One of them—probably the shoulder—knows that the Greeks gave women nine-tenths of sex (isn't that who was meant by *the unmoved mover, producing motion through being loved*). The other one thinks he's invisible.

Somehow, these accidents rattle the car. Bodies bruise bodies, shoes pierce shoes. Up on the roof, two rows of handles rock noiselessly back and forth. Nobody uses them; nobody reaches up there.

* in which one who previously swallowed invisible desserts happens upon a weapon with which to conquer the tyranny of consequences.

THOUGHT EXPERIMENT: MARY IN THE BLACK-AND-WHITE ROOM (PART II)*

The difficult years began and continued with nobody much the wiser. Sleep with its cumulus backdrop was what they craved. One by one, the nuclear members fell from the center like spores; a certain din remained to feed their rules.

Following them, the council met atop a granite rock. The agenda, extracted from street-corner surveys and anonymous calls, was soaked in ambition. When the gavel fell, all hypotheses were sacrificed to their interpretations.

The eldest elder held up the meeting with an unheard-of sob of regret; the rest joined in, despite the passage of time (Proposition Zero). By high noon, one family came to blows and descended, cursing the painted sun as their daughter Scarlet burned in the third person.

* in which a colorless Mary, having read up on red, abandons herself to her newfound omnipotence by taking up the pen.

74

RICHARD EOIN NASH

Mister Equanimity

One cold bright February morning, Mr. Equanimity decides to go fishing off the Coney Island Pier. He walks because he does not drive. He enjoys the exercise and feels a quiet pleasure when he reaches the boardwalk and continues down the 400-foot-long pier. Unpacking his tackle and preparing his line, he barely registers the presence of his fellow fishermen—Sadness, Disgust, Bitterness, Despair—their faces so familiar to him, though he does not know a single one of them by name. He casts forth into the sea and waits.

A great time passes. The others around him, more agitated than he, reel in and cast out, reel in and cast out, reel in and cast out. Not he. Morning unflappably becomes afternoon.

Suddenly he registers a distinct cry amid the general cackle of the beach. Scanning the horizon he sees nothing. His eyes trail along the water back towards the pier. Fear. About fifty feet from the edge of the pier Fear is caught in his line. He grows concerned: is she hooked on his barb? No, the hook is too deep in the water, of course. Fear's foot, or wing perhaps—yes, it is her wing—is ensnared. The harder she flaps, the tighter his line wrapped around the wing.

His companions gather round him, silent and nervous. Mr. Equanimity reaches over the railing, grasps the line in his gloved hands, and hand over hand begins to draw Fear in. She flaps wildly, beseeching him to release her. His pace does not change. Although almost exhausted by the struggle, she continues to flap, sporadically now, jerking the line—Mr. Equanimity continues, unrelenting. Drawing Fear across the waves

—as smoothly as she will allow—until she is directly beneath him, he begins to hoist her aloft. Feeling the strain of gravity now, Fear renews her struggle and Mr. Equanimity continues his methodical elevation.

As Fear reaches the level of the boards on which he is standing, Mr. Equanimity can see how large she is—a wing span he estimates, in a flicker of calculation, to be at least six feet. Three more draws on the line and she is at the level of the railing. Holding her aloft with now just his left hand, extended as if in a salute, he gazes on her. Inspecting her, perhaps in the manner of a butcher inspecting a freshly shot goose. He takes Fear by the neck with his right hand, grasping firmly.

With his left hand he slowly unravels the fishing line from around Fear's wing. One turn, a second, then again and again, unspooling the snare. The wing comes free. She flaps once, then again. Mr. Equanimity holds her torso now in both hands, Fear's beak only three, four inches from his nose. He stays there, holding his ground for second after second. Suddenly he casts her out away from him and Fear flies directly into the setting sun, joined in her flight by her relieved companions.

75

JOSIP NOVAKOVICH

My Son's Views

Until getting up on the CN Tower in Toronto and walking on the thick glass floor which gave him an illusion of walking on air 1500 feet above the ground and a thrill of peril, my son's favorite buildings were the World Trade Center. Joey found it scary to be sitting perched in the glass and did not want to be pushed, as though he could fall through the glass. But he liked that fear, and seeing helicopters and airplanes fly below us made him laugh.

We walked up on the top in heavy wind, looked at the Statue of Liberty and Ellis Island. I told Joey how his great-grandfather had passed through that station on false papers, an Austrian cow's export certificate, to enter the States. But this made no impression on him. Before World War One, border crossings in Europe were loose, so Grandfather got away with that. To Joey, the story didn't mean anything—borders, papers, what was all that compared with the grand vision we were having?

He recognized the Empire State Building and the Chrysler Building. We had gone as high as we could on the Chrysler but the top was private. Those wood-paneled elevators were beautiful, as was everything about the building from far, near, and inside, which could not be said about the Twin Towers. Still, the magnetism of gleaming metal surpassed everything in the city for him, and I must admit, for me. On my first visit to the States at the age of 18, I had a picture taken with the towers and my head only, so that as much as possible of the building could fit in the image. The kind passerby who took my picture understood what I wanted and had kneeled on the pavement to look up, and to get nearly the whole building with my beheaded version.

After enjoying the sinking sensation in the swift elevator ride, we walked around the towers, and my brother who was also with me then and I marveled at the sheer size. When these buildings become too old and decrepit, how will people take them down, Ivo and I pondered. Should they use helicopters, starting from the top? They couldn't just implode the buildings, could they? Maybe it would take as much work to take them apart as it had to put them together? Did the architects think of that when designing the monsters?

We went to the Border's Bookstore in the underground complex beneath the towers, on the subzero floors which later would be destroyed as well. In the bookstore we got a few books, including the elongated *Skyscrapers*, mimicking a profile of one of the WTC buildings. Joey was surprised that there were buildings taller than the WTC: in Kuala Lumpur, the Patronias Towers. Joey learned the top ten buildings, with their sizes in feet and meters. For a whole year after touring the tall buildings in New York, my son made many drawings of the Twin Towers, the Empire State, and the Chrysler. He loved New York. When people asked him where he was from at his preschool in Cincinnati, Ohio, where we lived at the time, he said, I am part North Dakota, part Croatia, and part New York. He was most proud of the New York part.

And now, four years later, when he is eight, I got a fellowship to live in New York City as a writing fellow of the New York Public Library. I thought my family would join me in the city, and instead of attending a regular school, Joey would be home-schooled, or rather, city-schooled. By seeing all the aspects of the city, and by getting top-level cello lessons, he would learn more in eight months than by sitting somewhere indoors, exposed to the terrorism of elementary school discipline. I thought we would start with the World Trade Center. Well, the first day of my fellowship fell on September 10. My family had wanted to finish up with music lessons and various other projects in Zagreb, Croatia, so they changed the original plan and did not come to New York City with me. If they had, we might have, in jet-lagged state, got up early the following day, and tried to be up there before 9 on the 11th.

On the eleventh, I was at the library, and after hearing what had happened and running out into the street to gaze at the growing cloud, I called home. I thought Joey would be devastated, he would cry, perhaps, the way he did when his pet turtle died, squashed by a rock. But he did not cry. He said, Yes, Dad, I know everything. I have seen the best details and what I haven't seen, Mom has told me. OK, Bye! He sounded thrilled, positively excited. I suppose he was excited by tall buildings because they were such a spectacle, and the destruction was an even greater spectacle. How could I blame him to be swept by fascination rather than sorrow?

I still don't know whether he is sad about it, I will ask him the next time I talk to him. Maybe a turtle has a soul. The building, no matter how big and fascinating, may not have had a soul but now many souls remain in its place, hovering somewhere above the ground. I am writing this at JFK, about to fly on American Airlines to Zagreb where my wife and two kids had remained, partly because of the World Trade Center disaster, partly because after staying there for a whole semester, they wanted to finish up their school year. I will ask Joey whether he misses the towers, whether he wants to play the cello for them, the way people played for Sarajevo during the siege. I think he should, he should sit in the pit, and play Bach, for the towers, for me, for us. It would be a beautiful sight, a frail boy in a black suit with long blond hair, like a small replica of Kinski, playing on the sad instrument.

76

DENNIS NURKSE

After a Bombing

1

Lovers who had separated
wrote and asked
are you OK? and reconciled.

Fathers who disowned their children
called and cried:
Thank God you were in Queens.

The one who was late
because of a lost key
felt good fortune on his shoulders
like a crushing weight,
a tower he'd have to carry:

the one who called in sick
wandered deeper into fever,
looking for suffering,
for a spring to drink from:

2

and the children drew the Plane,
sticking out their tongues, pressing
hard with crayons, never looking up,
as if they'd seen it all their lives:

the Tower—a huge box:
the Fire—an orange flower:
God—a face bright with tears
appalled in the margin:
the sun with nine spokes:

the Fireman in his smudged hat
running with outstretched arms
up a flight of endless steps
that veered suddenly off the page.

77

GEOFFREY O'BRIEN

A History

1.
In the middle of drinking wine
and of studying the curve
of the companion's shoulder,
curve defined by angle and her distance
from the light source, in the middle
of the middle—

2.
Afterwards
there will be the memory
of the exploded room,

a space of perfect freedom.

3.
They had forgotten what city they were in.
So temperate the day
they had forgotten almost their names
for as long as it took the sun,
shifting from faucet
toward the casual heap of cotton and leather,
to catch a zigzag stitch.

4.
Woke to the taste of ashes.

5.
The ancient world
of breached walls and famine tactics—
spies who hid in the gully—
they were living in it
and surrounded by it.
The position of the city in the river.
From those moorings
they traced a history of unladed bolts
of silk, stacks of etched boxes.
Wet stones, an air of arrival.

6.
The ancient world
of stolen glimpses. Outriders
describe the shapes of things.

Bulked masses,
what light hits from a distance.

The ancient world of borders.

7.
"And if I could invent
the air of that room, spin it
out of myself

like the gold thread in the story,
the room
to be made a permanent resort,

its windows guarded, and point of entry
hung with ornament—

what days would be celebrated,
festivals of breath
not written in any history—"

8.

A piece of wall
having had time to lose its markings
is border. Market in another city,
shored up by eroded diggings.

The wall ends
where something ended
to make place for river light
shifting through the accumulated passages.

One city resembles another
as one day resembles another,
as one face resembles itself
in an altered light.

9.

The room.
A view of buildings and water.

LARRY O'CONNOR

78

The Pond

Not far from our editing operations in Building 4 of the *Wall Street Journal's* temporary corporate headquarters in South Brunswick is a pond. Each morning I like to leave for my break by a side entrance. As the managers and department heads grapple with the future of the company, I make my way across a wide expanse of grass toward a bench near the water where I sit under some trees. The air is fresh and bracing, the sky cobalt blue. But I don't look up as I go. I have to watch my step to avoid the goose scat.

Before September 11, I would rise at 7:30 A.M. and be at my desk at One World Financial Center at 8:30. I took my first break with my Page One friend, or strolled to the Winter Garden and sat on a bench and looked at the palm trees. Now I wake up at 5:30 to be at work at 8, and leave for my first break two hours later. The ride in the company van from Brooklyn is slow, but not traffic-snarled as it can be for people going to New York City.

If we take Fourth Avenue to the Verrazano bridge, we pass Nice and Necessary, the pharmacy and beauty aids shop. John, the oldest driver, prefers the shadows of Third Avenue. Around Thirtieth and Third, a man comes outside of a car wash with a long pole, a large American flag at its end and plants it into a hollow base. Next door is Pleasure and Paradise, private viewing booths. Cafe Gowanus. On the Verrazano itself, I watch a jetstream in the morning sky and wait for the explosion, the end of the perfect white line.

Usually, the geese and I have the green space to ourselves. But as I settle into the bench, I am startled to see three Australian shepherds running toward the flock. Their noses thrust forward like racers, the shepherds run alongside a man driving a golf cart at its top speed. For days I'd watched as Canada geese gathered near the pond in ever-increasing numbers. Perhaps because I am originally from Canada, they evoke home. Now at least one hundred of them are in flight to get away from the dogs and a man in a golf cart, hurtling around the pond.

The geese circle high in the air, but then slowly coast their way back to the surface of the water. I can't get a good look at the man inside the golf cart, but he is big and dressed in green from head to toe. The man and the dogs circle the area one more time, forcing the last goose into the air and onto the surface.

Next, man and dogs stop at the water's edge. The man takes a thin plastic bag and opens its mouth to the autumn breeze. It fills in an instant and he ties it securely, then tosses the ash-colored balloon onto the pond. The bag rolls like tumbleweed across the surface toward the geese. The man fills another bag and tosses it as well, and then another, until a phalanx of inflated bags march on the floating geese. Suddenly, as one, the birds beat the air with their wings and honk in fright, flying away, the pressure of a wild thing on a sleeping chest. The man and the dogs dash off, too, to gather up the bags which were rolling in the wind beyond the softball diamond where at the post–September 11 company picnic the technical workers edged the news staff, 10 to 9.

I sit on the park bench a little longer. My break is over and I need to get back to work. There are stories that need editing, supervisors, with deadlines approaching, who are beginning to wonder where I am. Perhaps the managers have returned from their meetings, to announce who would be staying in South Brunswick, who would be returning home. It is time that we all should learn what the future holds.

Now empty, devoid of the birds, the man and the dogs, the grass expanse and rippled water look as eerie as an unsold postcard at the turnpike. A cloud covers the sun for a moment and I shiver and stand up to go. That is when I notice the pond, without the birds, the dogs, and the man in the golf cart. I get up on the seat of the park bench for a better vantage point and can see what had escaped me before. There is no doubt. The pond is built in the shape of the state of New Jersey.

79

ROBERT POLITO

Last Seen

I remember my father strapped to the bed, repeating "God-Oh-God," the only other sound the ping of the life-support.

I remember Mark climbing up into his blue truck for the drive back to Marion.

I remember stopping at the door, and waving to my mother. She would be released from the hospital on Monday.

I remember Arthur at my mother's funeral, an oxygen canister beside him in the aisle of the church.

I remember listening to Mark talk about his book—a chapter on each of his ten favorite songs, including Elvis Costello's "King Horse"—and the lesions on his tongue, his joke about the coincidence of his drugstore canker medicine, Cank-aid, and AIDS.

I remember thinking how tired he looked, as I put Jimmy into a cab outside the movie theater where we had just seen *Vanya on 42nd Street.*

I remember Elvis trying to stand and greet Dr. Russo.

▪

There are terrible spirits, ghosts, in the air of America, D. H. Lawrence wrote in 1923.

I thought of Lawrence's ghosts often those early days after the towers came down, particularly when the flyers of the missing—always "the missing"—started to cover Lower Manhattan, most spectacularly throughout Union Square, but also on nearly every wall, store front, telephone booth, lamp pole, and tree south of Fourteenth Street. Some of the flyers were plain as a wanted poster—a black and white photograph; minimal docket of vital statistics. But the images on the flyers of the missing usually were in color, and caught the loved one during passages of conspicuous happiness—a wedding, graduation, or party—and attired in celebratory, often formal dress, tuxedos and gowns. Many cradled babies in their arms. And nearly all carried a prominent scar, mole, tattoo: *5'11" 184 lbs. Blue Eyes Tattoo of Bulldog on Shoulder Last Seen 1 WTC 102 Floor Please Contact . . .*

You needed to imagine a legion of the missing—5,000 those first weeks—wandering New York, lost, amnesiac, waiting for someone to recognize them from their photo and life story, and send them home. *Those that are pushed out of life in chagrin*, Lawrence continued, *come back unappeased, for revenge.*

▪

A beautiful fall morning, perhaps still more beautiful because of the quiet. During the brief space between the moments the planes hit and the towers fell, I kept running down to the street to stare again at the flames, twenty blocks away, as if to prove this wasn't a TV spectacle. Sixth Avenue was a scene from a monster movie—hundreds of silent men and women moving uptown, all of them walking unnaturally fast, or unnaturally slow, craning their heads back over their shoulders for another look.

80

NELLY REIFLER

A Plague

1. We remembered that we had lived our lives before, but we didn't remember how we had lived our lives before. We remembered that we had known a kind of lightness, but we also remembered that we hadn't known that the lightness was there, and we couldn't remember what the lightness felt like. We cursed ourselves for not memorizing the feeling of lightness.

2. Where did it come from? Had it been hiding in the earth? Had it dozed in the soil for centuries? Or did it come from above? Was it borne on some thick and heavy storm? Or maybe it sweated from the leaves and buds of the orchard. Or maybe it crawled from the river. Or maybe it came in with a stranger. Or maybe . . .

3. Neither of our village doctors—father and son—knew what to do. The younger one suddenly became religious; the older plied his patients with useless medicines.

A specialist was called in from the city, where he was head of his department at the university hospital. The specialist took a train to the next town over from ours. There, he was met by the knife man in his red step-truck. The knife man dropped the specialist at the edge of our village, where he was greeted by the sheriff and the older doctor.

The specialist stopped at the inn just long enough to splash some cold water on his face and hang up his change of clothing. Then he followed the older doctor to his office, where the specialist set up a makeshift laboratory. After that, they were off again.

They spent the rest of the afternoon visiting the homes of afflicted villagers. When they rang the first doorbell, the specialist smiled to himself—he hadn't made a house call for, he calculated, at least twenty years.

He stopped smiling when he saw the patient.

Late that evening, he looked at the samples he'd taken. The older doctor watched from a chair in the corner as the specialist bent over the microscope. The specialist almost gasped at what he saw—not from horror, exactly, but from admiration (the two aren't as far apart as you think).

This was an organism of great beauty: silky and motile, it danced on the slide, slowing down, speeding up, then whipping around to the point that it just started to break apart . . . and then stopping and resting before it began its dance again.

4. When you're trapped, you want to flee. You try to flee. But when you're trapped, there is no escape. A trap—by definition —is something from which you can't escape.

We learned that the most unbearable kind of trap is one in which no one has trapped you. In this situation, there is no one to outwit, no one to beseech, and no one to hate.

5. The land flourished as the people faded. The earth was black and moist. In early spring, you could squat down in a field, choose a single pale green sprout, and watch it grow before your eyes. By midsummer, the fields were tall and lush, the orchards were in full bloom. In autumn, the overripe apples fell. The ones that were not carried off by birds and field mice rotted, giving off a sweet and drunken perfume. The living watched from inside their houses.

81

ROSE-MYRIAM RÉJOUIS

Keeping Vigil

One fall morning, I awoke to find my car missing. How would I get to work in Westchester on Monday, I thought. After my husband called the police to make sure it hadn't been towed, we went downstairs and learned from a man with a clipboard and a two-way radio that our white Chevy had been moved by the crew of *Law and Order*. I didn't see any cameras or actors, just yuppies in dark Patagonia rain jackets, guarding the entrance to our building in Inwood, in northern Manhattan. I suppose they were shooting a scene that required the violation of a home: the discovery of a dead body on the kitchen floor, the pursuit of a "perp," or the badgering of a reluctant witness. *Law and Order* was in my neighborhood—not to set anything right (after all it's just a TV show), but to take advantage of the fact that some things here "look wrong," that some gritty quality made our block an appropriate setting for the mock-violence and mock-despair of a police drama.

The show's encroachment triggered a familiar pang about the distance that has grown between me and the world of my parents. Mine is a hyperactive world that is perpetually trying to stave off boredom at any cost (which in this case meant making a new episode of *Law and Order*). Theirs is a world with little leisure and few shortcuts, a world where faith is supposed to set things right.

In Haiti, where my parents and I are from, religion (Catholic, Protestant, Voodoo) works overtime, stretching to fill the gaps created by poverty and political unrest. As a boy, my father raised pigs to buy books and his first pair of shoes while teaching himself to read. My father's favorite memory of these hardscrabble days in the village of Touin, near Léogane, is accompanying his mother on her prayer rounds: "She would lay her hands on the sick and the troubled," he told me, still awestruck by the woman he would usually describe as having been too old to take care of him, her twelfth child. "People would call for her from near and far." Tagging along whenever he could, my father would walk for miles at all hours. A few years later he won a scholarship to attend a Nazarite Seminary in Port-au-Prince.

Although he often has trouble admitting it, things haven't worked out as planned by my father. Seven years after we had left Haiti for France, he decided to follow in his mother's footsteps and leave for the next best thing to Haiti: Miami. In France, where we reached middle-class bliss within three years (a big house in a safe suburb, with swings in a garden), he worked for a large accounting firm. He never managed to explain what he did there. Itching to lay his seminary-anointed hands on an ailing community, he talked the family into leaving *Douce France* for blistering Miami.

In Florida, we immediately joined the ranks of illegal Haitian immigrants since the local culture overlooked our French citizenship. Then we joined the ranks of the poor, when following bad advice, my father opened a shoe and toy stand at a local flea market which was supposed to run itself with a little help from an enormously friendly and talkative lady, my mother. The stand failed a few months later, taking with it most of the savings from the sale of the house in France. After that, my father began to drive a taxi while my mother divided her time between staying in bed and rehearsing with my grandmother the things she would tell my father when he would come home: How could you do this to us? How could you do this to *me*?

Though my father still drives a livery car six days a week, six to twelve hours a day, things are better at home. My mother left her bed and then the house to get her GED and Nurse's Aide certificate. But the best news for them is that they have finally reconciled the need to take care of the self with the desire to repair the world. A year ago, they got a house with a garden and founded a church. Their congregation meets every Sunday in a room borrowed from an Episcopal Church. And on weekday mornings at 5 A.M., my parents make prayer rounds. They go to the home of a sick or troubled "brother" or "sister in Christ" to lay hands on someone's head or shoulders.

In Haiti, they call these morning prayers "sentinelles," my mother gleefully told me over the phone. Gleeful about the gathering (as she is about all gatherings) and gleeful about the word (as she is about any rare three-syllable French word). *Sentinelle.* I say that word to myself sometimes, when I start worrying about my parents. *Sentinelle.* It is a word I carry with me as I commute from Inwood to Sarah Lawrence College, where I teach.

I have had to move several thousand miles north to pursue my vocation, spending the last decade far away from my family. But finding the crew of *Law and Order* on my block seems a better measure of the distance that separates me and many others from a point of origin. It's the distance between a place where people still try to make a fire that will keep the body warm, and the slick police dramas which fetishize cold D.O.A.'s bathed in fluorescent light and surrounded by workaholic professionals.

Many of us shuttle between these two places as easily as we do between home and office. We take it for granted that, no matter what, we will always be warmed by our own good intentions. As a writer, my hand has not yet healed anyone, besides myself perhaps. But it is seeking its way, past the drone of cultural white-noise, to a tradition of vigilance, of *sentinelles.*

82

APRIL REYNOLDS

River

But then in late April, with spring struggling to arrive, it began to rain.

When it came, without rumble, sharecroppers and owners alike were thankful. Cotton cultivating only mere weeks away, they had grown worried for what generally was a rainy winter had turned stingy in early November, cracking low tide creeks and withering gardens. Back-breaking work would become even more so and foolishly every farmer between Cornith and Pascagoula prayed for just three days of rain: the unceasing, rolling kind, so that by May the earth would fold up and over like cloth. And at the end of April, their prayers were answered. When one day turned into two, which flashed into three, something not quite far from pride soaked inside the tenants of the Sillers plantation. Hadn't they prayed and He delivered? They began plotting how many days would it take to cultivate so many acres, and planned visits to far away relatives. Even when the rain stretched to days four and five, they refused to be troubled. "Didn't we ask for rain? Can't look God in the mouth, now," they all murmured over late dinner. But by the end of the week, the sly comments stuttered to a close, and even the old couldn't stamp out general concern, "Ain't studying no rain. Week worth of rain ain't nothing." One week slid into two, and now when children tucked in their chins and raced to gather kindling out of the wood bins in the morning, top soil greeted them at their front door. Dogwood blossoms and trumpet honey suckles drowned on the vine. And without being told, the sharecroppers knew their prayers had turned into a curse, that now with almost a full month of rain, acres of land were too wet to cultivate and even the stubborn, who thought: you want to rain? Gone rain then, and soaked themselves through while dropping cotton seed in the ground had their efforts cleanly swept away.

But a respite came in the middle of May. Sudden and harsh, it stopped. For five hours, nothing stormed down and Mrs. Hubbert swept puddles of muddy water off her porch. But before her neighbors could finish their collective grateful sigh intermingled with, "That sho was close," it began again, drowning marigolds and day lilies, and if anything, it rained harder. Two more weeks full of rain went by, and now Mrs. Hubbert didn't leave the house at all, since rumors now floated around the Sillers plantation that farther north, everything that had the misfortune of being still was in the midst of being drowned. And now instead of planning visits to far-away relatives, conversations curled around the strength of the nearest levies, man-made structures that kept the river in its place. Many thought they should gather what they could and travel as far east as possible, but sunk so far into debt with Mr. Sillers no one could travel even to Jackson, Mississippi. Gossip surfaced that Mrs. Sillers and her children had left for New York weeks ago.

And so they gathered. Concern and dread licked at their feet at night and no one wanted to say aloud what floated in front of their minds: that this was the ONE, the culmination of God's wrath that would wash away all the sinners and if true, they were the damned since there wasn't a Noah among them. Hadn't He said forty days and forty nights? A month ago they were sure. Thirty-four days tumbled into thirty-seven, but then those five hours crept between them and God's fruition. Mrs. Hubbert swore she counted out the hours—from one to six o'clock. Others weren't so sure of the lapse: wasn't it just as long as it take to get on dinner? But Mrs. Hubbert held fast to her godless knowing—five hours, no more, no less. And her certainness filled the Sillers' tenants with fear, since to admit she was right was to concede that they were not the destined; they were just unlucky.

"Well, shit," Mr. Hubbert said. It became clear to everyone congregated that it was time to leave.

But then it happened. And the mules knew it first. Aware that they were on the verge of being swept away, the mules quickened their clip, clip, flanks tightened. Chess heard it next, or rather his persistent dreaming heard it before him—a long gathering and rolling that caused him to look away from his neighbors and stare behind them, almost chanting: well, here it comes. Yes, sir, it sho is coming, not even warning his parents that he heard what he did not hear—the galloping of water all around him, that would crash and drown everything within moments. Finally his grown people neighbors heard what made the mules lift their lips, snorting within their rigging. But by then it was too late—the rising Mississippi River broke another private levy sixty miles away creating a gash in the man-made structure. Everything, water swept. Chess, his parents and those neighbors in the wagon with them could only look on as the two wagons traveling with them drowned. Now, now everyone in Mr. Hubbert's wagon thought: this is the ONE. We just didn't see it until now, and Mr. Paw we threw away. Later, Chess would only recall the sound: Ahhhhhhhhhhhhhhh and then the noise sliced away, like a spigot being turned off.

83

ROXANA ROBINSON

Christmas Music

At Christmas, in New York, music is everywhere. It blares through loudspeakers overhead, from the stalwart Salvation Army soldiers, in shops and malls and elevators. It is part of the air, the scene. This music is traditional and familiar, the whole point is that it's familiar, that this is music that reminds you that it's Christmas. We know these formal English verses, these solemn ecclesiastical melodies. If we grew up here, we know them all by heart, no matter who we are. And if you know something by heart, it is part of you, you feel you own it. So we've come to own these quiet hushed melodies, sung for centuries in the high dark spaces of English cathedrals. And we own these ancient Middle Eastern images: bearded men in robes, flocks of sheep in the rocky desert, the camels, the bright stars in the high dark sky. These are ours.

The carols are so much part of the season that yesterday, when I started down the subway stairs at 68th street, as soon as I heard music I knew it was Christmas music. Down on the platform I saw the players: two men in their late forties, playing an accordion and a saxophone. They looked Russian, with pale skin and dark hair. They hadn't shaved. The accordion player was plump, with a round face and close-cropped hair. He was sitting on a stool, with a towel over his knees. He wore a sweater with a leather vest over it, and before him, on the pavement, was a leather satchel, open for business. The saxophonist had a square face and longish hair. His black moustache was ragged and thick and dashing. His dark coat was buttoned to his neck, and at his throat a scarf was tightly knotted. On his head was a very black felt hat. His eyes were closed, and he was clasping his instrument to him and leaning into the music.

It wasn't Christmas carols. Often, at this station, there are jazz musicians, and for a moment I tried to make it into jazz. The notes were sliding and lilting, more urgent and engaging than Christmas carols, but it wasn't jazz either. I moved a few steps down the platform, listening, and saw a woman approaching me and them, her face a stony New York mask. I watched her walk over to them and lean down to speak. As she spoke she smiled at them, and dropped a bill into the satchel. When she turned back to the rest of us, the smile still echoed across her features. Everyone on the platform was listening.

The music was quick and melodious, plaintive, yearning. I kept expecting it to slide into "Those Were the Days, My Friends," that rhythmic song that makes everyone start longing for Mother Russia no matter where you came from. But it didn't do that. The saxophonist swayed, his black-hatted head cocked, his eyes still closed in sweet contemplation. Listening, I next began to think it was Gypsy music: it reminded me of those violinists in restaurants, leaning over your table and drawing out a haunting nostalgia with their bows. Maybe it wasn't Mother Russia we were all longing for, but Mother Rumania instead, and before that, Mother India.

We weren't all from Rumania, though, or from India, so what was the hold this music had on us? Why did it make everyone on the platform smile to themselves, even if they were not looking at the accordion-player, leaning back on his stool, his arms wide apart, the pleated accordion stretched soulfully out across his chest to the very limit of its possibilities? Or at the saxophonist, his black moustache embracing the mouthpiece, his chin lifted high under his black hat? Why was it that we were all listening, all smiling privately and tapping our toes inconspicuously, and thinking of somewhere we'd never been?

It was wild and sweet and strange, that music, and it reminded me of something else, but what? After a moment I remembered: just last night, in the street. A white van from New Jersey had driven around and around in our neighborhood. On its roof was a lit-up menorah, and the black-bearded driver spoke into a loudspeaker, exhorting us to light candles at Shabos. Between the exhortations there were recordings of Hannukah music. And that music, I remembered now, had the same penetrating minor chords, the same yearning, haunting, Eastern quality that made the spine straighten and the blood quicken. And listening now to the two Russians, I felt a thrill at the recognition, at the wide, wild, ancient connections I was hearing.

So this is how it is, now, at Christmas in New York. We're all Russians, Americans, Jews, Gypsies, Christians. Nothing is simple now, nothing can be taken for granted, and nothing belongs to us alone. Everything comes from somewhere else; we're part of a great web of connections, ancient, complex, intricate. We're in a shared, wider, more complicated place now. We're living our lives to the music of the world, and this is haunting and strange, thrilling, with a relentless beat that stirs our pulses and challenges our hearts and urges us on and on, to somewhere we've never known, but which somehow we remember.

84

AVITAL RONELL

This Was a Test

Testing opens up the site that occurs, Nietzsche suggests, after Christianity has fizzled, arriving together with a crisis in the relationship of experience to interpretation. No longer is it a question of interpreting one's own experience as pious people have long enough interpreted theirs, namely, "as though it were providential, a hint, designed and ordained for the sake of the salvation of the soul—all that," Nietzsche says, "is *over* now." Now we godless ones test, we rigorously experiment. *That cannot be what W meant when he finally came out that evening, after the inexplicable time of concealment, and said that we are being tested, can it?* He had at once invoked and scrambled the codes by announcing, on the evening of 9/11, that the attack on the World Trade Center was, in his words, a test. How does his language usage work here? When he introduced a new rhetoric of justification for imminent military action, the president in fact reverted to a citation of pretechnological syntagms that capture the auratic pull of the test. In this context this term sparkles as an anointment; the president bears the mark of election by virtue of the test. If a few months earlier he was elected by dubious political means, he is now elected by divine mandate to meet the demands of a terrific test in order to create history, which he begins to do by reinscribing the crusades. Still, why did he revert to the figure of the test that evening?

To be sure, testing did not emerge as an event one day; it did not arise cleanly from the ashes of a vital and present Judeo-Christian tradition but occupied a place prior to technological dominion. Let us consider the sacred inventory of trials and the requirements that serve to mark the exulted status of the one chosen for testing. God had been testing his nearest and dearest all along: Abraham, Job, Christ, and my mother were constantly being tested, and not all of them chose to remain mute about having their patience tried. Saying that the terror attack was a test, President Bush leaves no room for the undecidability of Abraham, the contestability of Job, or the intricated martyrdom of Christ in the desert or on the cross. Disturbing the codified usage of the trial to which "the test" alludes, the utterance subverts the condition of *being tested* by offering that, at the moment of its mention, the past had been passed. The test will already have made sense and turned in the result: one would not have been chosen to withstand, the logic goes, if one had not *already passed* the test of history, countersigned, in this case, by God. Reinscribing and repeating the wars of his father, this little Isaac jumps at the chance to return to traumatic sites. Like Isaac, neutralized and silenced by the father's package deal with the sacred, this one wants to dig into the earth, signing a legacy to which he was and was not called.

Another version of Isaac, W also wants to be Abraham but persistently falls short of the paternal mark. When Abraham was tested in his faith, the test itself remained hidden. Privileged and close enough to God to be worthy of the test, Abraham, for his part, must not *know* it is a test. If Abraham had known it was a test, the answer would have been at hand. God did not announce that "this is a test, this is *only* a test of the emergency broadcast system. If this were a real emergency . . ." until Abraham had made the grade. Abraham could not know until the ordeal was over, which means that it had and had not been a real test, but becomes one only after its aggressive question has been effectually answered.

With the spread of technology, testing lost some of its auratic and exceptional qualities and started hitting everyone with its demands, that is, anyone who wanted to gain admission anywhere, and all institutions started testing to let you in and let you out. Yet the scrambling device installed by W splices incongruent moments or scenes from both epochs of testing that depend for their relation to truth on diverging registers. Pretechnological traces indicate a different, at once more hidden and dramatic rapport to the predicament of testing. These traces, sometimes found in old books, tell us that testing, a sacred assignment, bespeaks an incomparable closeness to the divine.

In the case of W, when he comes out swinging at the elusive enemy, he knows, he claims, that he is being tested. Had he however truly been tested, he would have been disabled from knowing, thrown off the cognitive trail. The false assurances plied by cognition are not entirely W's fault. They merely exhibit his membership in the age of technological dominion: we think we know about the test and its eventuation even where it holds us unconsciously.

85

DANIEL ASA ROSE

Upon Seeing a Shooting Star on the Lawn at Tanglewood Two Days after the World Trade Center Disaster

After yapping with one's estranged parents about the
imminent collapse of western civ
There is still this:

A lawn full of shell-shocked souls dining upon pails of
carry-out salad from Guido's (three bean and lobster
tortellini and chicken with raisins)
3000 subdued strangers spread out before trembling
candelabrum atop dewy patchwork blankets
The occasional pop of champagne corks muzzled by linen
napkins as the Prokofiev begins humbly to expound upon
the crickets edging the lawn on
all sides and everyone lies back to lose themselves straight,
mercifully, upwards

Then four minutes into the reverie, as if on cue and not on
cue at all, a shooting star

Corny at first gasp but it grows, and grows
A radically candid star with a tail and a fiery tale to tell
Traveling from one end of blue-black sky clear across to the
other

Long enough for people to jab each other, acknowledge the
 jab, and jab each other back
Long enough for people to be conscious of the thought:
 "I am witnessing an amazement"

And still it arcs on, sputtering, streaking

Long enough to feel a civilization palpitate
To feel 3000 private wonderments across the lawn respire in
 and out and out again

And afterwards, to breathe a collective murmur
 that fills the space between the music

A different kind of music—

The hush of human hearts enlarging.

86

JOE SALVATORE

Postcard

Postmark: 31 October 2001

Here's the way it looks now, since I know you'd want to know, since you're the reason I moved here, since it was you who loved cities and tall buildings and myriad faces, and since it was you who said go to the Big Apple, get that degree, but don't forget to write. I didn't forget. I sent something off to you. And that, too, was a postcard. Just before you went into the hospital for good, remember? It was a picture of those two big buildings, the ones we had stood atop, you pointing your shaking finger north to Boston, saying, I think I see the Prudential. All around us was sky. You told me how you took Mom to its top, to cure her fear of heights.

Let me tell you how it looks now. Where I'm sitting, on Bleecker and MacDougal, you'd never know by merely looking (though if your eyes were closed and you breathed in, you'd know something had happened here). But today there is no sign of any of it anywhere, no rubble, no trucks, no bucket brigades, none of that awful white dust. I can't even spot a flier. Just tables and chairs—a bit emptier than usual, but out and open for business, as everyone keeps saying. There are some little kids in costumes—though rarely without an adult hand hovering nearby. And seeing them made me think of you, the time you were here last, in '98, when you came to visit me before I graduated. We walked past the apartment in the Village where your brother had lived back in the forties. It took you a while to remember its location. You said it was because the city was different then. How changed it all seemed to you now.

We sat here, at this café. We waited twenty minutes for a table; today I'm the only customer. We sat and drank coffee as black as your eyes, and, though your memory was starting to go in that awful way it would go, you told me stories, you loved stories, you had hundreds of stories, they all seemed to tie into each other, digressing into other narratives with similar points of ingress. (I guess I'm guilty of that, too. All I seem to do these days is babble.) You repeated your Prudential story about Mom and her fear of towers, and I pretended it was the first time I'd heard it; and that story led to another story, about the last time we had stepped atop those two towers a year before in '97, looked out across this island, directed our eyes north through the clouds, north to Boston, back to where the others had boarded those planes, planes bound for a heaven that would contain both them and you. (Am I romanticizing it? I need a place to remember you, is all.) And that's when you suggested we go there again, remember? We waved to the waiter and you spoke Italian to him, and although I couldn't fully understand what you were saying, I saw him laugh, his moustached mouth spreading east and west, and you looked at me, your eyes glinting, as if proving to me that you could still make contact with this world. We paid Carlo in cash; I dropped an extra dollar, if for nothing more than his smile. And we set off for the tip of Manhattan. As we walked down Church Street, I recited from memory Whitman's *Splendid Silent Sun*, and although you didn't fully understand what I was saying, you smiled when I finished and said, "Good boy, well done, you have an excellent memory." And you reached out and shook my hand like a man trying to hold tight on to something. Then you were silent for awhile, looking fearlessly ahead. We were both silent for awhile, just the two of us, together, walking south, the sun at our backs.

87

GRACE SCHULMAN

In the Foreground

In Monet's painting, men building a pier
stand out, their forms reflected in the water
while houses of Parliament dissolve in fog.

Workers cast images that say it twice:
No law, no sovereign power, can be as clear
as planks sanded to make a wharf, each log

raised up a ladder thin as a bracelet.
No act passes as calmly as a barge
sails under a bridge in daybreak's lavender.

His Paris at war, Monet fled and stared
through a window at the Thames. In his vision,
life in the foreground outshines large decisions.

Here at the shore, a swan skimming the bay
goes double, mirrored upside down in water.
Two trees bend, unlike towers that might have swayed

or not. No tragic account is as clear
as lines reeling out silver from a pier,
or a surfer rising to stand in wind,

no rubble plainer than shadow-pocked sand.
The dream you wake from is another dream.
Horror to peace. A swimmer heads home,

a sailor unfolds canvas. A cormorant
spreads wings like vestments for the eucharist.
The terns fall silent now as sun-clouds darken,

and in the city, where smoke-clouds still hover,
a woman looks skyward, hoping for rain.
Up front—pier, ladder, barges—things are clear.

88

LYNNE SHARON SCHWARTZ

Near November

The terrible mocking blue sky is finally gone and we are all glad, even the obedient ones who have taken up their daily rounds, pretending life will be as before. The sky has paled, the warmth drained from the air, and still we come each morning with our boxes of chalk, our knee-pads, our goggles. We need to be down here; it's where we belong, we're pulled to the barricaded streets. The foul air makes us cough but the searing in our throats spurs us on. The first morning after, only a few of us came, all with the same idea, to write in big letters on the streets. With every passing morning, those blazing azure mornings, others joined us. At first the police looked askance, then decided we were harmless. People stop to ask why we are down on our hands and knees, why months later we keep writing on the streets. Often they join us.

We write the same thing each day: I was in my car, on the bridge, I saw . . . On the bus, a woman on a cell phone started screaming . . . I was feeding the baby, I had the radio on . . . The phone rang, it was my sister-in-law, my girlfriend, my downstairs neighbor, my ex-husband . . . I was in the coffee shop, at the office, at the dentist, in class, from my hospital bed I saw it all out the window . . . I was in Honolulu, in London, in Paris, in Sydney . . .

The city sent people to question us. They were gentle, at least at first. Everyone was gentle, at first. We were breaking no laws. It is not yet against the law to write on the streets. It would be hard to arrest us anyway—we are too many. Now at night, to deter us, they hose the streets down. (It seems never to rain anymore, as if the sky holds back its tears.) See, they say, your writing is washed away. No matter. We'll write it again: The butcher's wife was in there. The girl in my yoga class was in there. The super's daughter. My daughter. My father. My wife.

A man from the city pleaded with us: Go back to your lives, he said. Or at least write something new.

We would like to write something new, we are very tired of our stories, but we don't know what the next sentence should be.

We have tried to proceed to the next sentence. But to write, you must know something, and we know nothing beyond the intolerable questions that assail us. Grief, at an infernal temperature, has burnt knowledge out of us. We try to write the next sentence, and senseless, contrary words come out, as if from a cauldron. What is the just path? Revenge is tempting, but also loathsome and useless. Can we love our country if we cannot love the voices that claim to be our country? Could this have happened? Look, over there, it happened. Terrible things have always happened to people. Why not to us? But why should such things happen to anyone? Who did it? Who are "they"? Who is innocent? Who is guilty? How can we tell? Is it war again? Then win the war. But don't kill anyone. Be prudent. No, be bold. No, a show of strength will only make things worse. The voices that blame us stir our rage—this is no time for blaming. The voices that extol us stir our rage—this is no time for smugness. Will some voice, please, speak an intelligent word in public? We long to hear an intelligent word. No, we long for silence. Enough words have been spoken. The words are ashes poured in our ears. Deafened, we seek the right path. But with our eyes coated with ash, how can we see any path, or truth, or justice?

We cannot write such sentences, made of useless words that seethe in the head. Of that blue and fire morning, we can only write what we know for certain: I would have been in there except I slept late . . . I had a toothache . . . I got caught in traffic . . .

But our sisters . . . Our brothers . . .

This we imprint on the streets, as if the soft chalk might cut grooves in the pavement. We cling to our stories, we take root in our stories like the nymph who took root in a tree and became its prisoner. Unlike her, we will regain our shapes—almost. We will do what is needed; we will write the next sentence. Only not yet, not here on the bleak brink of November.

89

DANI SHAPIRO

Now They Are Leaving

The birds are nestling closer. She noticed them two winters ago—the winter after she moved into the Brooklyn house with her husband and infant son. First only a few fat ones were perched atop the brownstone across the street. The next time she glanced out the window of her study, there were many more. Some were still, frozen against the white sky. Others seemed to be pacing back and forth, as if impatient, waiting for something to happen.

Three years earlier, when she moved with her family into the brick townhouse at the end of a row of darker, more ornate Victorians, she thought they would live there forever. As the men tilted the piano through the doorway, their muscles bulging and straining, the armoire up the steep staircase, her husband's cumbersome desk over the delicate old railing, with each safe arrival she breathed a sigh of relief and thought to herself: *we will never leave here.* She pictured her son as a teenager bounding up those stairs. Her husband, middle-aged, raking leaves in their small garden. And she—she would become like the older women in the neighborhood, with their shorn hair and dangly earrings, their comfortable, baggy clothing, laugh lines around their eyes. Happy, content city creatures. Gnarly, weather-beaten, like small dinosaurs in a museum.

It has been no time, really. An inhale, an exhale. And now they are leaving. Her study is filled with boxes. The bookcases are empty. The house—she can now finally say it—has felt wrong to her, practically from the beginning. She has felt, the entire time she's lived in this place, as if someone or something has been watching her. Just yesterday, one of the birds flew straight into the closed window of her study, with a dull thud and the papery rustle of feathers. Stunned, it settled on the wide brick ledge outside her window, one black eye trained, or so it seemed, on the interior. What did it see? A woman in a bathrobe hunched over her desk. A man hauling boxes—optimistically—down the narrow flights of stairs. A young boy asleep in his room, a boy whose first words were *bus* and *park* and *fire truck*, urban words which will remain tucked somewhere in his memory as they are paved over with new words—rural words—like *tractor* and *blue finch*, *daffodil* and *mountain hike*. Today, another bird settles on the ledge. This time a flesh-colored bird, an ugly, monochromatic bird with tumorous bulges along the sides of its neck.

"Go away!" She swats at the window, but the bird doesn't move. If anything, it presses closer against the glass. "Disgusting thing!"

"They're only here to warm themselves in the sun," her husband says. It is nearly spring and the light in the sky has shifted, it's true. She wants to believe her husband. He sees the same things she does, after all.

"But why only on our house?" she asks her husband.

He shrugs, by way of an answer. He doesn't believe in omens.

"Why our house?" she repeats. She hates the tone in her voice. She is whiny and afraid.

"Why not?" Her husband says as he bends down to pick up yet another box. And she knows he wonders: in the new house, will she find new signs? The ladybugs, perhaps? The dead trees lining the driveway?

90

AKHIL SHARMA

Bonus

Before September 11th, Weinstein was already complaining to Dyer, the global head of investment banking, about being bored with work. Weinstein was the biggest rainmaker in Media and Telecommunications and the complaints were partially to suggest to Dyer that it was time to push out Lethem, the head of M&T and one of those bankers who have a few good repeater clients but who mostly sit on many internal committees. After September 11th, Weinstein stopped complaining. He had teared up in front of Lethem while discussing his daughter, who was born in August. Weinstein worried that Lethem might say to Dyer, Weinstein looks ready to bolt and become a teacher or, like that VP in fixed income, go to film school. This could mean Weinstein's bonus, which he expected to be three and a half million, might be cut in half or even down to a million.

Weinstein was thirty-nine and a former linebacker from Rutgers. He had short black hair and a rectangular head with a chin like a heel. He was famous for ripping apart analysts' cubicles. As the analyst who had disappointed him worked frantically, Weinstein would yank big black aluminum drawers out and throw them across the aisle. He'd grab the cubicle's walls and with two or three pulls drag apart the glued and taped joints. The last time Weinstein had done this was a couple of years ago. But he started doing it again to show that he was as aggressive as ever.

In October when Enron started going through its troubles, Weinstein tried to get hired by Enron to divest their bandwidth trading unit. He failed and immediately switched to soliciting a possible buyer whom he could represent. The presentation to get this business was not complicated. But the analyst working on it was not the brightest star in the sky. Even after three months, she still used a mouse instead of keyboard commands. Once she stored files on her personal drive and not the shared drive. She was black though and probably thought she could get away with it. One morning when a pitch wasn't ready to be printed—all the bitch had to do was slap on a logo, Cntrl F for the name of the client they had last used the pitch for, and send it to Print Production—he began tearing her cubicle into pieces. She kept quiet, as did everyone in the nearby cubicles and the bank of offices that lined the outside of the floor, until her monitor began sliding off the desk. Then she hopped up and yipped, "This is a hostile work environment."

"Fuck you," he answered, moving past her to the keyboard.

But she went to Human Resources. Soon an officious and perky thirty-year-old woman came down to see Lethem. Lethem was on the minority hiring committee and this looked bad for him, so he scolded Weinstein for his Management Skills, one of the line items in the 360 evaluation form sent out before bonuses.

Then the *Wall Street Journal* reported that the commercial bank that owned the investment bank was in talks with Enron to buy the bandwidth trading unit Weinstein was trying to drum up interest for. Some of the clients they had solicited with the presentation complained to Dyer.

In December, gaps grew in the schedule of meetings as CFOs and CEOs went skiing. Weinstein took two weeks of "maternity" leave. He called it "maternity" leave because it was better to make fun of himself than to have someone else do it.

Lying in the tub with Eliza on his chest, Weinstein watched her trying to pick up water. Her whole fist was no wider than his thumb. She put her hand in the water, closed it, lifted it, and then put the hand in again. He considered quitting investment banking. He thought about this every year before bonuses. He already had seventeen million invested and an apartment on Park Avenue that he had bought in 1993 for a million and which might be worth four. Weinstein considered starting a fund to invest in high-yield telecommunications debt, but he liked deals and the idea of taking trading positions seemed boring. Suddenly a wave of pity shook him. All his life, he had only wanted a little piece of luck. He kissed Eliza's bald and pink head.

Dyer called him to a seven-thirty meeting. Over the last week, a few senior bankers had already met with Dyer to be told what kind of haircut they should expect on their bonuses and how much the firm loved them. Waiting outside Dyer's office for a conference call to end, Weinstein said to Sheila, one of Dyer's two secretaries. "You do a good job, but everybody has his own ideas." Sheila nodded. She had a telephone head set on and was fluffing the flowers that had just arrived for Dyer's office. Weinstein showed her a photo of Eliza.

The conference call ended and Weinstein went in. Three of the walls were glass. Snow drifted over silent and dark Broadway.

Lethem was resigning, Dyer informed Weinstein. Bonuses had not been announced so this meant Lethem was being fired. Weinstein and another banker would become co-heads of Media and Telecommunications. The first thing Weinstein felt was fear. The target on his back had stretched out like an enormous sweat stain.

Only that night, in the town car home as he passed the glowing shops of Madison Avenue, did Weinstein become giddy and laugh.

91

SUZAN SHERMAN

Nurse

Before the realtor had showed James his apartment, she had ventured to mention that it was located squarely across the street from the hospital. The view from the apartment was no view at all, unless one considered gazing directly into a wall of hospital rooms a view—the long, incessantly bright tubes of fluorescent light, and the televisions casting their hazy blue glow as they are flicked on and off by the impatient and infirm who lay motionless in their beds, festooned by wilting flower baskets and ridiculous helium balloons emblazoned with the words Get Well Soon! If one didn't mind the endless, blaring sound of the ambulances screeching to a halt in front of the hospital, their red lights flailing within feet of the apartment, gurneys being rushed into the emergency room, the people laying on them barely clinging to life, then it was indeed the perfect apartment. Of course it was perfect. What could be better? Except maybe an apartment in the hospital itself, which of course was not an option. James had taken out his checkbook on the spot—with the harbored hope that some members of the hospital staff might be his neighbors. To have a nurse for a neighbor—he could borrow sugar from her to bake a cake, or at least pretend he was baking to borrow the sugar. Together he and as many as a half dozen nurses could share the small, intimate space of the elevator for minutes at a time, their shoulders squeezed together, breathing the same air as they are transported higher and higher. His mind spun with all of the wonderful, endless possibilities that his new apartment held for him.

But despite the apartment building's size, James had not seen a single person enter or leave it in the two months he'd been living there. It was as though James was its only inhabitant, though he did smell meals being cooked behind closed doors, meats mostly, and the apartment next to his emitted the distinct aroma of gardenias and baby powder—but when would life ever emerge?

Sometimes he considered planting himself in the apartment building's lobby, in the faux brown leather sectional, until he saw someone besides the mundane trio of FedEx man, postman, and doorman. How he loved the lobby, where it seemed that no one had ever seated themselves before. Next to the sofa was an end table with a remarkable orange and magenta tropical flower bouquet made from silk—its petals leapt up in the air in a variety of exotic poses, screaming for attention. James imagined holding a party in the lobby space—there was certainly plenty of room—and so convenient to the hospital right across the street.

And then one afternoon, as he looked out his window, he had spotted her walking out of the hospital. She was different than the others he had observed in that she wore a white cape, and a little white cap with a red cross emblazoned on the front of it. That she was wearing such an outfit was almost absurd: it was so far removed from the more contemporary nurse uniforms which were merely a simply cut, comfortable pair of white slacks and a white shirt to match. A few weeks before he'd been lucky to get a glimpse of a nurse in a full white skirt which went down to her ankles, though she quickly disappeared into the subway and hadn't resurfaced since then. But James had never, ever, seen one in a cap. It was fantastic, something out of a World War II film or an Ernest Hemingway novel. He imagined her capable hands tending to the rows and rows of wounded GIs. For months these men had experienced the horrors of living in the trenches, and now, as she cupped their bloody heads while bandaging them, they couldn't help but feel a quiver beneath their uniforms. Those that would return home in one piece might share their newfound fascination with their wives. Some would be accepting and fasten the little white cap onto their heads with bobby pins, while the other veterans would be forced to hide their tattered nurse uniform catalogues beneath their beds.

James saw that the nurse was crossing the street now, she was walking towards the building. He immediately rushed out of his apartment, and to his great fortune the elevator was waiting on his floor for him. As it lurched down the seven stories to the lobby he attempted to straighten his hair in the odd, convex mirror which seemed to be in every elevator, and made his nose look exceptionally large. But his hair refused to cooperate, the part in it was not a clean line, but more closely resembled a jagged lightening bolt.

The nurse was probably not heading for his apartment building anyway, but had merely walked past it to the Dunkin' Donuts next door, which the doctors and nurses commonly frequented—they ate more sugar than anyone, even children, they were absolutely the most unhealthy people. By now the nurse had probably come and gone, toting a jelly donut in a pink and orange waxed paper bag back to her shift in Intensive Care.

But no. He couldn't believe it, there she was, in his very lobby, standing next to the wall of mailboxes with a set of keys. She was jingling them, and they made a wonderful little tune in her hands. He realized that he too had his keys on him, and had not yet retrieved the day's mail. He walked over to his mailbox, not far from where she stood, and inserted the key into the proper slot and turned. One envelope, a bill, fell into his hand.

JENEFER SHUTE 92

Instructions for Surviving the Unprecedented (Break Glass in Case of Emergency, If Glass Is Not Already Broken)

Protocol 9, Section xi: For Those Who Live Alone

1. You will hear the news from people living thousands of miles away, people in other time zones. People who watch TV and know what is happening in your city, your neighborhood, before you do.

2. You will gradually become conscious of the sirens, the never-ending scream and wail, the lament of the sirens, more sirens than you have ever heard. Afterwards, this sound will fill you with dread.

3. The phones will go dead. All the phones. You will not understand this at first and will keep trying different phones: cell phones, neighbors' phones, even the payphone on the corner, where people are queuing up, numbly, though all the phones are dead.

4. The reporter on the radio will sound puzzled at first, stumbling incredulously over his words, then afraid. His fear will infect you. You will feel the first inklings of the unprecedented, a vertigo of the whole body, a speedy, queasy weightlessness. You will quash it.

5. You will respond inappropriately (how else to respond to the unprecedented?). It will not occur to you at first that your world has changed, that it's being blown apart, that you might be in danger. You will think of what is happening, at first, as some kind of spectacle unfolding in your backyard. You will feel a slight, illicit thrill. You will continue blindly with your plans for the day. You will see no reason not to go uptown.

6. You will do stupid things: you will leave the house, as planned, heading for the subway, until you hear on your Walkman that all the subways have been closed. You will head towards the scene with your camera, swimming against the tide of people fleeing, the silent masses swarming up the empty avenues, the ash-covered army of the living dead. Only later will you think about things like smoke, fumes, explosions, collapsing buildings and tunnels, flood and fire, nerve gas, toxins, viruses, spores. Only later will you realize that you should have stayed home.

7. At home you will feel trapped, isolated, useless. Once inside the door—as after a divorce or separation—you will not know what to do next. Somehow it will be impossible to absorb this alone. You will need to be part of a narrative. You begin to understand what language is for, what other human beings are for. But all the phones are dead.

8. Your 83-year-old neighbor, when you go across the hall to check on him, will be so unresponsive, so preoccupied with something in the kitchen, that at first you will think he hasn't heard the news. Only later will you understand that he was in shock.

9. You will want to do something. You will make a nuisance of yourself in the streets and at the hospitals, with thousands of others, trying to volunteer, trying to donate blood. The

impulse behind this will not necessarily be altruism. It will be fear.

10. You will end up doing what everyone else is doing: you will watch TV. The repetition of images will not dull their impact: the repetition of the unthinkable, at first, renders the unthinkable more, rather than less, unthinkable. You will understand nothing. You will have no ideas, no opinions, no analysis. You will keep saying, "Oh, my god."

11. You will end up spending the day with some unlikely person, because the people you really want to be with are out of reach. You will be grateful to this person and his giant TV. You will drink whatever he has in the house—cheap sake, leftover liqueurs. After about eight hours, you will emerge, shakily, like invalids, in search of food. The streets will be deserted. The shops will be shuttered. The city will be silent, except for the never-ending wail. But one Indian restaurant will be open and packed, glittering with light, as if a party is going on. People will talk animatedly, eat voraciously. No one will be alone.

12. You won't sleep well. You'll keep getting up in the night, to turn on the news, to see if your email works.

13. The next day you will have no reason to go out but you will go out anyway. You think perhaps you should stock up on something. The air will burn your eyes and throat and lungs. You will smell things you've never smelt before, chemical things and biological things. You won't allow yourself to think about what they are. You will see people wearing masks; their eyes will meet yours, over the masks, solemn and grim. You will buy yourself a surgical mask, a pack of ten. You will feel stupid; you will put the mask on upside down. The sight of masked people on the streets, masked children, will frighten you more than the police barricades and the military jets, more than the mass of smoke over the mutilated skyline, more

even than the sirens' never-ending wail. Because you know the masks are useless.

14. You will see, on a lamppost near your house, a poster for a missing person. It will break your heart. Then, in the next few days, you will see thousands. They will all break your heart. After several months, they'll still be there, tattered and rain-streaked, but you won't see them any more.

15. You will come home to find an enormous flag on the front door of your building. You will feel violated, misrepresented; you will think, no, this isn't what I want to say. But you will understand why it's there. The super has put it there. He's an immigrant. He's afraid.

16. You will feel sad that no one calls to check up on you, even though all the phones are dead.

17. You will understand that you live next to a vast charnel house, that your city has become a necropolis.

18. You will go to a square where people have lit candles and left bouquets, where crowds are standing silently and studying the posters for the missing and the dead, the messages that others have written on scrolls upon the ground. Someone will hand you a felt-tipped marker. You will kneel. You will write: "Words Fail Me."

19. Months later, they won't.

93

HAL SIROWITZ

The War at Home; What to Save for Death

THE WAR AT HOME

Your great grandfather was born in America,
Father said, which makes you the fourth generation
to be born here. So don't worry
if your friends keep asking why
I didn't fight in the Second World War.
Just because I didn't serve abroad
doesn't make me less of an American.
You can't be less of what you already are.
I had to stay home to take care of my sick parents.
I did my share of fighting. "Dad, it's not cheaper
not taking your medicine," I had to keep saying.
"If you get sicker it'd cost even more." "Mom,
I couldn't just marry a rich woman. Making money
that way will make me lose my self-respect."
It was a struggle. They fought me tooth & nail.
I'd rather have fought a real enemy.
It's always harder fighting your own kind.

WHAT TO SAVE FOR DEATH

You should be thankful you're alive,
Father said. No matter how bad you're feeling
it could be a lot worse when you're dead.
No one knows what that may feel like.
That's why you should take advantage
of nature—the sun on your shoulders,
the wind in your hair—because once you're dead
you may never get that opportunity again.
You may have plenty of time to indulge
in your own thoughts when you're dead.
That may be the only thing you could do.
You won't be able to walk in a meadow
if your legs don't work & your eyes stay closed.
So if I were you I'd do more physical stuff
while you're still capable of doing it,
& save the thinking for when you're dead.

94

PAMELA SNEED

Elvis

As an avowed feminist, intellectual,
writer, and professor
in a privatized city college
One thing I don't allow is
bible thumping, proselytizing,
no Jesus or Judaism freaks
wanting my students to reach,
explore different terrain,
and branch out from their often religious upbringing
I say sternly of religion
"there are places for that."
a comment which sometimes causes
an explosive reaction—
So given this,
you can imagine my dismay the other day
in one of my speech classes
comprised of English as Second Language students
when one of my students from Pakistan
who looks like a Muslim Elvis Presley
with exquisitely arched Black eyebrows and
hair a bit too high
like someone caught between his country and ours
whose assimilation is a little askew
does a presentation on an unexpected topic
without confirmation or consent on my part
choosing to talk about Islam, as a religion of peace.
I am aghast

and find his speech more rambling and less cohesive than others
though it's the semester's end
I admonish him on how poorly put together it is
saying he should have checked with me about the topic first.
Yes Miss he says in stumbling but firm english.
I am afraid to speak here.
Afraid of talking about my religion—
Some of my professors are upset and won't let me speak
and I've seen what they are saying
about Muslims on TV
Oh, So this is really about September 11th
and the United States' war on Afghanistan, I say
and your needing to defend yourself and your religion.
Well, that's important, you should have said that first.
Yes, he says, overriding my comment
They say we hate women
but two women in my country have become prime ministers.
No woman has ever been elected president in America
That's a point and I agree.
It's also terrible how the U.S. is bombing Afghanistan
and scapegoating Palestine.
Yes, he responds,
The television isn't talking about how the U.S. is arresting and detaining
Muslims here.
In the stores and streets they are yelling epithets
and saying I should return to my own country—
Muslims are leaving America, though generations of their sons and daughters
were born here.
I am afraid Miss.

Afraid of speaking out.
Yes, I say looking at the five other students in
class,
ranging from China, to Russia, Columbia, and American
born Chino-latino
you are not safe
that is reality
but don't be afraid
speaking is your god given right
too bad about your teachers,
you must speak and we must hear,
our conversation carries from the classroom to the
street
until parting we come to a traffic light—
I warn him against religious dogma
but confirm he must speak
and we must hear
walking away—he says in that potent kind of ESL way
language that cuts straight to the core
without mincing the way native speakers do
their juxtapositions are much more risky and
metaphoric
which makes ESL students always my favorite as a poet
Thanks Miss
I happy.
You give courage.

95

CHRIS SPAIN

Hinge

November going on December, end of the tree man's year. That late fall tilt to the earth knocking the light down early. White horizons so there is no near and far. Working in a drizzle, wet to his pockets, he's almost finished dismantling what's left of this old silver maple, taking it down in chunks, dropping in a day what it took a hundred years to build.

He kills the saw, rests it on his thigh. Steeped in a cut-wood smell. As if he's on some kind of island, as if he's been washed up on a shore, waterlogged, arm heavy, a shipwreck. Feeling buoyant though, the way he gets when he's worked himself close to exhaustion. That chemistry of the blood. Or maybe it's just being up so high, about as far from the grief of the ground as you can get.

A clump of birch behind the derelict pool. Something about birch in winter. Peeling bark like tattered clothing, the bare wood beneath. He's never known war but they look like what he imagines refugees from a war would look like.

What disaster has been visited on this place? None of the ornamentals wrapped, dead weeds fallen over in the cracks of the pool walk, the grass looking like it never saw a mower all season. No pool cover on the pool, the deep end clotted with leaves. Chalk lines on the tennis court long faded, the net sagging between posts. As if a big wind has left everything out of kilter. Flags up everywhere for the last year, but not here. Just the lines and rusted rigging. Probably an old widow alone. Probably just that most natural of disasters, the unrelenting storm of time.

She called last night, her voice almost lost in the wires. A tree broken under the weight of its years. The electric company had the lights back, but they told her what was left of the tree wasn't safe. Could he come out.

The drizzle has turned to snow. Wintertiming. It was his boy who said that once. His boy. Just yesterday or a hundred years ago.

He drops out of the sky with the snow, unclips his harness, gathers the tether, walks the fifty feet to a gaunt spruce giant, ties what's left of the maple against a backfall. The stubborn Stihl coughs, sputters, dies. He yanks the rope again and this time the saw catches. An old tree, canyons in the bark. He notches it in the direction of the fall, first from one side, then the other, sights a retreat, just in case the maple decides not to cooperate, draws the guide bar across the trunk, begins his felling cut. When he completes the hinge it starts over slowly at first, as if dropping to its knees, then faster, gravity calling harder.

He sees her then, walking toward him through a day all but buried already. She stops twenty feet away, tilts her head back, looks up at the empty air, at the space where the maple just was. Even from a distance, even in this tired light, you can see the meagerness of her. So thin she couldn't be long for the world. A birch in winter.

He quiets the Stihl.

—You were right, it had to come down, he says.

It sounds like a shout.

Little hisses from the spark arrestor when the snow lands on it.

The smell of two-cycle exhaust.

She holds out a hand, palm up, as if she has just noticed the snow. Behind her, in silhouette, the bare trees don't look dead but like some kind of eastern writing telling a story. Perhaps she has forgotten how to talk.

He sets down the saw, walks toward her, connects the dots of her.

She is young.

She is young, and she is weeping.

She covers her face with her hands, turns away.

—I'm sorry, she says. I'm sorry.

No sweater, just thin cotton, what is left of her all bone. Pale, almost purple skin. Like one of those people who can't get enough oxygen, like a boy he once knew with a hole in his heart.

—There was no safe way to save it, he says.

—It was the only thing to do, he says.

—I'm sorry, she says. I'm sorry. It's not the tree.

She looks windblown even though the snow falls straight down. She wipes her eyes, turns back to him.

—I don't even know why I'm crying.

She wipes her eyes again.

—I guess it's too late to ask you not to fall.

Almost a smile, quick and gone.

And then it comes to him exactly the way a fall comes, as if he has lost his purchase, slipped from a branch, has to grab for something to save himself. Her story writes itself in this moment. An hour from the city, right on the train line, Wall Street money, the place a year and more let go. He is certain of it.

She is crying again, and this time she doesn't turn away, doesn't wipe away her tears.

—We are asked to accept such losses, she says.

—I'm so sorry, he says. I'm so sorry.

She hugs herself, as if she has just felt the cold.

The edges of their breath clouds mixing.

—They say it never goes away, but that it gets better, she says. That one day you want to get out of bed, want to eat, want to talk to people, want to laugh, want to listen to music.

His heart unraveling, and he is not sure toward what end.

He almost reaches to hold her, but he has only known her these seconds.

The gravity of grief.

The ache of this light.

The useless and feeble things we say. Silence would be better. And yet.

—I think those things are true, he says. I think it never goes away, but one day you'll want to hear music again.

The thinnest copper wire of words, telegraphed across the half dark.

And the rest of the world falls away, leaves them the last two people on a tiny planet of dirt and grass and log jumble.

96

ART SPIEGELMAN

Re: Covers

What is the half-life of memory? My September 11th is finally dimming down to a shadow of itself, to a few compulsively retold anecdotes and a vivid image or two. As a citizen of Lower Soho, on the outskirts of Ground Zero, I had a ringside seat to the calamity, and so my perspective has been slower to shift back to narcotized normalcy than some. If it wasn't for a tremulous inner voice, singing off-key along with "my" government's self-serving reminders to Stay Afraid, I might be able to reduce my memory of the vaporized towers down to size, to little more than last season's most compelling media event.

Everyone around the world with access to a television set saw the cataclysmic destruction of those towers, saw it in constant replay, burning—and burning itself into our collective retina. What slowed down my own amnesiac responses is simply that I first experienced those events unmediated by television.

Those towers had been our taken-for-granted neighbors, always picture-postcard visible a mile south of our front stoop. On the morning of September 11th my wife, Françoise Mouly (the covers editor of the *New Yorker* magazine) and I had just stepped out to vote in the mayoral primaries. We heard the plane roar above us and heard a crash as we walked north. The stricken expression on the face of a young woman facing south convinced us that it might be worth turning around, that this crash might be more than some big rig navigating the potholes of Canal Street. The scale of the disaster was at first unclear: as many have since observed, it seemed "surreal"—and we had to get over our stunned disconnect to realize that this was no movie, and that our fourteen-year-old daughter, Nadja, was in the heart of the growing pandemonium.

Nadja is a freshman at Stuyvesant High School, right below the towers. A half-hour after the first blast we had made our way into the lobby of the school to find her. It took over an hour to locate her among the 3000 disoriented students in the ten-story building. Some of her classmates had parents who worked in the towers; some had seen bodies falling past their windows. While we were there, the building momentarily lost its power and shook, as the south tower crumbled right outside. We got Nadja out a few minutes before the school decided to evacuate and we made our way home on the promenade alongside the Hudson. We turned back to see the north tower tremble. The core of the building seemed to have burned out, and only the shell remained—shimmering, suspended in the sky-before ever-so-slowly collapsing in on itself. Françoise shrieked "No! No! No!" over and over again. Nadja cried out: "My school!" while I stared slack-jawed at the spectacle, not believing it real until the enormous toxic cloud of smoke that had replaced the building billowed toward us.

We began planning how to get uptown to get our ten-year-old son, Dash, out of the United Nations School he attends. We stopped at home long enough to retrieve some phone messages and heard, with relief, the voices of some friends who lived under the towers and whom we had feared dead. Among the messages were several from the *New Yorker*, telling Françoise to make contact, that a new magazine, with a new cover, had to be put together in the next three days. That too seemed surreal.

▪

Whenever I walked north in the hours and days that followed, I turned back—as if toward Mecca—to see if my buildings were still missing. Not especially well equipped to help in the search for survivors, I applied myself to searching for an image of the disaster. Despite what felt like the irrelevancy of the task, it gave me a way to fend off trauma and focus on something. I wanted to find the awful (and awe-filled) image of all that disappeared that morning.

I tried to juxtapose the deadly blackness of the event with the wondrous crystalline blue sky that underscored the surrealism of that bleak day. I sketched the towers, shrouded in black as if by a Christo in mourning. They floated against a tranquil Magritte sky above a Lower Manhattan cityscape. But Surrealism was inadequate to that moment, and the vividness of the color seemed to obscenely mock the blackness at the heart of the picture. I scanned the sketch into my computer, and gradually desaturated and darkened the color of the sky and cityscape until my screen was virtually black. Only when my picture all but disappeared did it accurately reflect the painful new emptiness I and many others needed to see. Ad Reinhardt's black-on-black paintings offered a solution.

When Françoise saw the phantom towers on my screen she knew well before I did that I'd found the *New Yorker*'s cover. My work ethic kept insisting that I still needed to render all the buildings that surrounded the World Trade Center, but ultimately, anything other than the most minimal gesture seemed to be an insult to that somber moment. The overwhelming response to the "black" cover—which only revealed its secrets as one's perspective and lighting shifted—indicated that I had succeeded in somehow channeling the toxic air around me into an image of the towers that helped people come to terms with their loss. The afterimage of the towers lingers, insisting on its presence through the blackness. But now, in the months of "new normalcy" that have followed, the rescue and salvage operation that continues near my front stoop has allowed me the luxury of trying to rescue and salvage my first image. I've "sandblasted" and scrubbed my first sketch and now, with some distance, that blue sky—on the cover of this book—seems at least a little more possible.

CATHARINE R. STIMPSON

97

Staffing

At church, when I see bishops, I get a little chuckle from their staffs, those sticks they carry, the ones with a crook at the end. They're supposed to remind me that the bishops are my shepherd and I'm a member of their flock. But my position is Administrative Staff, Grade 13, and if I protect anybody, it's my boss, who's nice to me, and whose wife can be pretty nice to me, and who doesn't cheat on his wife, unlike most of the bozos around here, and who takes care of me if one of the bozos hits on me.

Some of the families are going to visit the office today. My boss'll meet with them in his office. After September 11, we put another American flag on his wall, to go with the American flag and the state flag on their stands by his desk. But he'll only meet with them for a minute or two. None of the families live in the district. Not even a cousin. I checked that out. Believe me, I checked that out. But he has to meet with them, because they are the families, and it would look awful if he didn't. It would be awful if he didn't. We all watched the towers burning on TV, and we all said America will never be the same, and he's a co-sponsor of the bill that says the state is going to crack down on people who cheat on their student visas and ask the state police to make colleges tell us who's really in class on those visas.

I will meet with the families after him. I don't think we're going to get any widows, and I'm glad about that. I don't have trouble talking to people, but meeting the widows, or any of the children, would put me into a meltdown, and I go into enough meltdowns as it is. It's so sad. It's really tragic. I feel so bad for them. I can't begin to describe my feelings. I think we are going to get a brother and two sisters of the victims, and a father if he can manage the trip.

It's going to be hard, very hard. We know what they want. They want September 11 to be declared a state holiday, like Memorial Day or Flag Day. We also put American flags on all the doors of the offices after September 11. But it's turning into a big deal. Yesterday, the boss met for an hour, a lifetime around here, with some constituents and major players. They were very respectful. They didn't want to look as if they were playing politics—god forbid—over the bodies of the victims. So all they said was that they were afraid of a state holiday. But they said it in that tone they use when they mean pay attention. The small business people are afraid of the money. I don't blame them. They lose money on state holidays, because the insurance people and the accountants and the little places have to close, unless they're in retail. And small business—that's mother's milk for us. The Bear himself told us troops that a state holiday would cost $25 million—$25 million—in holiday bonuses for state employees. And I know the staffer who came up with that figure. He doesn't fool around. And then the unions would demand the day off, and that would just mean the usual table-pounding and shouting.

The leadership says we should tell the families that we'll guarantee a Day of Remembrance. I have made up a list of Days of Remembrance for them. Pearl Harbor is right there. A Day of Remembrance has dignity, and before September 11, Pearl Harbor was the worst thing any enemy ever did to America. I agree with the boss here. I'm protecting him on this one because I really believe it, and you can believe me, I know the difference between protecting him because I have to because I'm a staffer and because I want to protect him because I believe in him. I'll listen to the families, and remind them of Pearl Harbor. The place where my mouth will stick is having to say that state holidays mostly suck anyway, obviously I'll say it nicer than that, that nobody cares about them except to go shopping and have barbecues. Have you ever seen a supermarket parking lot before a state holiday, before Memorial Day? Nobody's buying books about World War I or World War II. They're buying nachos. But it's going to be hard to say that, because I can't look as if we don't respect Memorial Day or Presidents' Day or Flag Day. And I'll promise the families that my boss will put a provision in the bill, he'll personally see to it, that all the flags on public buildings will fly at half-mast on every September 11 forever and ever. I'll make a Day of Remembrance a great memorial, and a state holiday a joke. But the gentlemen, as they call themselves, in the other chamber say that September 11 was so big and so awful that it has to have a state holiday. We won't remember it unless there's a holiday. Funny, isn't it, to have a holiday so we can think about dead people and debris and the War on Terror. One of them actually saw the towers collapse, and he's impossible to talk to about the issue. His guys say a state holiday would only cost $5 to $8 million. Only $5 to $8 million.

In this job, you've got to learn to count the votes. I often tell my boss I'm going to save all the little pieces of paper where he's scratched down names and how they're going to vote. I tell him they look like betting slips, and he asks me how I know about betting slips. A good question. My Granddad would have to answer it. This is what is going to go down. Our chamber will pass a bill for a Day of Remembrance. The other guys will pass a bill for a state holiday. And if it gets on the news, and if it's more than an inside story in the *Times*, which our constituents don't read, we'll look damn stupid—again. But if it's only an inside story in the *Times*, the leadership will try to strike a deal—although it's hard to make a deal because of the guy who saw the buildings go down, and some of the other guys who actually knew people who were victims. And, I don't want to be crude about it, because evil was done on September 11, but we don't exactly have the same constituencies.

So I'll put on my black suit, with the skirt that goes below my knees, and listen to the families. I'll show them the old copy of the magazine I keep in my desk drawer, with the black cover, where you can just see the outline of the towers in black. I feel for them, I really do, I believe in a Day of Remembrance, for all America. And why not for all the world?

98

LIZ SWADOS

Shakespeare & Punk

I was in Paris during September scoring a production of Shakespeare's *Merchant of Venice*. Andrei Serban was directing at the Comédie Français. He wanted to bring out the skinhead, neo-Nazi aspect of the revelers, and also deal with the hint of homosexuality between Antonio and Basanio by placing the first scene in a sizzling steambath with men gently whipping each other with flayed branches. Shylock was portrayed as a Wall Street trader, in a three-piece suit, on several phones at once, a calculator in his hand and a deal-a-minute in his Jewish head. There was a lot of discussion as to whether Serban's portrayal of Shylock was more or less anti-Semitic than Shakespeare had intended. Was the presence of Ku Klux Klan costumes pro or against racism? Should the girls wear revealing underwear? Needless to say, the show was highly provocative, though I'm not sure what the theme behind the provocation was exactly. But I was afforded the opportunity to compose a wide range of styles musically. I did hard-core head banging themes, bee bop, medieval fairy tale music, klezmer, and Aryan nationalist music, mystical new age music for the lovers, and magical-forest-type music, Jewish cantorial music and Arabic and Spanish steaming gay bathhouse music. The responsibility for interpreting my themes lay with two Parisian male musicians—a synthesizer player and a percussionist who, at every opportunity, demonstrated their doubts that a woman composer could handle the complexities of the task at hand and, therefore, rewrote, rearranged, and sometimes discarded my compositions entirely. There were several intense, emotional and intellectual confrontations about the meaning of theater and music, but having learned from experience I settled stylistic differences by threatening to fire them if they didn't play what I wrote. This tactic soon had them behaving very nicely. I don't know what happened once I left Paris. For all I know, they could've gleefully made up a new score every night.

I was a CNN junkie while in Paris. News makes me less homesick so, within hours of the attack of the World Trade Center, I was seeing it on my small TV set in my hotel. I was too numbed to be horrified. I remember that the stuffy French concierge was much nicer to me that day and that several French guests expressed very sincere condolences, which was both touching and completely bizarre. My partner and I tried to get through to New York—we live downtown—but it was impossible. We ran to an Internet café nearby and stood with a crowd of Americans, hoping someone's e-mail would go through. After many scary hours someone could e-mail their family in Northern Michigan who could contact a friend in New York. We got scraps of stories, some comforting—others terrifying: French actors had heard that a plane had been shot down by the U.S. Army because it was heading for a nuclear plant. After a day, the stories became more or less uniform. We made contact, but didn't know the fate of four young businessmen who lived in our co-op building. It turned out one of them had died in the disaster. Then, all one could do was hang out at the TWA office as if waiting for tickets to a World Series game or Shakespeare in the Park, and then spend hours pacing at the airport.

But the crux of this story is about my dogs—Valentine, a ten-year-old Bijon Frisé and Tootsie, a six-year-old chocolate standard poodle—and their walkers. An elderly friend was sleeping at our loft and we had hired a young husband and wife to walk the dogs. These dog walkers were Goths who own and ran their own music label, supplementing their income by a newly discovered talent—that they were good with dogs. They dressed in black, layers, rags, combat boots and had piercings in their eyebrows, nose and lips. The young husband could talk non-stop about the need for integrating truth into the alternative music movement. For some strange reason, this gave me confidence that they could handle routine walks with my dogs. They were, after all, obsessively dedicated music people with dyed black Rasta dreads and had to be devoted to animal life and spiritual consciousness. In the beginning they were dedicated professionals and I was at ease knowing that my two gorgeous, spoiled, and somewhat neurotic dogs were getting the love they deserve. But after the disaster, my two electric-fried messengers of punk changed. The air where I lived had become thick with an acrid smell. If the wind blew a certain way, there was the frank smell of death. People were encouraged to wear surgical masks. Rumor has it that the Goth dog walkers became frantic about air quality and were anxious about nuclear and biological doom—as Goths are wont to be. They took to walking our dogs while wearing fully appointed World War I gas masks. I'm surprised my poodle didn't attack them, since she is afraid of Halloween masks, large hats, and feather boas. Two dull green, oversized insects had to be disconcerting. After two days, the Goths, without a word and without returning my deposit, disappeared. Luckily, several of my students pitched in; then, within 42 hours of the abandonment, I was home. Given the extraordinary tragedy of the time, my story is a trivial testimony about 2 freaks and odd behavior. But when I think about September 11th with all its horror and rage, I also have this picture of a large sleek poodle with a small fluff ball being led through the smoke-filled streets of downtown New York by two Gothic punk rockers in World War I gas masks. There is dread and hope in that image.

By the way, the show in Paris became a huge controversial success. But I have this uneasy kind of magically inspired guilt that maybe September would've been different if I hadn't been involved, as a Jew, in such a blatantly anti-Semitic play. We all have our own Voodoo.

99

LYNNE TILLMAN

Save Me from the Pious and the Vengeful

for Joe Wood 1965–1999

Out of nothing comes language and out of language comes nothing and everything. Everything challenges the tenuous world order. Every emotion derails every other one. One rut is disrupted by the emergence of another. I like red wine, but began drinking white, with a sudden thirst, and now demand it at 6 P.M., exactly, as if my life depended upon it. That was a while ago.

What does a life depend upon? And from whom do I beg forgiveness so quietly I'm never heard? With its remarkable colors and aftertastes, the wine, dry as wit, urges me to forgive myself. I try.

Life's aim, Freud thought, was death. I can't know this, but maybe it's death I want, since living comes with its own exigencies, like terror. In dreams, nothing dies, but birth can't be trusted, either. I remember terrible dreams and not just my own. Memory is what everyone talks about these days. Will we remember, and what will we remember, who will be written out, ignored, or obliterated. Someone could say: They never existed. It's a singular terror.

The names of the dead have to be repeated daily. To forget them has a meaning no one understands, but there comes a time when the fierce pain of their absence dulls and their voices become so faint they can't be heard.

And then what do the living mean by being alive, how dare we? The year changes, the millennium, and from one day to the next, something must have been discarded, or neglected, something was abandoned, left to wither or ruin. You didn't decide to forget. People make lists, take vitamins, and they exercise. I bend over, over and over.

I'm not good at being a pawn of history.

The news reports that brain cells don't die. I never believed they did. The tenaciousness of memory, its viciousness really —witness the desire over history for revenge—has forever been a sign that the brain recovers. But it's unclear what it recovers.

Try to hang on to what you can. It's all really going. So am I. Someone else's biography seems like my life. I read it and confuse it with my own. I watch a movie, convinced it happened to me. I suppose it did happen to me. I don't know what I think anymore. I don't know what I don't think. I'm someone who tells things.

Once, I wanted to locate movie footage of tidal waves. They occurred in typical dreams. But an oceanographer told me that a tidal wave was a tsunami, it moved under the ocean and couldn't be seen. This bothered me for a long time. I wondered what it was that destroyed whole villages, just washed them away. In dreams, I'm forced to rescue myself. This morning's decision: let life rush over me. The recurring tidal wave is not about sexual thralldom, not the spectacular orgasm, not the threat of dissolution and loss of control through sex—that, too—but a wish to be overcome by life rather than to run it. To bc overrun.

I don't believe any response, like invention, is sad. The world is made up of imagining. I imagine this, too. Things circle, all is flutter. Things fall down and rise up. Hope and remorse, beauty and viciousness, and imagination, wherever it doggedly hides, unveil petulant realities. I live in my mind, and I don't. There's scant privacy for bitterness or farting or the inexpressible; historically, there was an illusion of privacy.

Illusions are necessary. The wretched inherit what no one wants.

What separates me from the world? Secret thoughts?

What Americans fear is the inability to have a world different from their fathers' and mothers'. That's why we move so much, to escape history.

Margaret Fuller said: I accept the universe. I try to embrace it. But I leave it to others to imagine the world in ways I can't.

I leave it to others.

Out of nothing comes language and out of language comes nothing and everything. I know there will be stories. Certainly, there will always be stories.

100

MIKE TOPP

Bad Luck

It is bad luck to drop a book and not step on it.
It is bad luck to bring a hoe into the house.
It is bad luck to sweep the floor before the sun rises.
It is bad luck to count the stars.

It is bad luck to comb your hair after dark.
It is bad luck to rock an empty chair.
It is bad luck to burn apple trees for firewood.
It is bad luck to eat only one helping of rice.

It is bad luck to look at the moon through branches.
It is bad luck to meet a left-handed person on Tuesday.
It is bad luck to watch a person out of sight.
It is bad luck for a black hen to come into the house.

It is bad luck to milk a cow on the ground.
It is bad luck to sell a crowing hen.
It is bad luck to wear a needle in your clothes.
It is bad luck to break a bird egg.

It is bad luck to spin a chair on one leg.
It is bad luck to dream of eating cabbage.
It is bad luck to see a pin and not pick it up.
It is bad luck to open an umbrella in the house.

It is bad luck to sit on a pair of scissors.
It is bad luck to see a cat's tail by the fire.

It is bad luck to sun bed sheets on Friday.
It is bad luck to sit on a trunk.

It is bad luck to be proposed to in church.
It is bad luck to carry eggs after sunset.
It is bad luck for a sick person to cut his fingernails.
It is bad luck to dream about eating white grapes.

It is bad luck to wear black at a wedding.
It is bad luck to be married in black.
It is bad luck to be married on Thursday.
It is bad luck to name a baby for the dead.

It is bad luck to change a baby's name.
It is bad luck to dream about rats fighting.
It is bad luck to wash new clothes before they are worn.
It is bad luck to sift through the ashes.

It is bad luck to prod the beach rubble.
It is bad luck to sneeze with your mouth full.
It is bad luck to have small ears.
It is bad luck to have sulfur in your shoes.

It is bad luck to see a candle go out.
It is bad luck to burn red candles.
It is bad luck to find a knot in a feather.
It is bad luck to not fold back the thumb.

It is bad luck to find a snake bone in your pillow.
It is bad luck to have a frog in your leg.
It is bad luck to hear a screeching owl.
It is bad luck if fruit trees bloom twice a year.

101

DAVID TRINIDAD

Skylines

Monday night, I took a cab to have dinner
with my father—in transit from Portugal to his home
in California—at a hotel near JFK.

From the BQE, the city was all imagery: the moon,
low in the sky, was a small slice of cantaloupe;
the bridge lights were strung, like diamond necklaces,

across the East River; and the Empire State Building,
so short now that it's the tallest, was a flag hung in sudden,
helpless patriotism. The skyline still beautiful at night,

though haunted by the absence of the Towers, by the
thousands of souls who perished so unexpectedly, so evilly.
New York seems less like home, somehow, since that morning.

I don't think I'll ever be able to look in that direction
without feeling a stab of sadness. Some of my happiest
nights in New York: walking downtown after a reading

or party and staring up at the lit Towers, marveling that I
lived under their shadow, that I lived in New York at all—
first five, then ten, then a dozen years—how truly lucky

I was.

102

VAL VINOKUROV

Concert at St. Paul's Chapel, Fulton St.; From the Other End

CONCERT AT ST. PAUL'S CHAPEL,
FULTON ST.

All of the city's American flags
have bivouacked in Lower Manhattan.

Outside: the symphony of concrete,
taxicabs, the tap shoes of high finance.

While inside St. Paul's Chapel—
restored into a marshmallow of pink
and white and baby blue—our bodies
are suffused with Schubert, Hindemith,
Beethoven. And the culture speculators
move slow, like convalescents, their mouths
agape from music or from before.

Health dictates I must unlearn the pleasures
of the pleasant, the plucking
of the holy and sublime, the fumes
of empathy, the chords of kindness.
Better to resound with the acoustics
of existence, the thud of bread and
peace, the click of urgent soles.

FROM THE OTHER END

Everyone is writing garden poems
and I want a garden poem of my own,
but all my arugula can think of is
sex—an orgy of little yellow flowers
for me to prune like a parent screening
phone calls.

My pot of herbs resides at the edge
of the wide, sloped window ledge;
if it slides in the rain and falls
on somebody's head, I'd probably
get sued.

There's something about Inwood that requires
a garden and its accompanying verse.
This finger of a neighborhood,
the Golan Heights of Manhattan, is wild
with trees and whalehump boulders that give
it mass as it seesaws on the island's
other end.

103

CHUCK WACHTEL

The Persistence of Who We Were

Downtown Manhattan: 9/16/01

Why don't my children take care of me? asks the baker, leaning against the end of the counter nearest the back. The woman he asks the question of says, in Spanish, Only God knows. The face of a newscaster, the attractive one whose blonde hair is cut in a straight line just above the dark rectangular frames of her glasses, is on the screen of a small black and white TV on a shelf behind the counter. The sound is turned off. Why don't they take care of me? he asks again, in English.

I have come in to buy bread and am looking at the loaves and rolls in the showcase beneath the countertop. It's usually so busy here you have to wait in line but this morning I'm the only customer. It's been less than a week since the attack on the World Trade Center and business is very slow.

I just don't get it, he says. And she, in Spanish, says, Only God knows why your children don't take care of you. Why do you keep asking me?

Because whenever your sister calls it's all you talk about. Does mom need this, does mom need that? That's why I'm asking.

The baker is in his mid-fifties, the woman somewhere in her forties. I imagine they've been speaking this way, in two languages, for so long they've become entirely unconscious of doing so. I think to myself, they are like a piano and a saxophone, but that is silly, and untrue, as are most thoughts that come when you imagine writing about a moment, or telling someone about it, while you're still inside it.

You got a problem with that? The woman asks the baker.

Of course not, he says, annoyed that she hasn't gotten his point.

On the right side of the split TV screen the second plane is hitting Tower One. On the left side is the still image of a young man wearing a Pep Boys T-shirt, holding a Styrofoam cup out in front of him, as if toasting the person taking his picture. There is nothing but sky behind him, but something in the light makes me think he is at the beach. I have seen this footage several times in the last three days and know we are hearing the voice of his mother, asking if anyone has seen him. He worked on the 89th floor. He has a tattoo on his left ankle, and on Tuesday he wore a yellow tie to work. And at this point she appears briefly on the right side of the screen, beside him, and as I watch her speak I realize that in remembering her words I have been speaking them to myself, and in this act: watching her, reciting with her, I realize that she has not only lost a son, she has had the substance of her own presence stolen from the words with which she speaks. He'd help others before he worried about himself, she says as the repeated footage of the second plane replaces her image, that's the kind of person he is.

We take care of my mother, the woman behind the counter says to the baker, and *my* children take care of me.

And you know what, he says, angrily, you don't even know how Goddamn lucky you are. And now, to me, somehow assuming I have understood her as well, he says, Don't you think she's lucky?

Thus, I have been invited into a conversation these two people would probably not be having had they not been confined together in the long hours of work on a slow day.

She is, I say to him.

Why does that make me lucky? She asks me in English.

Because your children take care of you? I say, in Spanish, stupidly, and as a question.

You see? the baker says. *He* hears what I'm saying.

That doesn't make me lucky, she says. That's just the way things are.

104

MAC WELLMAN

from HOWLER

1.

Just because you achieve some great end
doesn't mean you know what you are doing.
For now you must grow a shell
and become turtle.
That hurts because shells offer
countless examples of spiral
Surfacery. Whorls and unfocussable
helices, a vibration of pinwheels.
The apparent Archimedean point
is a dizzying
froth. What
to do now? In and of itself
the panorama circulates,
a litmus for the aggrieved to, to cry
out. Each one
A different kind of frog. Things
are unique before they are alike,
And the battle for the center stays
away;
stands selfishly on the rim. Rime
world ubiquity, as
cozily ensnared as a coat-tail rabbit,
all silk and paradiddle.

The diesel debops de strange chamber
and hems in him, for

that "just because" gives evidence
of inept quotation, like Settler Joe
[Settiform Settigerous Djo]
did, the dumb dong dreadful, because. Because
He gives evidence that follows
from other pieces of evidence and wood
—would, I mean, not "wood"—
be proved along with their proof
if he did not just sit here like this,
a rascal on the lam.

2.

For I abide my time.
I byde
I byde it
I byde my time
Innocenter patienter constanter.
O, the pain of being blown through the
        pane of glass,
as if I never knew the greats . . .

OWEN WEST

105

A Terror for Terror

Special Agent Trista Delgado's hip buzzed with electricity when she turned the corner of the running path in front of the Holocaust Museum in Battery Park City. She thought a bumble bee had flown into her running shorts. Trista was allergic to bee stings. She yelped, dropped her walkman, and swiped at the waist band of her shorts, considering a jump into the Hudson River as she convulsed. Her hand found the offending intruder—the Motorola pager the FBI required her to wear even during a workout—and she giggled with relief. She unclipped the pager and sat on the seawall reading the message. Her stomach roiled for the second time. She knew the call-in procedure for an "All Call" message but she had never actually seen one. She read it again, hoping that she had somehow memorized the phonetic code words incorrectly.

ALL CALL—ALL CALL—ALL CALL: FBI EYES ONLY. DO NOT BREAK CONTAIN. SUITCASE NOVEMBER WHISKEY EN ROUTE TO MANHATTAN. DELIVERY VEHICLE UNKNOWN, DRIVER ARAB MALE. PACKAGE LIKELY 250 LBS. DELTA FOXTROT AUTHORIZED WITH CONFIRMATION. MOVE IMMEDIATELY TO ASSIST NYPD AT LIKELY ENTRANCES AND TARGETS.

Her gun was locked in a safe in her apartment, two miles away. It wouldn't do any good against a November Whiskey—a nuclear weapon—but she would need it to stop the driver. Deadly force was authorized. Trista sprinted north along the esplanade toward the World Financial Center, cognizant of the families and strollers and bikes she passed. She thought of her own family.

She ran between the volleyball nets at the south end of the tiny man-made inlet that served as a harbor for some big yachts that specialized in tourist cruises. Moran's, the big bar next to the Mercantile Exchange, was brimming with people tipping bottles of Corona. The roar of the happy hour crowd was magnified by the surrounding buildings that trapped the echoes, sending conversations bouncing back and forth. Trista ran up to two cops offloading a refrigerator from a white yacht that advertised dinner cruises on its gunwale.

"You guys get the word?" she panted, noticing they were Arab and then feeling guilty for noticing.

"What word?" asked the fat one as he pulled the loaded dolly up the gangplank and onto the concrete landing.

"An All Call went out two minutes ago."

The other cop brushed past her and backed his police cart up next to the refrigerator. He was not wearing his nametag. The fat one, whose tag read Azzi, said, "Who are you?"

"Oh, right. Sorry. My name's Trista Delgado. I'm a fed."

"A fed? Listen, we have work to do here. Wait a few minutes and we can help you with your problem."

She thought she heard the cop without the nametag hiss at her, but she wasn't sure. It might have been a light cough. Her heart was already beating hard and now it felt as if a small rabbit was trapped under her breastbone. She had always explained away her father's passionate belief that a human being could actually sense danger to some kind of shell shock from Vietnam. Until now.

"Okay," she said, pointing at Moran's. "I'll be up there."

Scott Duffy was seated at a table with three of his buddies from the trading floor when he saw her. He put down his beer, the fifth of the afternoon, and brought his hand up in a half-salute to block the sun. "Yo. Check this out," he said. He combed his hair with his fingers.

A good-looking woman wearing black running shorts and

a white sports bra jogged up to the table and stood over them. Scott saw a rivulet from her sweaty brow drop into the beer bucket. "My name's Trista Delgado and I'm an FBI agent. I need a cell phone right now."

Four phones were snatched from four different pockets and extended. She chose Scott's and in his buzz he took it as some kind of positive sign. "You have to dial one if . . ."

"I know how to use it. Listen to me. If anything happens to me down there I want you to go to the first police officers you see and tell them those men are smuggling the weapon they're looking for. See that refrigerator they're loading?"

Scott followed her finger toward the harbor and squinted. "Yeah."

"If you don't find an officer, you four need to keep it here until one shows up."

"But those are cops right there."

"No they're not."

She dialed and turned away from the table. Scott watched her jog down the steps with the phone in her ear. One of his friends, he wasn't sure who, said, "Is she for real? If not, she's got your cell phone, dude."

The two cops hopped into their overgrown golf cart and started to drive away from the boat. Scott watched the woman sprint in front of the vehicle, an arm extended to halt it. Now she was slapping on the plexiglass windshield and shouting. The cart was still moving and seemed to crawl up the woman's leg. She balled herself into the fetal position and leaned into the tire even as it peeled her sports bra from her body.

"Oh my God!" shouted Scott. "Are you seein' this?"

As he was running alongside his friends, Scott saw one of the cops shoot the woman in the head. He jerked her body out of the tire well and hopped in the back compartment with the refrigerator. The cart leapt forward toward West Street.

And the World Trade Center.

(This text was written in April 2001.)

106

RACHEL WETZSTEON

A Trampoline in Wayne

September twelfth. Strange doings out at school:
two undergraduates are jumping on
a trampoline that's suddenly appeared
on campus. As the bustle of the day
gets underway (bells tolling; freshmen late
for chemistry; briefcases built for speed)
the girls bounce up and down as if the earth,
grown weary of the pain that makes it spin,
has stopped. Their motions grace a different world.

Whatever twist of fate has brought them here—
perhaps I'll open up the student paper
and read of some unorthodox class project
or learn the circus is in town—I watch
their fertile energy with stinging eyes
and think back to the chaos in Manhattan
(proud towers turned to Wheat Chex, autumn air
stinking of flesh and flame, downtown a wound
uptown gives blood to), and next thing I know
I'm telling stories, I'm inventing ways
the carefree girls are comments on the carnage:
however high we build our clever hopes,
some smiling villain sends them tumbling down
to smithereens. Or else, more happily:
though buildings are more fragile than we could
have guessed (one shape descends), our lust for life
(another rises) makes a foiled ghost of

each suicidal pilot who believes
we'll go down, scorched and beaten, with the towers;
when one strong healthy body crashes down
the other, just as strong, pops up again.

But these girls are adventurous; their leaps
are every bit as varied as their plummets,
and no trim definition—allegory,
parabola, plunge, surge, drop—holds them all.
There will be time for metaphor. For now
it is enough to watch them on this crisp,
peculiar morning and remember that
what's obvious is often what we need
reminding of: to be alive is to be
capable of jumping on a makeshift
trampoline in New Jersey for no reason;
though downcast moods like mine may fence them in,
people will keep inventing crazy schemes
and leaping high as long as there is blood
flooding their cheeks, fire burning in their eyes.

107

SUSAN WHEELER

[The movie set on the horizon glows]

The movie set on the horizon glows
  all night *as well, seeking strength in spirit*
beyond the Kohn-Perderson-Fox monolith
  novitiate *there were large-scale failures*
priorly a stub below the real. It was
  Prior *just one challenge*
who buggered hard in his fiancée's wake,
  and a *United Airlines Flight 175*
bee that in the sink tonight
  I stubbed. *Still, the incredible feat—*
All this is true and will you make
  it false. *Empire once fought the*
True-dat, not-true-dat: they played
  this game—*officials will—*
on radio before gangster rap
  was banned. *As one official put it—*
To be a movie set the tarps went up
  like gaffs *220 pounds*
in the sharp morgue scent—*acrid* not
  true dat—*former jet pilot Donald*
the rid in putrid truer and I want it false.
  Für Elise *dragnet for America's*
was Ludrid deaf when first he
  heard it? *Military installations*
Patois, tonight, shouts from the park—"he
  president" *U.S. service members*

and then the wash of flesh in air hard
    sinking, *that came upon America*,
on, the furry lungs in-taking, true
    dat was *a command post at*
that the *sharp* of acrid—glow burning—It is
    Steve McQueen—*Congress, perhaps*
it's Lubitsch————It is undone
    by grief. *I was just incredulous.*
This is all true. The city is deaf
    in grief. *Wascom said the airlines*

O will they come 2 hear him. *Pocketknife and corkscrew*—
O U that turned and saw. Turned stone.

U.S. News and World Report, September 24, 2001

108

PETER WORTSMAN

New York Does Not Exist

ode on a city-state of mind

"I ain't gettin' off! I ain't stayin' on!"

—Anonymous New Yorker, male, circa 13, hanging out between subway cars

The crumpled letter lying on the platform preserves the anger of an absent hand.

▪

Directly opposite me on the subway sits your prototypical New Yorker in a narrow-brimmed, non-descript gray felt hat and a London Fog gray trench coat huddling behind a newspaper. Could be my late father, himself a master at folding his *Times* with crisp pleats into ever narrower vertical wedges to fit the shrinking elbow room at rush hour. Thus immersed and anesthetized into a soothing numbness by the tabloid tragedies of his fellow man, the New Yorker preserves the illusion of privacy by never looking a fellow human in the eye.

Whenever I pass a certain subway stop, though my Dad's been dead and gone for two decades and counting, I still scan the platform half-expecting to spot him leaning against a pillar folding his *Times*. Every platform harbors its resident ghosts.

This particular nocturnal commuter makes no pretense of scanning the day's news. It's too late for such a charade, the 9-to-5'ers being long since planted before their TV screens feeding on the evening news. My man, as I only now notice, is gripping the paper upside-down in his trembling white knuckles.

But why?

Presently, as the train screeches round a hairpin curve, his hat tilts first into, then out of the turn, the blocked felt hesitating for a fleeting instant, till finally, no longer able to resist centrifugal temptation, it tumbles into the mess of renegade objects on the floor: lost buttons, razor blades, pennies, hypodermic needles, cans and bottles. Dropped accidentally or intentionally discarded, this lawless collection is free to indulge the wild delinquent desire to roll. No New Yorker in his right mind would reach his hand out to retrieve a fallen object, however precious, from the vicious snouts of that savage horde. For the subway floor is off-limits, a precinct of virtual infection not even the clean-up crews dare sweep. Oblivious to prudence and propriety—must have been out of my mind—I reach for the hat, and not a moment too soon, for a gang of broken bottles is already hurtling my way.

"Your hat, Sir!" I cry out above the screech and clatter.

"Thanks!" comes the muffled reply, more echo than now.

And then, like a secret grown sick of itself, the newspaper falls, revealing the absence of a face. No nose, no eyes. Holes instead. Flaps of skin where ears ought to hang, and in the middle, a horizontal slit twisting upwards into a grinning crescent.

1. GOING NOWHERE IN A HURRY

Newly migrated to the New World, still wet behind the ears like so many greenhorns before them, my parents passed their first New York rite of passage. After ceremoniously tasting and gagging on root beer, they parted ways at the tip of the Flat Iron Building to find work on either side, only to meet up again, newly employed, at its flat end.

And now that I am a father and breadwinner, I feel duty-bound to reiterate this vital bit of information (of which we children were informed every time we passed the crossroads of Broadway and Fifth) to my own son and daughter as we trundle by in a downtown bus, lest by failing to re-tell the tale I undo the spell of the past and so unravel the linked double-helixes of my own and their begetting.

A mere landmark to most out-of-towners, lofty in its heyday—a bonsai skyscraper dwarfed by the subsequent spatial expectations of a restless city—the Flat Iron Building keeps pressing out destinies.

It was here, too, that I found my first publisher in a narrow triangular corner office on the seventh floor and signed my first book contract on a desk wedged into the narrow rounded tip, cross-eyed, with my right eye full of lofty illusions of Broadway and beyond, my left fixed clearly, realistically, on the hopeless tangle of traffic choking lower Fifth Avenue.

JOHN YAU

109

The Morning after That One

The telling will go on for many years until the last one who was there expires. There is here. Here is the gridded set of coordinates by which you will tell where in the there you learned that time had been slowed down. The story begins with coordinates, with the measures and markers one used to deduce one's movement toward and away. Unable to stop, to come to a point of rest, one became the mind and body of a gyroscope.

How many orbits did anyone of us find ourselves in? This is the gravitational pull of that day's persistent questions. Where in relation to what? Where in relation to where? Could one account for all one's pronouns?

The telling of the story begins with the intersection of geography and time, where and when. Of this story there are many tellings. This one begins before the 6:20 Silver Meteor departs for Miami, stopping at Baltimore. The hours between departing and stopping is when he sleeps.

Somewhere past Wilmington he wakes up and sees little puffs of fog hugging the still wet grass. And this one begins around 10:00 A.M., on a subway to Penn Station. A description of the woman who helps you lift the baby carriage onto the platform.

These stories meet in a present whose boundaries keep moving past the horizon, as you and I become silhouettes sitting in someone else's house, watching the story begin again and again. Impossible to leave this room which is inside a room whose air is burning. Beneath sky's black roof time both starts and stops, spirals back on itself, becomes a wheel spinning back to the first moments of that day, coffee's heated molecules dispersing into the air, garbage truck engine idling as its hydraulic gears lift a sheet metal container briefly skyward. Sky still dark, streets still empty.

I was alone that morning, you were across the river, with the baby. Many hours later, the sky black once more, we would meet on the edge of a town I hadn't been to in over a decade, near where you teach, in a house we had never been to before, guests of someone I had never met and you knew only slightly. This is one side of the telling.

▪

How close or far is the answer that asks to be told. The question is unspoken, need not be asked, is in the air between. One hesitates to ask more, knowing more will come. Of when and where one first saw or learned what others were seeing. Of these minutes. One has to see them passing. One has to see them again. One does not ask how long it will take to remember what one has watched and watched again.

For months afterward she would talk about the sculptor who said the events of that day would not affect his work. Her story includes his story, but she realizes that his story does not include hers. She can neither accept nor understand this.

I place these smaller stories, these shards, in front of the larger one and ones. I do not offer them as offerings.

110

CHRISTOPHER YU

Two New York Memoranda: October, 2001

1. Epitaphs (On the Death of Rehavam Ze'evi)

"Perfection, of a kind, was what he was after."
—Auden

Remorselessly, the news reports today
that gunmen have slain, in the name of revenge,
Israel's tourism minister,
a man who once referred to Palestinians as "lice."

As has been its habit of late,
Israel will retaliate
by sending missile-launching helicopters
and tanks to the West Bank. Perhaps before dawn
or in the torpor of mid-afternoon,
Palestine's children will die in the streets.

I turn down the radio,
but cannot halt the recitation
of dates, statistics, accusation
and counter-accusation, hostilities and lies.

Meanwhile, the image persists of
reputable bureaucrats with the poor and powerless
conferring civilly, at last, only in the grave.
Is this what the philosopher meant by banality?

Lord, if you exist,
if your eyes have known pity,
enlighten me, please. Tell me, if you can,
how does your New Jerusalem differ from the old?

2. Commuting

Rushing crosstown one evening after work,
while you traverse the bustling throng of woes
and every thought of debt or grievance grows
as a lean shadow lengthens toward dark,

you feel a shock—what lately in New York
unnerves—of something harder than surprise
that could translate the glitter, stench, and noise
into a legible design or mark:

one voice sings from a window high above.
And like a blow suffered amid the crowd
or recognition of an estranged face,

that human outcry fixes you in place
with the suggestion, more acute than loud,
of a desire as obdurate as love.

ABOUT THE CONTRIBUTORS

HUMERA AFRIDI is working on an M.F.A. in Creative Writing at New York University, and is currently at work on a novel, *Asymptotes.*

AMMIEL ALCALAY is a poet, critic, translator, and scholar. His books include *After Jews & Arabs, the cairo notebooks,* and *Memories of Our Future: Selected Essays, 1982–1999.* His translations include *Sarajevo Blues* by Bosnian poet Semezdin Mehmedinovic, and *Keys to the Garden,* a collection of Middle Eastern writing.

ELENA ALEXANDER is a poet and writer living in New York City. Her poem, *How the Lurking,* was recently chosen to be on a poster for "The Arts Respond to 9-11."

MEENA ALEXANDER's new book of poems is *Illiterate Heart.* She is currently at work on a commission from the Royal Festival Hall, London, to compose a poem on New York for Poetry International 2002. She is Distinguished Professor of English and Women's Studies at Hunter College and the Graduate Center, City University of New York.

JEFFERY RENARD ALLEN has published the novel *Rails under My Back,* and will publish two collections of short stories, *Radar Countries* and *The Green Apocalypse,* and a collection of poems, *Stellar Places.*

ROBERTA ALLEN is the author of *The Traveling Woman, The Daughter, Amazon Dream, Certain People, Fast Fiction, The Dreaming Girl,* and *The Playful Way to Serious Writing.* She is also a visual artist in the collection of The Metropolitan Museum of Art.

JONATHAN AMES is the author of four books, the most recent being *My Less Than Secret Life.*

DARREN ARONOFSKY is a director and writer. His *Requiem for a Dream* was nominated for a Golden Globe, and he was awarded the Sundance Film Festival's Director's Award for *Pi*.

PAUL AUSTER is a writer of novels, essays, poetry, and translations including *The New York Trilogy* and most recently *Timbuktu*.

ULRICH BAER is the author of *Remnants of Song: Trauma and the Experience of Modernity in Charles Baudelaire and Paul Celan* and *Spectral Evidence: The Photography of Trauma*. He teaches literature in the department of German at New York University.

JENNIFER BELLE is the author of the novels *Going Down* and *High Maintenance*.

JENIFER BERMAN is a writer and editor living in Brooklyn.

CHARLES BERNSTEIN's books include *My Way: Speeches and Poems* and *With Strings*, from the University of Chicago Press. He is the director of the Poetics Program at SUNY–Buffalo.

STAR BLACK is a poet and artist who has published several books of poetry including *Balefire* and *Waterworn*, and co-edited *The KGB Bar Reader*.

BREYTEN BREYTENBACH at present teaches part of the year at New York University as a Distinguished Global Professor. He is also the executive director of the Gorée Institute in the Bay of Dakar. His most recent publication is *Lady One (Of Love and Other Poems)*.

MELVIN JULES BUKIET is the author of six works of fiction including *Strange Fire* and *Signs and Wonders*, and the editor of *Neurotica: Jewish Erotic Writing* and *Nothing Makes You Free: Stories by Later-Generation Holocaust Survivors*.

PETER CAREY's books include *Bliss, Illywhacker, The Age, Oscar and Lucinda, The Tax Inspector, The Unusual Life of Tristan Smith, Jack Maggs*, and *The True History of the Kelly Gang*.

LAWRENCE CHUA is the author of the novel *Gold by the Inch* and the editor of the anthology *Collapsing New Buildings.*

IRA COHEN is a pioneering poet, musician, and photographer who recently published a collection of poetry, *Poems from the Akashic Record.*

IMRAAN COOVADIA recently published his first novel, *The Wedding.*

EDWIDGE DANTICAT was born in Haiti and has written the novels *Farming of Bones, Krik? Krak!*, and *Breath, Eyes, Memory*, and edited *The Butterfly's Way: Voices from the Haitian Diaspora*, and *The Beacon Best of 2000: Great Writing by Women and Men of All Colors and Cultures.*

ALICE ELLIOT DARK is the author of the recent novel *Think of England* and two collections of short stories. She lives in Montclair, New Jersey.

ERIC DARTON, author of the novel *Free City* and *Divided We Stand: A Biography of New York's World Trade Center*, teaches in Goddard College's M.F.A. Creative Writing program.

LYDIA DAVIS is the author of the novel *The End of the Story* and the story collections *Break It Down, Almost No Memory*, and most recently, *Samuel Johnson Is Indignant*, which was a VLS Favorite and an American Library Association Notable Book. Her translation of Proust's *The Way by Swann's* is forthcoming from Penguin UK in the fall.

SAMUEL R. DELANY is the author of *They Fly at Ciron, Equinox, The Mad Man*, and *Times Square Red, Times Square Blue*, published by NYU Press, among other books.

MAGGIE DUBRIS is the author of *Weep Not, My Wanton.* She is also a 911 paramedic who responded to the World Trade Center disaster on September 11.

RINDE ECKERT is a singer, composer, actor, dancer, writer, and director whose solo pieces and collaborations, including the acclaimed *And God Created Great Whales*, have been performed throughout the United States and abroad.

JANICE EIDUS, twice winner of the O. Henry Prize, is the author of two story collections, *The Celibacy Club* and *Vito Loves Geraldine*, and two novels, *Urban Bliss* and *Faithful Rebecca.* She is currently in the process of adopting a child.

MASOOD FARIVAR, a reporter for Dow Jones newswires, was a member of the anti-Soviet resistance, the mujahideen, in Afghanistan.

CAROLYN FERRELL lives in the Bronx and teaches creative writing at Sarah Lawrence College. She is the author of the story collection, *Don't Erase Me.*

RICHARD FOREMAN has received a MacArthur Fellowship, has recently won the PEN Master American Dramatist Award, and has written and/or directed over eighty plays around the world. His own Ontological-Hysteric Theater is located in the St. Mark's Church in New York City.

DEBORAH GARRISON is a poet. She is the author of *A Working Girl Can't Win.*

AMITAV GHOSH is the author of *The Glass Palace*, his most recent novel.

JAMES GIBBONS is a short-story writer and Assistant Editor at the *Library of America.*

CAROL GILLIGAN's most recent book is *The Birth of Pleasure.* She is currently adapting *The Scarlet Letter* for the theater and is at work on a novel.

THEA GOODMAN is an author of short stories and poems published in *Confrontation* and the *New England Review*. She is currently writing a novel.

VIVIAN GORNICK is a memoirist and literary critic whose books include *Fierce Attachments, Approaching Eye Level*, and *The Situation and the Story: The Art of Personal Narrative.*

TIM GRIFFIN is the art editor of *Time Out New York*. His poetry has appeared in *Purple*, *Lingo*, *Explosive*, and *Kiosk* and is forthcoming in *Hat* and *Fence*.

LEV GROSSMAN is a staff writer at *Time Magazine* and the author of the novel *Warp*.

JOHN GUARE is a playwright whose work includes *The House of Blue Leaves*, *Six Degrees of Separation*, and the screenplay for the film *Atlantic City*.

SEAN GULLETTE is a writer, actor, and filmmaker. This year he will direct his screenplay *Monopolis*, a psy-fi thriller set in a Manhattan skyscraper in 1960.

JESSICA HAGEDORN is the author of *Dogeaters*, *The Gangster of Love*, *Danger and Beauty*, and *Burning Heart: A Portrait of the Philippines* (a collaboration with photojournalist Marissa Roth).

KIMIKO HAHN is the author of *Air Pocket*, *Earshot*, *The Unbearable Heart*, *Volatile*, and *Mosquito and Ant*.

NATHALIE HANDAL is the author of a book of poems, *The NeverField*, a poetry CD, *Traveling Rooms*, and editor of the Academy of American Poets bestseller, *The Poetry of Arab Women: A Contemporary Anthology*.

CAREY HARRISON's poetry, plays, and fiction—including *Richard's Feet*, *Cley*, and *Egon*—have been published by Holt and Viking in the United States, and by Penguin, Heinemann, and Oleander Press in the United Kingdom, and have been translated into nine languages. He teaches at the City University of New York.

JOSHUA HENKIN is a short-story writer and novelist whose works include *Swimming across the Hudson*, and the forthcoming *The Flourishing Senescence of Professor Nate Hammond*.

TONY HISS's books include *The Experience of Place* and *Building Images: Seventy Years of Photography at Hedrich Blessing*.

DAVID HOLLANDER is the author of the novel *L.I.E.* He currently teaches writing at Sarah Lawrence College and at various New York City public schools. He lives in Brooklyn.

A.M. HOMES is author of the forthcoming, *Things You Should Know*, and the novels *Music for Torching, The End of Alice, In a Country of Mothers*, and *Jack*, as well as the short-story collection *The Safety of Objects*, and the artists' book *Appendix A*. Her work has been translated into ten languages and is much anthologized. She is currently a fellow at the Center for Scholars and Writers at the New York Public Library and teaches in the Writing Program at Columbia University.

RICHARD HOWARD is a poet and translator. He teaches literature in the School of the Arts (Writing Division) at Columbia University.

LAIRD HUNT is a former UN press officer and is New York correspondent for London's *Mouth-to-Mouth* magazine. He is the author of *The Impossibly*, a novel.

SIRI HUSTVEDT is the author of the novels *The Blindfold, The Enchantment of Lily Dahl*, and *Yonder*. She is also the author of a book of poetry, *Reading to You.*

JOHN KEENE is the author of *Annotations*. His poetry, fiction, essays, and reviews have appeared in an array of periodicals and anthologies. He currently teaches at Brown University.

JOHN KELLY is an experimental theater artist who creates both solo and ensemble works that incorporate choreography, visual design, film and video, and song.

WAYNE KOESTENBAUM is the author of *Andy Warhol* and *Jackie under My Skin: Interpreting an Icon*. He has also published three books of poems: *The Milk of Inquiry, Rhapsodies of a Repeat Offender*, and *Ode to Anna Moffo and Other Poems.*

RICHARD KOSTELANETZ is a writer, musician, editor, and

translator whose works include the *Dictionary of the Avant-Gardes.*

GUY LESSER lives and works in Brooklyn.

JONATHAN LETHEM is an award-winning novelist whose work includes *Motherless Brooklyn*, and *As She Climbed across the Table.*

JOCELYN LIEU is a fiction writer whose work has appeared in the anthology *Charlie Chan Is Dead* and frequently appears in various literary journals.

TAN LIN is a writer and artist. He is author of *Intelligent Dance Music.* His movie-book *Disco M Figure* is forthcoming.

SAM LIPSYTE, the author of *Venus Drive* and *The Subject Steve*, lives in Queens, New York.

PHILLIP LOPATE is a fiction writer and essayist focusing on urban New York stories. His works include *Writing New York: A Literary Anthology* and *Portrait of My Body.*

KAREN MALPEDE has written twelve plays produced in New York and a film script "I, Emily," to star Calista Flockhart. She recently directed and co-adapted Victor Klemperer's *I Will Bear Witness* for the stage.

CHARLES McNULTY is a short-story writer and a theater critic at the *Village Voice* whose theater reviews and essays have appeared in *Modern Drama, Variety, American Theater*, and *Theater.*

PABLO MEDINA's work includes the collections of poems, *The Floating Island, Pork Rind and Cuban Songs* and *Arching into the Afterlife*; a memoir, *Exiled Memories*; and the novels *The Marks of Birth* and *The Return of Felix Nogara.*

ELLEN MILLER is the author of the novel *Like Being Killed.* At work on her second novel, *Stop, Drop, Roll,* she lives in New

York City, where she was born, has lived her entire life, and suspects she always will.

PAUL D. MILLER is an artist, writer, and musician whose work has appeared in the *Village Voice*, *Artforum*, *Rap Pages*, and other periodicals. As "DJ Spooky That Subliminal Kid," he has released numerous records and articles. He is completing a novel entitled *Flow My Blood the DJ Said* and collaborating in different projects with writer Margo Jefferson, dancer Francesca Harper, and architect Bernard Tschumi. An anthology on sound art and multi-media entitled *Sound Abound* is forthcoming.

MARK JAY MIRSKY is the editor of the magazine *Fiction*. His work includes the novels *Thou Worm Jacob*, and *Blue Hill Avenue*, a collection of essays, *My Search for the Messiah*, and *The Absent Shakespeare.*

TOVA MIRVIS is the author of a novel, *The Ladies Auxiliary*. She lives in New York City and is writing a second novel.

ALBERT MOBILIO's most recent book of poems is *Me with Animal Towering.*

ALEX MOLOT is an author of short stories. He lives in New York City.

MARY MORRIS has written several novels including *House Arrest*, and *Acts of God*. She teaches at Sarah Lawrence College.

TRACIE MORRIS is from Brooklyn, New York, and works with page and sound-based texts. She teaches at Sarah Lawrence College.

ANNA MOSCHOVAKIS moved to New York from Los Angeles in the early 1990s. She works as a freelance editor and translator.

RICHARD EOIN NASH is a writer and performance artist. He is the author of four plays: *for quite some time now*, *Heartbreak*

City, *Mister Happiness*, and *Party Animal*; all of which have been scheduled to be produced in New York.

JOSIP NOVAKOVICH, a native of Croatia, was a writing fellow at the New York Public Library in 2001-02; he teaches in the M.F.A. Writing Program at Penn State. His book, *Salvation and Other Disasters* won an American Book Award. This fall he will publish a new book of nonfiction, *Plum Brandy: A Croatian Sojourn.*

DENNIS NURKSE is a poet and the author of *Voices over Water, Staggered Lights, Shadow Wars,* and *Isolation in Action.* He is Brooklyn's Poet Laureate.

GEOFFREY O'BRIEN's books include *Castaways of the Image Planet*, *The Browser's Ecstasy*, *Dream Time: Chapters from the Sixties*, and *Floating City: Selected Poems 1978–1995.* He is Editor in Chief of the Library of America.

LARRY O'CONNOR is a writer for the *Wall Street Journal.* He has published a memoir called *Tip of the Iceberg.*

ROBERT POLITO, poet and biographer, directs the Graduate Writing Program at The New School.

NELLY REIFLER's fiction has appeared in various magazines and journals. Simon & Schuster will publish her short-story collection, *Splinter*, in 2003. She lives in Brooklyn.

ROSE-MYRIAM RÉJOUIS teaches Caribbean and African Francophone literature at Sarah Lawrence College and has translated (with Val Vinokurov), *Texaco* and *Solibo Magnificent* by Patrick Chamoiseau.

APRIL REYNOLDS is professor of creative writing at New York University's Gallatin School for Individualized Study. Her novel *Red Ribbons and the Broken Memory Tree* is forthcoming.

ROXANA ROBINSON is a novelist, essayist, biographer, and Guggenheim Fellow.

AVITAL RONELL's works include *The Telephone Book, Crack Wars*, and *Stupidity*. She is currently adapting the relation of Eckermann to Goethe for the theater. She teaches critical theory at New York University.

DANIEL ASA ROSE is arts and culture editor for *The Forward*. He is the author of a memoir, *Hiding Places: A Father and His Sons Retrace Their Family's Escape from the Holocaust;* a novel, *Flipping for It*, and a collection of short stories, *Small Family with Rooster.*

JOE SALVATORE is a faculty member at The New School. His work has appeared in *Open City* among other journals. He lives in Brooklyn.

GRACE SCHULMAN's new poetry collections include *Days of Wonder: New and Selected Poems,* and *The Paintings of Our Lives*. Earlier books of poetry include *For that Day Only*, *Hemispheres*, and *Burn Down the Icons*. She lives in New York where she is Distinguished Professor at Baruch College, CUNY.

LYNNE SHARON SCHWARTZ is the author of fifteen books, most recently the novel *In the Family Way: An Urban Comedy*, and *In Solitary*, a collection of poems.

DANI SHAPIRO is the author of three novels and a memoir. Her new novel, *Family History*, is forthcoming.

AKHIL SHARMA's stories have appeared in *Best American Short Stories, O. Henry Award Winners*, the *Atlantic Monthly,* and the *New Yorker.* He is the author of the novel *An Obedient Father.*

SUZAN SHERMAN's writing has appeared in *The Mississippi Review,* mrbellersneighborhood.com, *BookForum,* the *New York Times,* and *BOMB,* where she is a contributing editor.

JENEFER SHUTE's work includes two novels: *Life-Size*, and *Sex Crimes.*

HAL SIROWITZ is Poet Laureate of Queens, New York, and the author of *Girlie Pictures*, *Happy Baby*, *Mother Said*, and *My Therapist Said*, among other books.

PAMELA SNEED is a writer, performer, and actress. She is the author of a book of poetry, *Imagine Being More Afraid of Freedom Than of Slavery*, and she is at work on a new collection of poetry, short stories, and political essays. Her recent work appears in *Role Call*, an anthology of political writings, and in *Brown Sugar*, an anthology of Black erotica.

CHRIS SPAIN lives in Katonah, New York.

ART SPIEGELMAN is a graphic novelist and designer. His publications include *Maus* and *Maus II*.

CATHARINE R. STIMPSON, a literary critic and writer, is Professor and Dean of the Graduate School of Arts and Science at New York University.

LIZ SWADOS is a writer, musician, and director. She is the author of six children's books, three novels, and two nonfiction books. Her most recent novel is *Flamboyant*.

LYNNE TILLMAN is the author of the novels *Motion Sickness*, *Cast in Doubt*, *Haunted Houses*, and *No Lease on Life*, the short-story collections *Absence Makes the Heart* and *The Madame Realism Complex*, and *The Broad Picture*, a book of essays.

MIKE TOPP was born in Washington, D.C. He is currently living in New York City unless he has died or moved. His work has appeared in *Exquisite Corpse*, *Lungfull!*, and *McSweeney's*. His most recent book is *I Used to Be Ashamed of My Striped Face*.

DAVID TRINIDAD is the author of *Plasticville*. His books include *Answer Song*, *Hand over Heart*, *Pavane*, *Monday, Monday, Monday*, and *Essay with Moveable Parts*.

VAL VINOKUROV is a writer, scholar, and translator. His translation (with Rose Réjouis) of Patrick Chamoiseau's *Texaco* won the American Translator Association's Prize for Best Book in 1998. He teaches at Eugene Lang College, The New School.

CHUCK WACHTEL's books include *Because We Are Here: Stories and Novellas*; the novels *The Gates* and *Joe the Engineer*; and two collections of poems and short prose: *The Coriolis Effect* and *What Happens to Me.* He teaches in the Graduate Program in Creative Writing at New York University.

MAC WELLMAN's plays include *Terminal Hip, Crowbar and Blowjobs, Sincerity Forever, Cleveland,* and *Murder of Crows.*

OWEN WEST is a former U.S. Marine and current commodity futures trader for Goldman, Sachs in New York City. He has published the novel *Sharkman Six.*

RACHEL WETZSTEON is the author of two collections of poetry: *The Other Stars*, and *Home and Away.*

SUSAN WHEELER's poetry collections include *Bag 'o' Diamonds, Smokes,* and most recently, *Source Codes.*

PETER WORTSMAN is the author of *A Modern Way to Die.* He has translated Robert Musil's *Posthumous Papers of a Living Author*, among other works.

JOHN YAU's most recent books are *My Heart Is That Eternal Rose Tattoo* and *Borrowed Love Poems.* He has lived in New York for more than twenty-five years.

CHRISTOPHER YU's poems have appeared in the *New Republic* and the *Paris Review*. His book, *Nothing to Admire: The Politics of Poetic Satire from Dryden to Merrill*, is forthcoming.

PERMISSIONS

All texts have been reproduced by permission.

Ammiel Alcalay's text is excerpted from a book-length poem *the warring factions* (Beyond Baroque, 2002); Jonathan Ames's text originally appeared in *Shout* and in his book *My Less Than Secret Life*; Peter Carey's piece is excerpted and adapted from a longer piece called "A Letter from New York," published September 23, 2001, *The Observer* (UK); Deborah Garrison's poem first appeared in the *New Yorker*, October 22, 2001; Amitav Ghosh's text first appeared in the *New Yorker*, September 16, 2001; Jessica Hagedorn's "Notes from a New York Diary" is excerpted from an essay included in a new edition of *Danger and Beauty* (City Lights Books, 2002); Tony Hiss's text was first published in the *New York Times*, September 16, 2001; A.M. Homes' text first appeared in the *New York Times*, Sept 26, 2001; Richard Howard's "Fallacies of Wonder" was first published in *CITE: The Architecture and Design Review of Houston* (Rice University); Phillip Lopate's text is adapted from an essay first published in *The Forward*, November 9, 2001; Dennis Nurkse's poem first appeared in *The Forward*, November 9, 2001; an earlier version of Art Spiegelman's text was published on the website of the *New Yorker* in September 2001; Val Vinokurov's "From the Other End" has appeared in *New American Writing*, June 2002.